EARLY CHILDHOOD EDUCATION SERIES

Beyond Compliance in Early Childhood Education: Centering Disability, Freedom, and Belonging
MAGGIE BENEKE & HAILEY R. LOVE, EDS.

Addressing Stress With Self-Compassion: A Guide for Early Childhood Teachers
DAVID P. BARRY

Teacher Well-Being in Early Childhood: A Resource for Early Care and Education Professionals
ANGELA C. BAUM & KERRIE L. SCHNAKE

Pro-Blackness in Early Childhood Education: Diversifying Curriculum and Pedagogy in K–3 Classrooms
GLORIA SWINDLER BOUTTE, JARVAIS J. JACKSON, SAUDAH N. COLLINS, JANICE R. BAINES, ANTHONY BROUGHTON, & GEORGE LEE JOHNSON

Seven Crucial Conversations in Early Childhood Education: Where Have We Been and Why Does It Matter?
NANCY FILE, NANCY E. BARBOUR, & ANDREW J. STREMMEL, EDS.

Supporting Korean American Children in Early Childhood Education: Perspectives From Mother-Educators
SOPHIA HAN, JINHEE KIM, SOHYUN MEACHAM, & SU-JEONG WEE

Relationship-Based Care for Infants and Toddlers: Fostering Early Learning and Development Through Responsive Practice
SUSAN L. RECCHIA, MINSUN SHIN, & ELENI LOIZOU

Infants and Toddlers at Work: Using Reggio-Inspired Materials to Support Brain Development, Second Edition
ANN LEWIN-BENHAM

Leading Anti-Bias Early Childhood Programs: A Guide to Change, for Change, 2nd Ed.
LOUISE DERMAN-SPARKS, DEBBIE LEEKEENAN, & JOHN NIMMO

We Are the Change We Seek: Advancing Racial Justice in Early Care and Education
IHEOMA U. IRUKA, TONIA R. DURDEN, KERRY-ANN ESCAYG, & STEPHANIE M. CURENTON

Young Investigators: The Project Approach in the Early Years, 4th Ed.
JUDY HARRIS HELM, LILIAN G. KATZ, & REBECCA WILSON

Emotionally Responsive Teaching: Expanding Trauma-Informed Practice With Young Children
TRAVIS WRIGHT

Rooted in Belonging: Critical Place-Based Learning in Early Childhood and Elementary Teacher Education
MELISSA SHERFINSKI WITH SHARON HAYES

Transforming Early Years Policy in the U.S.: A Call to Action
MARK K. NAGASAWA, LACEY PETERS, MARIANNE N. BLOCH, & BETH BLUE SWADENER, EDS.

Music Therapy With Preschool Children on the Autism Spectrum: Moments of Meeting
GEOFF BARNES

On Being and Well-Being in Infant/Toddler Care and Education: Life Stories From Baby Rooms
MARY BENSON MCMULLEN

Principals as Early Learning Leaders: Effectively Supporting Our Youngest Learners
JULIE NICHOLSON, HELEN MANIATES, SERENE YEE, THOMAS WILLIAMS JR., VERONICA UFOEGBUNE, & RAUL ERAZO-CHAVEZ

Resisting the Kinder-Race: Restoring Joy to Early Learning
CHRISTOPHER P. BROWN

Reshaping Universal Preschool: Critical Perspectives on Power and Policy
LUCINDA GRACE HEIMER & ANN ELIZABETH RAMMINGER, WITH KATHERINE K. DELANEY, SARAH GALANTER-GUZIEWSKI, LACEY PETERS, & KRISTIN WHYTE

Pre-K Stories: Playing with Authorship and Integrating Curriculum in Early Childhood
DANA FRANTZ BENTLEY & MARIANA SOUTO-MANNING

Ready or Not: Early Care and Education's Leadership Choices—12 Years Later, 2nd Ed.
STACIE G. GOFFIN & VALORA WASHINGTON

Teaching STEM in the Preschool Classroom
ALISSA A. LANGE ET AL.

High-Quality Early Learning for a Changing World
BEVERLY FALK

Guiding Principles for the New Early Childhood Professional
VALORA WASHINGTON & BRENDA GADSON

For a complete list of series titles, visit https://www.tcpress.com/ece

continued

I0805946

Early Childhood Education Series, *continued*

Leading for Change in Early Care and Education
ANNE L. DOUGLASS

When Pre-K Comes to School
BETHANY WILINSKI

Continuity in Children's Worlds
MELISSA M. JOZWIAK ET AL.

The Early Intervention Guidebook for Families and Professionals, 2nd Ed.
BONNIE KEILTY

STEM Learning with Young Children
SHELLY COUNSELL ET AL.

Courageous Leadership in Early Childhood Education
SUSI LONG ET AL., EDS.

Teaching Kindergarten
JULIE DIAMOND ET AL., EDS.

The New Early Childhood Professional
VALORA WASHINGTON ET AL.

Teaching and Learning in a Diverse World, 4th Ed.
PATRICIA G. RAMSEY

In the Spirit of the Studio, 2nd Ed.
LELLA GANDINI ET AL., EDS.

Exploring Mathematics Through Play in the Early Childhood Classroom
AMY NOELLE PARKS

Becoming Young Thinkers
JUDY HARRIS HELM

The Early Years Matter
MARILOU HYSON & HEATHER BIGGAR TOMLINSON

Thinking Critically About Environments for Young Children
LISA P. KUH, ED.

Standing Up for Something Every Day
BEATRICE S. FENNIMORE

FirstSchool
SHARON RITCHIE & LAURA GUTMANN, EDS.

Early Childhood Education for a New Era
STACIE G. GOFFIN

Everyday Artists
DANA FRANTZ BENTLEY

Multicultural Teaching in the Early Childhood Classroom
MARIANA SOUTO-MANNING

Inclusion in the Early Childhood Classroom
SUSAN L. RECCHIA & YOON-JOO LEE

Moral Classrooms, Moral Children, 2nd Ed.
RHETA DEVRIES & BETTY ZAN

Defending Childhood
BEVERLY FALK, ED.

Starting with Their Strengths
DEBORAH C. LICKEY & DENISE J. POWERS

The Play's the Thing
ELIZABETH JONES & GRETCHEN REYNOLDS

Twelve Best Practices for Early Childhood Education
ANN LEWIN-BENHAM

Big Science for Growing Minds
JACQUELINE GRENNON BROOKS

What If All the Kids Are White? 2nd Ed.
LOUISE DERMAN-SPARKS & PATRICIA G. RAMSEY

Seen and Heard
ELLEN LYNN HALL & JENNIFER KOFKIN RUDKIN

Connecting Emergent Curriculum and Standards in the Early Childhood Classroom
SYDNEY L. SCHWARTZ & SHERRY M. COPELAND

Infants and Toddlers at Work
ANN LEWIN-BENHAM

Educating and Caring for Very Young Children, 2nd Ed.
DORIS BERGEN ET AL.

Beginning School
RICHARD M. CLIFFORD & GISELE M. CRAWFORD, EDS.

Emergent Curriculum in the Primary Classroom
CAROL ANNE WIEN, ED.

Enthusiastic and Engaged Learners
MARILOU HYSON

Powerful Children
ANN LEWIN-BENHAM

Supervision in Early Childhood Education, 3rd Ed.
JOSEPH J. CARUSO WITH M. TEMPLE FAWCETT

Guiding Children's Behavior
EILEEN S. FLICKER & JANET ANDRON HOFFMAN

The War Play Dilemma, 2nd Ed.
DIANE E. LEVIN & NANCY CARLSSON-PAIGE

Playing to Get Smart
ELIZABETH JONES & RENATTA M. COOPER

The Emotional Development of Young Children, 2nd Ed.
MARILOU HYSON

Young Children Continue to Reinvent Arithmetic—2nd Grade, 2nd Ed.
CONSTANCE KAMII

Bringing Learning to Life
LOUISE BOYD CADWELL

Bringing Reggio Emilia Home
LOUISE BOYD CADWELL

Beyond Compliance in Early Childhood Education

Centering Disability, Freedom, and Belonging

Edited by Maggie Beneke and Hailey R. Love

Foreword by Tran Nguyen Templeton

Teachers College Press
Teachers College, Columbia University

Published by Teachers College Press,® 1234 Amsterdam Avenue, New York, NY 10027

Front cover illustration by Helen Stebakov / Shutterstock.

Library of Congress Cataloging-in-Publication Data is available at loc.gov

ISBN 978-0-8077-8662-8 (paper)
ISBN 978-0-8077-8663-5 (hardcover)
ISBN 978-0-8077-8284-2 (ebook)

Printed on acid-free paper
Manufactured in the United States of America

This book is dedicated to the young children whose resistance to compliance has taught us so much about disability, freedom, and belonging, and to those mentors whose shoulders we stand on. We are grateful.

Contents

Foreword

For 11 years, I lived in the space between resistance and compliance, first as a special education teacher and later as a school director. While I rejected conventional classroom structures and rigid behavioral expectations, I was still tethered to a deeper form of compliance—the relentless institutional pursuit of normalcy. Every intervention I implemented, every curriculum I differentiated, was aimed at one destination for the children in my care: the mainstream, inclusive classroom. Like many special educators, I understood my role as "supporting" disabled children to adapt to existing systems rather than questioning why those systems demanded such adaptation in the first place. While disability studies in education has long offered tools for examining such compliance-based approaches, many of us in special education remained distant from these perspectives. This edited volume illuminates the path from where many of us begin to where our field needs to go.

Early in my career, I picked up the phrase "worry about yourself" from my first mentor teacher. When children expressed concern for their peers, this teacher redirected them to focus on their own tasks, their own behaviors. I tried this approach briefly—along with other practices that reflect dominant behaviorist and developmental frameworks—but it felt increasingly discordant with my growing understanding that we should be learning to "worry about each other" and that classrooms should reflect our fundamental interdependence. In less than a decade, Maggie Beneke and Hailey Love have theorized and expanded this insight far beyond what I could have imagined. They articulate across their bodies of work and now as they gather diverse voices how seemingly innocuous practices (like a simple phrase) reinforce capitalist, colonial, white supremacist systems of compliance and isolation.

As I see it, this volume embodies multiple liberatory possibilities. The chapters amplify those often relegated to the margins in early childhood special education: disabled children themselves, multilingual/multidialectical families, Indigenous familial voices and stories, educators reimagining practice. The voices of family members, elders, children, preservice teachers, special education teachers, and researchers expose and challenge how developmental frameworks and standardization in early childhood have historically and contemporaneously served to label, sort, exclude, and erase. Yet what makes this collection powerful is not only who speaks but how they speak. The authors present their commitments through art, images, narrative, dialogue, pedagogical documentation, and other forms that challenge traditional academic conventions—reflecting Beneke and Love's commitments to dismantling not just what counts as normal but also what counts as knowledge in early childhood education. The chapters in this text show us what becomes possible when we embrace disability justice and center wholeness, interdependence, and the relational pedagogies of those most impacted by the restrictive carceral systems dominating the field.

After reading this edited collection, I walked into my early childhood special education assessment course the next day and reimagined how to teach these processes that the students anxiously sought to understand. Instead of positioning assessment as a tool for measuring children against normative standards, we explored how each step could honor different ways of being and knowing. How might assessment practices center the relational pedagogies that families and communities already engage in? In feedback to students' reports, I gently nudged preservice teachers to document children's capacities without defaulting to deficit-based comparisons of age-based stages. What would it mean to document children's capacities through recognizing their wholeness rather than their proximity to developmental norms? This immediate shift in my teaching practice exemplifies what Beneke, Love, and the contributors to this volume offer: More than a critique of existing systems, they create pathways for "imagining otherwise," showing us how to move beyond that space between resistance and compliance toward something far more liberatory.

—Tran Nguyen Templeton
Assistant Professor of Early Childhood
Faculty Co-Director of the Rita Gold Early Childhood Center
Teachers College, Columbia University

A Letter to the Reader

December 21, 2023

Dear Reader,

We write to you from unceded Coast Salish and Ho-Chunk homelands (territories in Washington and Wisconsin states, respectively), on the heels of a mass-disabling pandemic that has brought so much loss and pain. Amid uprisings for decolonial and racial justice. Amid climate crisis and genocide. First and foremost, dear reader, we hope you are okay.

As we write on this darkest day of the year, we see young children playing outside, mesmerized by the winter frost crystallizing on glittery grass. We honor these Coast Salish and Ho-Chunk homelands with gratitude, knowing young children's bodyminds[1] are not separate from their environments, knowing that most Indigenous languages do not have a word for disability that carries the deficit connotation perpetuated by the Western world (Krawek, 2022).

We share this book with you as two scholars and former early childhood teachers whose scholarship has long centered on disability[2] and young children. Maggie is a white woman who was labeled with a disability as a young child. She experienced special education intervention as lessons in conformity and knows that her whiteness protected her from being further pathologized. As an early educator she wrestled with her own complicity in reinforcing early learning standards that perpetuate a culture of compliance. Hailey is a Black, nondisabled woman. Her schooling experiences were characterized by adherence to compliance as a protective measure. Yet as an early educator, she witnessed the limits of this strategy as Black, Indigenous, Latine, Asian, and/or Pacific Islander children with disabilities were ostensibly included into general education settings while being further labeled, denied affirming learning opportunities, and marginalized by racism, ableism, and classism. These experiences and social locations inform our efforts to resist ableism in our work and lives.

Here, *ableism* refers to the "system of assigning value to people's bodies and minds based on societally constructed ideas of normality, productivity, desirability, intelligence, excellence, and fitness" (Lewis, 2022). In our previous work, we have written about ways ableism intersects with myriad oppressions (e.g., racism, cisheteropatriarchy, linguicism, xenophobia) to uphold compliance in early childhood (Beneke & Love, 2022; Love & Beneke, 2021). Indeed, models of "inclusion" often require young children with disabilities, their families, and their teachers to conform to and comply with ableist notions of normalcy (e.g., expectations for typical development, norms for family engagement, curricular standards) (Ferri & Bacon, 2011). As a result, even in so-called inclusive settings, young children with disability labels experience limited freedom (Baglieri et al., 2011). That is, children's and their family's agency is systematically and institutionally limited as their abilities are differentially ranked, categorized, and pathologized (Lewis, 2022; Pérez et al., 2016). What might it mean for young children with disabilities to experience freedom and belonging from their earliest moments in school?

As we ask this question, we feel societal commitments to compliance with normalcy deepening. Narratives widely circulate around children's pandemic learning loss (e.g., NY Times Editorial Board, 2023) alongside pressures to increase interventionist approaches (e.g., Fuchs et al., 2023). We see these narratives manifesting in our work with families, in our research in classrooms, and in our coursework with teacher candidates. For example, preschool teachers with whom we collaborate feel pressured to spend the majority of their days teaching academic skills in the name of kindergarten "readiness." To achieve such a feat with groups of wiggly 3-, 4-, and 5-year-olds, teachers increasingly engage in top-down classroom management techniques, labeling children as "unready," "at risk," or having a disability. Even as teacher candidates' commitments to educational justice sharpen through their coursework, they feel constrained to deviate from curricular scripts and standards. Further, racialized families we work with are making difficult decisions about whether to homeschool their children as a form of protection.

We recognize how compliance in schools has long constricted children's freedom and is indicative of the ways ableist and racist notions of normalcy are maintained. And yet we also are motivated and bolstered by children's, families', and university students' resistance. For instance, in response to discourses about "learning loss," families are reminding school administrators of the valuable learning that takes place outside of school walls (e.g., McKinney de Royston & Vossoughi, 2021). Teacher candidates and graduate students are protesting unjust policies locally and nationally. And multiply marginalized young children continue to express themselves as whole beings, enact their cultural and linguistic identities, and boldly play.

We believe that to cultivate freedom and belonging in early childhood, the field must center disability and face the ways ableism operates. By questioning norms, refusing compliance, and elevating the perspectives of multiply marginalized children with disabilities and their families, we can create expansive alternatives to standardization. That is what this book is about.

FOCUS AND ORGANIZATION OF THE TEXT

This edited volume offers critical perspectives on disability, drawing from disability studies in education, disability critical race theory, and disability justice movement work, among others. Each contributing chapter considers how such critical perspectives can inform work with children with disabilities, their families, and teachers in early childhood contexts, moving beyond compliance and cultivating freedom (Hayes, 2023; Pejcha & Wang, 2021). Across this book, we seek to counteract understandings of the child rooted in white, nondisabled ways of knowing and being. Chapter authors

- make visible the history and contexts of ableism in early childhood;
- affirm and support positive disability identity in early childhood;
- highlight interdependence and relationships of support with and between children in early care settings;
- recognize children's varied social–emotional expressions as legitimate;
- cast light on children's expansive, multilingual, and multimodal meaning-making in the context of standardized academic goals;
- honor marginalized families' priorities, engagement strategies, and meaningful resistance; and
- integrate Indigenous, Black feminist, and/or disability justice perspectives in teacher education.

Moreover, the text aims to resist compliance with normative structures, processes, and genres of academic writing that narrowly construct "what counts" as knowledge. For example, throughout, we encouraged authors to integrate creative elements within their writing, pushing back against restrictive forms of presenting data.

The chapters in this volume present conceptual and practical innovations in teaching and learning that center disability across a variety of early learning contexts (e.g., Head Start, community-based centers, public classrooms, home visiting), disability labels, and geographic locations (e.g., United States, Brazil, Australia). Across the chapters, you may see variation in the use of language. As editors, we deferred to and honored authors' choices regarding the naming of disability identity (e.g., Autistic child) and racial groups (e.g., Latina mothers, Children of Color). As we organized this volume, we sought to resist categorical approaches to disability that often essentialize young children's ways of being. Instead, we structured the book according to the primary types of contributions each chapter makes in an additional effort to shift the field beyond compliance with normalcy. Together, the four sections of the book offer the interweaving of research, theory, and practice necessary to more fully understand relationships between ableism and compliance in early childhood settings, and to imagine beyond such framings moving forward.

As a collective of editors and authors, we raise our voices together. In doing so, we articulate how refusing compliance with dominant notions of normalcy in early childhood contexts can create space for young children with disabilities to be their fullest selves, and to experience freedom and belonging on their own terms.

OVERVIEW OF THE BOOK

Our collection opens with a section titled "Cultivating Relationships With and Between Young Children," wherein authors showcase how ableism operates in the construction of relationships in early childhood, as well as how teachers and young children in their classrooms might imagine beyond such ways of relating to one another. April Coloma Boyce and Malcom L. King begin with a historical account, tracing reverberations of eugenics-era ideologies in present-day early childhood reform efforts. Next, M. Nickie Coomer, Teukie Martin, William Proffitt, and Colleen Campbell consider how young children labeled with "emotional difficulties" and their caregivers narrate their early learning experiences. Bárbara Baptista de Oliveira and Ana Luisa Gediel end this section by presenting a case study of a Black, Deaf, and Autistic child in Brazil, highlighting the child's "escape routes" as resistance to discipline, body control, and the pursuit of standardization.

In the second section, "Enacting Pedagogical Resistance in Early Learning Contexts," authors describe how teachers, teacher educators, and early childhood programs might pedagogically resist ableism. Devanshi Unadkat and Caroline Cuenca open this section by describing how they resisted standardized literacy approaches and supported a neurodiverse child, Kit, to position himself as "creative" and belonging in the classroom. Next, Kathryn M. Meyer, Rosie Tuffour-Mercedat, Elizabeth A. Barcay, Brianna Doherty, A.R.Shearer, and Jasmin Stoffer discuss ways of resisting the pervasive erasure of disability identity and history in early childhood curricula. Ame Christiansen concludes this section by sharing pedagogical narration within an Australian nature-based preschool, making visible how children with disabilities engage in relational ways of knowing and being.

The third section, "Prioritizing Families' Perspectives and Stories," offers theoretical and practical contributions that strengthen current conceptions of partnerships with families of young children with disabilities. Christine L. Hancock and Chelsea W. Morgan open this section by presenting discursive strategies that families of infants and toddlers use to enact resistance during decision-making with Early Head Start home visitors. Then Jie Y. Park highlights how Latina mothers created a pedagogy of relationality and interdependence for their young children with disabilities as they navigated remote education during the COVID-19 pandemic. Rae L. Begaye-Tewa, Elizabeth A. Ruiz, and Nicole S. Begay conclude the section with a conceptual framework rooted in Indigenous storywork and knowledges, elevating families' perspectives about inclusive early childhood education.

In the fourth and final section, "Engaging in Critical Praxis in Educator Preparation," authors describe how faculty working in early childhood preparation programs might sustain commitments to centering disability, freedom, and belonging. We (Maggie Beneke and Hailey Love) begin with a dialogue, using principles from disability justice and abolition to expose our own compliance with early childhood pedagogical "scripts," and imagine beyond these scripts in our roles as teacher educators. Lilly Padía and Christasany R. Turner then discuss how early childhood teacher education praxis might be rooted in Black feminist thought and disability critical race theory. María Rosa Brea-Spahn and Xigrid Soto-Boykin provide a snapshot of their critical praxis, offering illustrative examples from their work in speech-language pathology to critically question what counts as "good" languaging. The book concludes with a discussion reflecting our (Hailey Love and Maggie Beneke) thoughts about ways of applying ideas presented within the book.

Reader, we offer our deep thanks to you as you read this work, knowing we are all holding so much and caring for so many. As editors, we feel fortunate to collaborate with such an incredible group of contributing authors, research partners, students, and colleagues. It is our hope that in reading this book, you can find ways to create spaces where young children with disabilities might experience freedom and belonging in your own realm of influence, and to sustain the work moving forward.

Take care,
Maggie and Hailey

Part I

CULTIVATING RELATIONSHIPS WITH AND BETWEEN YOUNG CHILDREN

This section sets the stage for the entire collection of chapters, providing an overview of the foundational ways ableism operates in perceptions of the child and the construction of relationships in early childhood. It also offers possibilities for how teachers and young children might imagine beyond such ways of relating to one another.

In Chapter 1, Coloma Boyce and King first critique how educational reforms aimed at addressing young children's social–emotional learning carry eugenic ideologies forward. They expose links between the eugenics era and compliance with current early educational practices that allow ableism to thrive. In Chapter 2, Coomer, Martin, Proffitt, and Campbell present the ways three young children labeled with "emotional difficulties" and their mothers narrate their experiences in classrooms. These narratives highlight social constructions of "good" vs. "bad" kids from children's first moments in school. Baptista de Oliveira and Gediel conclude this section in Chapter 3 by offering alternate conceptions of inclusion and belonging, grounded in understandings of children's agency, through a case study of a young Brazilian child (Sofia). They highlight how Sofia—who is Black, Deaf, and Autistic—strategically resists physical inclusion into spaces of discipline, body control, and academic standardization.

Each of these chapters invites readers to question existing norms, practices, and educational models, particularly from the perspectives of young children with disabilities themselves. In doing so, they urge us to move beyond compliance with the status quo and imagine new ways of relating to children, ones that reject prescriptive educational approaches and honor each child's gifts and insights.

Under the Circle Time Rug

The Eugenic Roots of Early Childhood Education

April Coloma Boyce and Malcom L. King

under the circle time rug

twisted rotten roots
concealed beneath the rug
prop walls that stand but crumble
tear out the roots so tightly clung
and watch the tower tumble

Finger-painted artwork strung across the room, "work hard" and "be kind" posters plastered on walls, children sitting crisscross applesauce on colorful squares, teachers smiling at well-behaved children—these visions of preschool are seemingly innocent but indicate principles of early childhood education rooted in a troubling past, often swept under the circle time rug. The theories, policies, and practices informing the field (e.g., developmental milestones, early intervention, behavior management) have deep roots in eugenics, and repercussions endure today despite decades of research calling for systemic changes toward equity and inclusion.

Racist and ableist underpinnings of eugenic logics manifest in educational disparities in the United States, where Black and Brown children are more often overrepresented in discipline outcomes compared to their total student enrollment in schools. For instance, according to the U.S. Department of Education Office of Civil Rights Data (2021), while accounting for only 9% of preschool enrollment, Black boys represented over 20% of preschool children receiving suspensions and expulsions during the 2020–2021 school year. In the same year, nearly 23% of preschool children with disabilities were served under the Individuals with Disabilities Education Act (IDEA) but were expelled at a rate 2.5 times higher than their representation in the total population (U.S. Department of Education Office of Civil Rights, 2021). To counteract these disparities, school leaders have responded with mandatory early educator training in "developmentally appropriate" approaches (Bredekamp & Copple, 1997;

Schwartz & McBride, 2021) and "evidence-based" practice (e.g., positive behavior intervention strategies and social—emotional curricula). However, these practices draw from research rooted in eugenic ideologies, often lack an intersectional framework, and fail to address the equity issues directly affecting Black and Brown children with and without disabilities (Baglieri et al., 2011; Ferri & Bacon, 2011; Newton et al., 2024).

In this chapter, we examine how the U.S. eugenics movement of the early 20th century has heavily influenced notions of normalcy in early childhood education, revealing the "cloak of benevolence" (Thorius, 2019) that maintains illusions of early childhood "best practices" as beneficial and necessary. The cloak—or in this case, the circle time rug—has concealed eugenic roots, allowing racism and ableism to proliferate and obstruct the field's potential transformation.

The medical model of disability remains dominant, positioning children with disabilities as problems to be cured or fixed. To counter this deficit model, we frame our critique of eugenic ideologies in early childhood education through the social model of disability (Oliver et al., 2012; Shakespeare, 2006), which instead discerns *educational barriers* as problems that contribute to the disablement of young children and must be fixed (see Figure 1.1).

While applying the social model can reframe deficit perspectives on disability, we recognize that experiences of disability can vary greatly based on gender, race, and other identities. Indeed, characteristics of "goodness" (Broderick & Leonardo, 2016) and "smartness" (Leonardo & Broderick, 2011) embedded within early childhood institutions are rooted in whiteness and ableism (Annamma et al. 2013a; Love & Beneke, 2021), leading to inequitable treatment of Black and Brown children with and without disabilities. We examine how worthiness has been co-constructed by racism and ableism and highlight eugenic ideologies that continue to harm multiply marginalized[1] young children (Artiles, 2009; Ferri & Connor, 2005).

Figure 1.1. The Medical Model of Disability vs. Social Model of Disability in Education

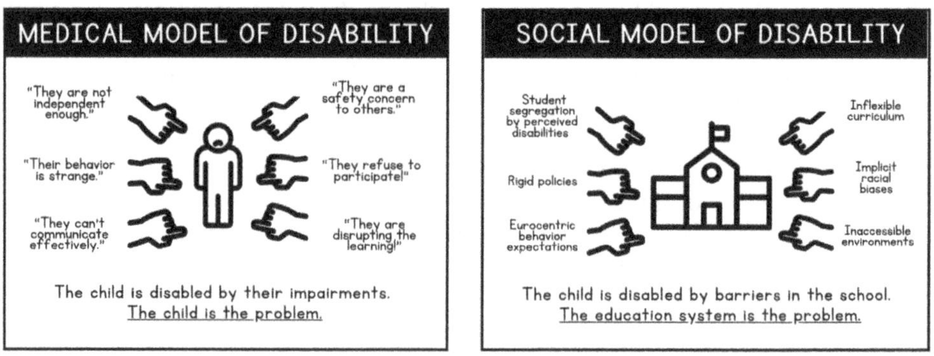

We also reflect on necessary paradigm shifts to move the field of early childhood beyond eugenic ideologies—beyond conformity, compliance, and false "inclusion"—and toward more liberatory ways of teaching and learning. We use language and images[2] to illustrate relationships between eugenics and early childhood across historical and contemporary contexts. Readers may find some examples offensive or triggering. However, we believe bearing witness to this harm and reckoning with the past are necessary to continue our collective work of building a liberated future.

THE TANGLED ORIGINS OF NORMALCY

> One cannot look at the history of U.S. slavery, the stealing of Indigenous lands, and U.S. imperialism without seeing the way that white supremacy leverages ableism to create a subjugated "other" that is deemed less worthy/abled/smart/capable. A single-issue civil rights framework is not enough to comprehend the full extent of ableism and how it operates in society. We cannot comprehend ableism without grasping its interrelations with heteropatriarchy, white supremacy, colonialism and capitalism. (Sins Invalid, 2019, p. 14)

From the early 20th century until the 1940s, eugenics was a social theory that gained popularity through U.S. scientific and government backing. Francis Galton—cousin of Charles Darwin—coined the term "eugenics" in the 1880s and spread the idea that the human population could be improved by controlling heredity (Bulmer, 2003). Coinciding with the Industrial Revolution, the theory held that people considered "fit," "intelligent," and "productive" were deemed "normal" and were convinced it was their moral obligation to reproduce as a means of enhancing the human species. Individuals considered "unfit," "unintelligent," and "unproductive" were discouraged from reproducing and were forcibly sterilized (Paul, 1995). Eugenic messages spread through public announcements and community events. An American Eugenics Society exhibit poster at a 1926 Philadelphia public fair (Figure 1.2) reads, "Some people are born to be a burden on the rest. . . . Every 16 seconds $100 of your money goes for the care of persons with bad heredity such as the insane, feeble-minded, criminals and other defectives."

At the time, eugenics was widely touted as a progressive science. It carried racist and ableist messages about undesirable individuals as financial and social burdens on society. Physician and defender of slavery John Van Evrie stated, "Since they belonged to a race inferior by nature, all blacks were necessarily inferior to (nearly) all whites. . . . Only disability might lower a white person in the scale of life to the level of a being of a marked race" (Baynton, 2013, p. 38). Similarly, immigrants who appeared, spoke, or behaved out of alignment with white cultural norms were perceived as inferior to their white counterparts. Such racist and ableist propaganda engrained societal beliefs that Black and Brown individuals with and without disabilities were "feebleminded." Based on

Figure 1.2. Photograph of Eugenics Exhibit at Public Fair, 1926

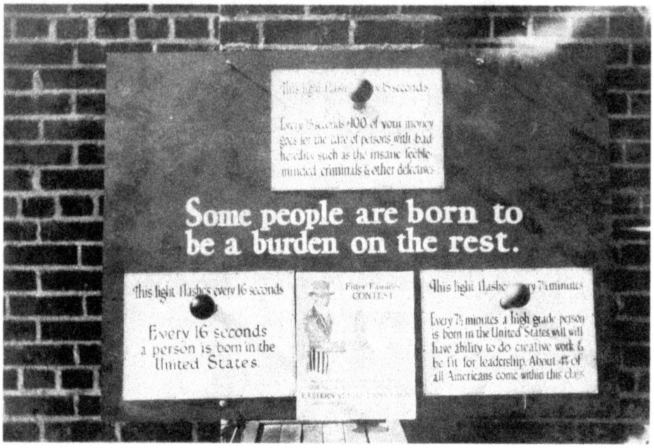

Note. From American Philosophical Society / Science Photo Library, Philadelphia, PA. https://www.sciencephoto.com/contributor/aps/

assumptions of racialized people's abilities, dehumanization through pathologization and institutionalization proliferated. Eugenic theories have since been discredited, but their legacy has left troublesome stains.

Eugenic Connections in Early Childhood Education, Past to Present

Concealed through claims of "improving the human race," eugenics was—and still is—about dominant groups controlling individuals and determining who deserves access to freedom (Paul, 1995). There is a misconception that eugenics is a shameful blip of the past, but deficit ideologies regarding race and disability persist today. In early childhood, these ideologies are masked under policies and practices designed to shape young children's bodies, minds, and behaviors. Here, we explicate how eugenic ideologies persist.

Black and Brown children continue to be marginalized and excluded in schools based on assumptions of "smartness" and "goodness." These ideologies can be traced back to the early 20th century, a time when white Americans sought to maintain property and power in response to an influx of working immigrants and African Americans, which intensified concerns about resource scarcity (Smith, 2023). In response, eugenic practices and policies, grounded in beliefs about heredity and disability, were developed by physicians and government officials. One notable example is the Intelligence Quotient (IQ) test developed by Alfred Binet (Figure 1.3).

The IQ test, developed to quantify intelligence, was used to categorize groups deemed unfit by those in power. Black and Brown individuals were

Figure 1.3. Schedule and Apparatus for Binet Test, 1921

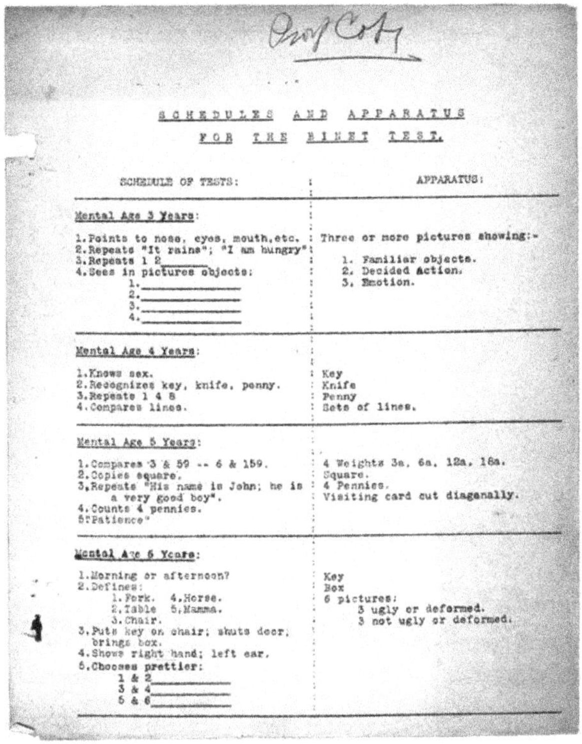

SCHEDULES AND APPARATUS
FOR THE BINET TEST.

SCHEDULE OF TESTS:	APPARATUS:
Mental Age 3 Years:	
1. Points to nose, eyes, mouth, etc. 2. Repeats "It rains"; "I am hungry" 3. Repeats 1 2 ______ 4. Sees in pictures objects: 1. ______ 2. ______ 3. ______ 4. ______	Three or more pictures showing:- 1. Familiar objects. 2. Decided Action. 3. Emotion.
Mental Age 4 Years:	
1. Knows sex. 2. Recognizes key, knife, penny. 3. Repeats 1 4 8 4. Compares lines.	Key Knife Penny Sets of lines.
Mental Age 5 Years:	
1. Compares 3 & 59 -- 6 & 159. 2. Copies square. 3. Repeats "His name is John; he is a very good boy". 4. Counts 4 pennies. 5. "Patience"	4 Weights 3a, 6a, 12a, 18a. Square. 4 Pennies. Visiting card cut diagonally.
Mental Age 6 Years:	
1. Morning or afternoon? 2. Defines: 1. Fork. 4. Horse. 2. Table 5. Mamma. 3. Chair. 3. Puts key on chair; shuts door; brings box. 4. Shows right hand; left ear. 5. Chooses prettier: 1 & 2 ______ 3 & 4 ______ 5 & 6 ______	Key Box 6 pictures: 3 ugly or deformed. 3 not ugly or deformed.

Note. From the Harry H. Laughlin Papers, Truman State University, papers C-2–4, 8. http://www.eugenicsarchive.org/html/eugenics/static/images/1102.html

targeted by these assessments and pathologized as "morons," "imbeciles," and "idiots," justifying their institutionalization in asylums or schools for the "feeble-minded" (Smith, 2023). A 1915 Virginia report (Johnstone, 1915) illustrated five stages of mental development (see Figure 1.4), with eugenicists linking feeble-mindedness to limited productivity and recommending segregation and sterilization.

Over time, policy definitions of feeblemindedness evolved to "mental retardation" in the 1950s to "intellectual/developmental disabilities" in 2010. Physicians and politicians, historically nondisabled white men, wielded significant power to label and oppress racialized and disabled people under the guise of more acceptable or scientific terminology, preserving dominant group privilege.

Historical practices of labeling, categorization, and segregation persist today, affecting how Black and Brown young children, in particular, are surveilled and assessed by physicians and early educators. We can see this in standardized

Figure 1.4. Steps in Mental Development

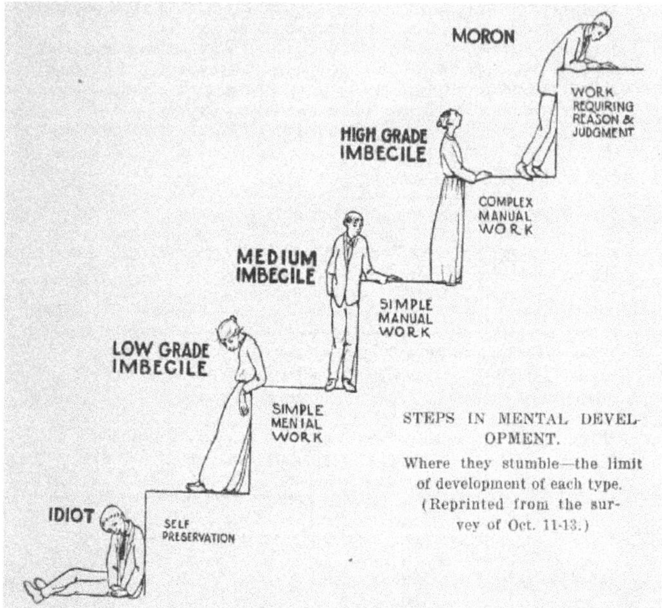

Note. "Steps in Mental Development" from the article titled "Exhibit of Work and Educational Campaign for Juvenile Mental Defectives," published in the October 11, 1913, issue of *The Survey*. From American Philosophical Society/Science Photo Library, Philadelphia, PA.

screening tests that evaluate children based on medicalized developmental milestones (Hagan et al. 2017). These milestones, assessed using tools that echo eugenic practices (Figure 1.3), categorize children by perceived intellectual and physical fitness, framing development as a stepwise progression toward increasing ability and productivity (Burman, 2015)—see Figure 1.5.

Further, through their "Act Early" program, the U.S. Centers for Disease Control and Prevention (CDC) urges families to continuously monitor their children's development using a tracking app and to seek additional screening and evaluation for children whose development seems atypical (CDC, 2024). This is just one way that Black and Brown young children are subject to excessive surveillance based on their perceived abilities.

Better Babies Contests and Intervention

The documented history of *Better Babies contests* in the early 20th century, founded on ideologies of "eugenic sterilization and race betterment" (Stern, 2002), explicates a racist and ableist history informed by "promoting ideas that only white babies could achieve perfection and symbolize the state" (p. 748).

Figure 1.5. Developmental Milestones in Early Childhood

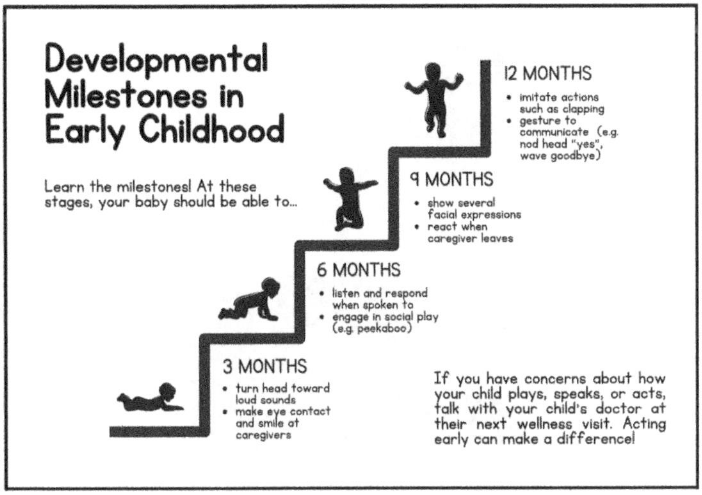

Note. An example of a guide for tracking young children's developmental milestones modeled after a similar resource developed in 2022 and offered to caregivers from a U.S. federal agency for health services.

Held annually from 1920 to 1932, Better Babies contests became prevalent at state fairs, touted as "a school of education in eugenics" (Dorey, 1999).

Addressing white mothers' concerns about their children's health, these contests systematically excluded disabled and non-white children, further reinforcing patterns of segregation and pathologizing diverse developmental trajectories. Because the contests took place at fairs, they were justified as professional medical endeavors and served as conduits for pediatric physicians and child psychologists to disseminate knowledge to parents from predominantly agricultural communities. Medical professionals used scorecards modeled after farm animal assessments to examine and evaluate infants' physical health, body proportions, and mental health. The contests "set the best standards of health before the parents that they may compare these with the actual condition of their child" (Stern, 2002, p. 749). Images of the "better baby" were embedded in advertising campaigns, influencing and rewarding prevailing notions of normality (see Figure 1.6).

While the Better Babies contests explicitly excluded Black and Brown families as well as disabled children, educational resources and assessment tools like the one depicted in Figure 1.5 subtly perpetuate white normative behaviors and expectations. By disregarding cultural diversity and socioeconomic factors (e.g., norms regarding eye contact), these resources position certain developmental milestones as the universal norm—ones generally more desired and achievable by non-disabled middle-class white children and their families. Like the

Figure 1.6. Better Babies Contestant, with Trophy, Louisiana State Fair, Shreveport

Note: From University of Tennessee, Knoxville, Mrs. Frank deGarmo Papers, MS #1879 (Circa 1910). http://www.eugenicsarchive.org/html/eugenics/static/images/2250.html

Better Babies contests, they also place responsibility for subsequently "tracking" children's development and seeking intervention on families (Erevelles, 2011).

Developmental milestones also shape early childhood environments in much of the Western world. They constitute benchmarks emphasized in caregiver resources (Figure 1.5), early learning standards, and teacher education programs, dictating understandings of "typical" behavior and how to label and treat children who deviate (Clark et al., 2022). Moreover, recommendations from local and national departments (e.g., U.S. Department of Education) and associations (e.g., American Academy of Pediatrics) emphasize closely monitoring developmental milestones before children enter kindergarten to identify and prevent disability (Lipkin & Macias, 2020). Thus, preschool teachers and caregivers are particularly implicated in flagging children who do not meet developmental milestones and socializing them to conform to "age-appropriate" norms through interventions (Timmer et al., 2022). This process is reminiscent of eugenic correctional efforts, ranking some individuals as valuable and others as defective.

Seminal educational research and theories often disseminated in early childhood teacher education programs are steeped in deficit perspectives, suggesting that academic achievement requires children's compliance (Burman, 2015). Biased beliefs about Black and Brown children's noncompliance lead to deficit-based practices of hyper-surveillance and hyper-labeling (e.g., Annamma & Morrison, 2018; Beneke et al., 2024), maintaining assumptions that multiply marginalized children need interventions. Subsequently, Black and Brown children are disproportionately labeled with conditions like "emotional and behavioral disorder" or "oppositional defiant disorder" and referred to interventionists for merely exhibiting behaviors that deviate from white, middle-class norms (Fadus et al., 2020). The opinions of educators and medical professionals shape and inform early childhood policies and practices, justifying assessments and interventions despite the harmful assumptions they carry.

The Cloak of Inclusion

Eugenic ideologies continue to prevail within early education in inconspicuous ways, maintaining objectives to categorize, pathologize, and criminalize children deemed unworthy. One such process is the ongoing segregation of Black and Brown children through special education placement. In 1975, the Education for All Handicapped Children Act (later renamed the Individuals with Disabilities Education Act) required public schools to provide free and appropriate public education to children with disabilities. Although *Brown v. Board* prohibited schools from segregating children by race and was used to establish legal rights for disabled children, separating Black and Brown children from their white peers because of perceived disabilities was justified under the cloak of including children with disabilities in physical school buildings (Thorius, 2019).

Of course, Black and Brown children were—and still are—pathologized and placed into segregated special education classrooms at much higher rates than their white peers (Artiles et al., 2010a; Cooc, 2022; Grindal et al., 2019). Conformity is reinforced when Black and Brown children disproportionately labeled with disabilities have to "earn" inclusion rather than it being assumed that they belong (Beneke et al., 2024; Meiners, 2017).

Early educational leaders have attempted to implement "inclusionary practices" (e.g., schoolwide positive behavior strategies, social–emotional curriculum) to include more children with disabilities in the general education setting, yet these programs still operate under the medical model of disability. Such approaches imply that Black and Brown children can be included *if* they adhere to white, nondisabled norms (Artiles et al., 2006; Howe et al., 2018). Rather than honor children's diverse experiences and strengths, schools continue to demand compliance and assimilation, maintaining hegemonic assumptions that children, particularly Black and Brown children, are "problems" that require intervention services to meet restrictive milestones and standards (Freidus, 2020).

Eugenic Tactics to Measure Achievement and Assign Labels

Eugenic ideologies persist through certain approaches intended to support inclusion (e.g., classroom management strategies), which often justify the disability labeling and exclusion of Black and Brown children based on perceived deviance (Baynton, 2013). Moreover, in an education system that devalues children based on Eurocentric measurements of normalcy (Annamma et al., 2013b), a logic grounded in eugenics, even those who do not qualify under a disability category still face ableism (Lewis, 2022). Schooling ideologically constructs some children as "smart" and others as "not-so-smart," entitling the former to cultural capital (e.g., valued learning opportunities) and limiting opportunities for the latter based on perceived intellectual inferiority (Leonardo & Broderick, 2011).

Notions of "smartness" are often conflated with "goodness," where being good is considered a prerequisite for being smart (Broderick & Leonardo, 2016). Consequently, racialized concepts of goodness disproportionately marginalize Black and Brown children, making them more likely to be labeled with a disability and excluded from privileges afforded to their nondisabled white peers. Standards of goodness and smartness are reinforced by frameworks like Social Emotional Learning (SEL) and Positive Behavioral Interventions and Supports (PBIS), which recycle deficit perspectives akin to eugenic approaches (e.g., differential valuing of white and normative abilities), pathologizing multiply marginalized children who resist compliance-focused norms (Kaler-Jones, 2020; Kim & Venet, 2023).

A core component of SEL is character education, in which topics such as respect, honesty, and responsibility are introduced to encourage prosocial development. One example, represented in Figure 1.7, is "whole body listening" (Truesdale, 1990). This strategy reminds children to be "good listeners" by

Figure 1.7. Whole Body Listening

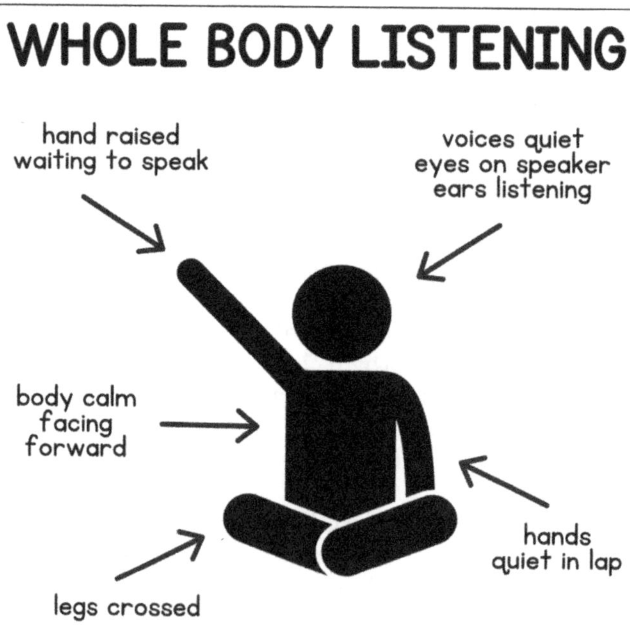

Note. Image of "whole body listening," a common term and visual aid found in early childhood classrooms to remind children of group time expectations.

sitting quietly, waiting for permission to speak, and making eye contact. When compliance with Eurocentric norms of goodness is rewarded, Black and Brown children and children with disabilities learn to mask nonnormative behaviors, as failure to do so leads to punishment or exclusion (e.g., Clark et al., 2022; Shalaby, 2021). As Dena Simmons[3] once stated, "SEL is white supremacy with a hug" (2019).

Classroom environments perpetuate expectations about behavior and conformity, with early educators positioned as key enforcers of these norms. Visual aids (e.g., Figure 1.7) reinforce eugenic ideologies by depicting behaviors associated with a "good" child, akin to the marketing of the "better baby" (Stern, 2002). Classroom management tactics, used to address negative behaviors (e.g., positive praise, sticker charts, group rewards), aim to assimilate Black and Brown children toward dominant ideas of normalcy (Casey et al., 2013; Shalaby, 2021). Even subtle gestures of power (Jackson, 1990) such as a teacher's facial expressions and tone of voice implicitly place value on "appropriate" behaviors. Additionally, evaluative processes for educators (e.g., required assessments, schoolwide PBIS expectations, and "zero tolerance" policies) encourage adherence to standards of normalcy. Consequently, even well-intentioned educators may pathologize Black and Brown children who resist these expectations, perpetuating eugenic objectives of discarding those deemed unfit. In sum, practices of labeling and exclusion—akin to eugenic-era propaganda and Better Babies contests—leverage ableism to control and oppress Black and Brown children.

PULLING BACK THE RUG TO UPROOT EUGENIC IDEOLOGIES

The eugenics movement of the early 20th century is a disturbing reminder of what happens when society fails to question and challenge research, policies, and practices brought about by dominant groups. Figure 1.8 depicts "the Eugenics Tree," an image designed for a brochure in the Second International Eugenics Congress of 1921. The caption states, "Like a tree eugenics draws its materials from many sources and organizes them into an harmonious entity." Eugenicists encouraged professionals across multiple disciplines, from medicine to education, to contribute, which is why the roots of eugenics remain stubbornly intact. The historical examples in this chapter illustrate just a snippet of the oppressions young Black and Brown children face the moment they enter the school system. Policymakers and early educators can continue to cover up racialized discipline and exclusion with new mandates and performative language, but pull back the rug and find that the roots of eugenics have created a fracture in the foundation—and the roots run deep.

Judy Dow, an Indigenous and French-Canadian activist, artist, and scholar, created the Witness Tree (Figure 1.9) in 2021 to counter the Eugenics Tree and conceptualize the "collective creation of an equitable and healthy world for all."

Figure 1.8. Eugenics Tree

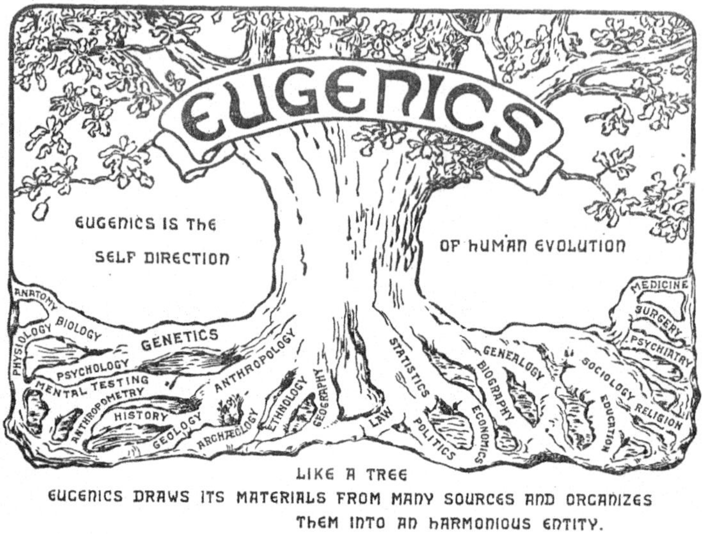

Note. "Eugenics Tree." From Harry H. Laughlin, The Second International Exhibition of Eugenics, held September 22 to October 22, 1921, in connection with the Second International Congress of Eugenics in the American Museum of Natural History, New York (Baltimore, MD: Williams & Wilkins Company, 1923), p. 15.

Figure 1.9. The Witness Tree

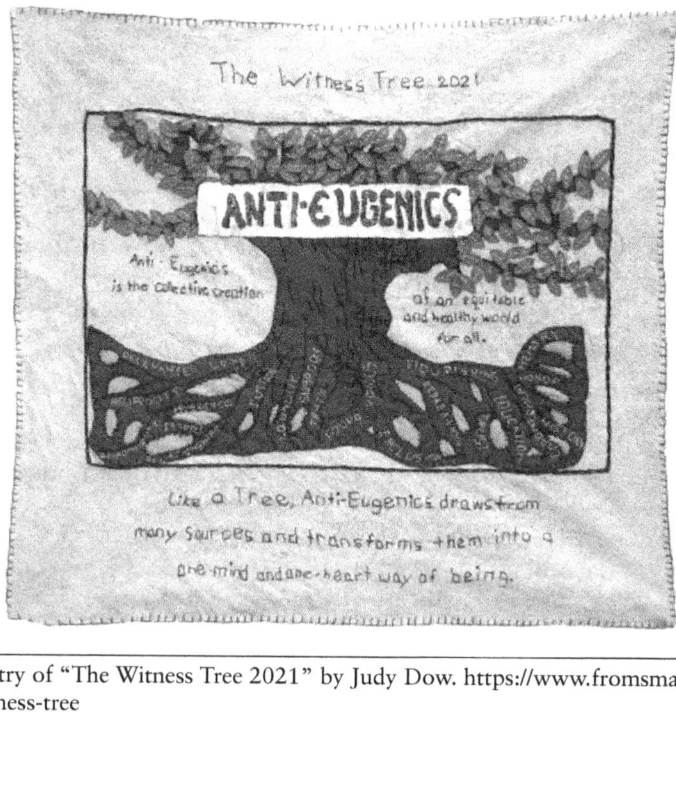

Note. Tapestry of "The Witness Tree 2021" by Judy Dow. https://www.fromsmallbeginnings.org/the-witness-tree

The tapestry reads, "Like a tree, anti-eugenics draws from many sources and transforms them into a one-mind and one-heart way of being."

Reflecting on her work, Dow explained:

> I have witnessed much after living for over 6 decades with the historical traumas caused by the beliefs named in the Founders' tree. A witness tree in nature is a tree that has lived a long life and witnessed many occurrences like border line changes, hurricanes, flooding and other traumatic events. They are the silent sentinels that document the many memorable episodes in life, both good and bad. The roots of the Witness tree reflect what needs to be in place to fight Eugenics for one hundred years to come. (Dow, 2021)

PLANTING SEEDS OF LIBERATION

Bearing witness to and grappling with the U.S. history of eugenics offers early educators an opportunity to critically reflect on policies, practices, and interactions with multiply marginalized young children. As early educators, we must reimagine classrooms beyond prescriptive curriculum, rigid standards, and performative posters—shifting away from eugenic logics toward more liberatory approaches for supporting multiply marginalized children in early childhood programs (see Figure 1.10).

These recommendations may seem daunting, as early educators are also subject to systems of control. But all it takes to contribute to the work of disrupting and challenging oppressive systems is a seed. Our small, everyday efforts fill the cracks in educational systems, allowing something new to emerge.

To cultivate liberation in early childhood, we can look to the children. Often disregarded for their presumed lack of knowledge, children's "natural processes are stifled by our narrowed understandings of the world" (Yoon & Templeton, 2019, p. 59). Noticing young children's motivation to seek connection, their innate curiosity and empathy for others, and their gift of imagination to envision alternative realities can support the revitalization of joy, hope, and purpose in a seemingly crumbling world. When we resist the dehumanizing processes in education by dreaming of classroom communities rooted in care, collective access, and solidarity with young children, we can begin to pull up violent eugenic ideologies and make space for something new to take root.

little heirlooms

seeds of liberation
tilled and buried no more
let their roots take hold
and from the rubble
watch a new world unfold

Figure 1.10. From Eugenic Logics Toward Liberatory Approaches

Supporting Multiply Marginalized Children in Early Childhood Programs		
Children with disabilities or perceived disabilities are pathologized and labeled.	→	Barriers are identified within school environments, and solutions are developed *with* children and families.
Decisions regarding interventions and children's "best interests" are determined solely by professionals.	→	Children and families' input is centered in the decision-making process.[4]
Multiply marginalized children are expected to conceal or suppress expressions or behaviors deemed "disruptive."	→	Conversations about disability and neurodiversity are ongoing for all children in the classroom. Diverse forms of expression and behavior are legitimized.
Black and Brown children with and without disabilities are pulled out of the classroom to receive intervention services, placed in segregated classrooms, or excluded if they cannot adhere to class expectations.	→	Teaching is differentiated in the general education classroom with accommodations made available to all children to increase accessibility. Children's resistance to class norms is understood as communication and respected as a form of self-advocacy.
Reward and punishment systems enforce rules and norms. Competition, individualism, and independence are valued as indicators of children's success.	→	Classroom communities are fostered through cooperation, collectivism, and interdependence. Behavior is guided by connection rather than fear or competition. No child is considered disposable.
Multiply marginalized children can only participate in general education settings if they can conform.	→	Disability is welcomed and affirmed. Classroom environments and curricula are designed to meet the support needs of all bodies and minds.

CHAPTER 2

Social Constructions of "Good" vs. "Bad" Kids

Understanding Children's Emotions and Behaviors Through a Mad Studies Lens

M. Nickie Coomer, Teukie Martin, William Proffitt, and Colleen Campbell

Emotional experiences and expressions are political. For those deemed outside the bounds of white, middle-class norms of thinking and feeling, to honestly and agentically experience emotions can be dangerous, even deadly. In early childhood, the power embedded in emotional expression, however, is often denied to young children in the interest of preserving the presumed logic of the adults around them. That is, children are subject to the interpretation—and scrutiny—of adults, particularly when their emotional expression serves to challenge status quo power relations. Accordingly, educational processes for interpreting children's emotions and behavior often rely on sanist[1] and racist interpretations of what normative, rational behavior should look like (e.g., Meerai et al., 2016; Thomas & Glenny, 2000). Relatedly, naming and interpreting children's emotions and behavior also relies on the teacher's position of power. Thus, young children are subject to the ways adults around them understand and narrate their expressions to others.

In school, children are typically subjected to the interpretations of white women, who comprise much of the teaching force (e.g., Bryan, 2017). It may come as no surprise, then, that Black and Brown children are disproportionately assigned stigmatizing disability labels (Banks, 2017; Harry & Klingner, 2022), punitively disciplined for behavior that is subjectively interpreted (Skiba et al., 2002), and more harshly disciplined for the same behavior as their white counterparts (Freidus, 2020; Morris, 2016). Teachers often uphold white, middle-class social preferences through subtle invocation and performances of "white civility"—the colonial establishment of white, middle-class beliefs, values, and behaviors as the normative standard to which all else is compared (Coleman, 1996; Hoffman, 2009; Massey et al., 1975). Teachers' subjectivities and white civility impede children of Color and working-class families from understanding and enacting their emotions and behavior in genuine, authentic ways. When children are treated as though they do not belong based on their emotions and behavior, not only are they subject to discourses of abnormality, but their agency in meaning-making, participation, and relationship is compromised.

In this chapter, we describe a study in which we talked to three children identified as having "emotional difficulties" and their mothers. We center their schooling experiences and perspectives on behavior and emotion to disrupt dominant narratives about children labeled in this way.

FRAMEWORK: MAD STUDIES AND TESTIMONIAL JUSTICE

Our analysis draws on mad studies (Price, 2009) and testimonial justice (Fricker, 2007).

Mad Studies

Mad studies is a form of activist scholarship that attends to the lived experiences, cultural histories, and epistemologies of *madness* (e.g., Le François et al., 2013; Menzies et al., 2013; Reaume, 2006). We use the word *epistemologies* to refer to how theories of and about knowledge and knowledge itself can be produced by those who exist in nonmainstream spaces. We invoke the word madness to reclaim and challenge ideas traditionally used to describe mental illness or mental disability. In this way, madness signifies empowerment and resistance, subverting negative, stigmatizing connotations associated with emotional and behavioral difficulties and disorders. Furthermore, the term *mad* is a broad and inclusive one that recognizes a range of experiences that might otherwise be marginalized (LeFrançois et al., 2013; Price, 2009). Although we use mad in the spirit of surfacing power imbalances that deem some people irrational, we acknowledge that not everyone adopts this label—particularly those who have not had the opportunity to engage with madness in the academic sense.

Hermeneutical and Testimonial Justice

The resistant and disruptive commitments of mad studies are the entry point through which we build on notions of hermeneutical and testimonial justice (Fricker, 2007). *Hermeneutical injustice* refers to ways individuals and groups are denied access to necessary tools when making sense of their experiences and communicating them (e.g., when adults perceive the behavior of young children as "irrational," and those young children are not taken seriously in explaining, describing, or narrating their experience). This denial, enforced by dominant cultures and groups, leaves communities and individuals labeled as "nonnormative" with only harmful, deficit frames for making sense of their experiences and themselves. *Hermeneutical justice*, therefore, can be realized when nonnormative groups (in this case, young children labeled as having "emotional difficulties") have access to alternative language and concepts that affirm, rather than pathologize, their experience.

Testimonial justice occurs when another person is trusted as a reliable narrator of one's experiences, especially when one is unfairly discredited due to racism, ableism, and sanism. In an early childhood education setting, this looks like an adult understanding a child's experiences as authentic, fair, and "rational," and responding to that experience with authenticity and empathy. This requires that both adult and child have the space and opportunity to be taken seriously so that they can both experience the agency embedded in the mutual empowerment that comes with authentic—and often vulnerable—relationships (see Jordan, 2017 for a deeper explanation of these elements through relational-cultural theory).

We contend that children labeled as emotionally and behaviorally difficult in school experience hermeneutical injustice and should be afforded testimonial justice. Young children's agency is limited by teacher evaluation and decision-making. In traditional teacher–child relationships, presumption of competence, logic, and reason are often afforded to the adults and withheld from children. This maintains power imbalances that make children vulnerable to the harms of schooling through their teachers' actions, biased interpretations, and communications. A mad studies theoretical frame that centers the lived and narrated experiences of multiply marginalized young children and their caregivers offers a pathway toward testimonial justice.

The Coloniality of White Civility in Evaluating Children's Emotions and Behavior in School

Schools act as colonial spaces in several ways: through curriculum and pedagogy that marginalize the histories, cultures, and contributions of nondominant populations; authoritarian power dynamics among schools, families, teachers, and children; and the marginalization of children and families who exist outside norms. Knight (2019) articulated how assumptions of children's linear progression, from one developmental stage to another with independence as the pinnacle of growth, reflect colonial logics. Children who do not develop linearly or who do not conform to colonial imaginations of childhood are then labeled as "problem children" (Knight, 2019). In this conceptualization, "white civility" acts as a vice, maintaining social rules that dictate which emotions and behaviors are acceptable and which are problematic. The preferred manners and etiquette of a given cultural space (e.g., the school) become indicators of "good behavior" and "moral superiority" of a "good child," while ignoring power dynamics inherent in colonial relationships (e.g., Broderick & Leonardo, 2016).

Drawing on these understandings, we asked:

1. How do the parents of children with emotional/behavioral difficulties and the children themselves narrate their experiences with the classroom?
2. What do these narrations reveal about the relationship between child identity agency and the ways in which "good" and "bad" behaviors (and "good" and "bad" kids) are conceptualized in school?

METHODS

We interviewed three children (Andrew Johnson, Kody, and Michael) identified as having "emotional difficulties" and their mothers (Mary, Laura, and Heidi) about their experiences in school. Andrew Johnson and Michael attend public schools considered "urban" due to their geographic location in a western U.S. city, Andrew Johnson's school is predominantly white and middle class, while Michael's current school is predominantly comprised of Black and Latinx children from working-class backgrounds. Kody is homeschooled, but he revisited his experiences in a public charter school in a southern U.S. state. All names of participants have been changed. However, on hearing his name would be changed when describing this research, Andrew promptly replied, "I want to be Andrew Johnson." Thus, in the spirit of giving credit where credit is due, we note that Andrew Johnson chose his pseudonym.

Participants (see Table 2.1) volunteered for the research by answering a call for participants posted to several Facebook parenting groups. Each dyad (mother and child) received a digital $20 gift card for their participation. Kody noted it was the "easiest 20 bucks (I) ever made."

We centered children's responses, considering responses from their mothers as contextualization of their child's responses. Each child was interviewed first, followed by the mothers; mothers also often clarified or added detail to their child's response.

Table 2.1. Study Participants

Child's Name	Child's Age	Child's Race	Mother's Name	Mother's Race
Kody	7	White	Mary	White
Andrew Johnson	8	Black	Laura	Black
Michael	7	Biracial (Black and White)	Heidi	White

We used a flexible, semi-structured interview approach to ensure topics of interest were covered while also allowing participants to extend the conversations in meaningful ways. For children, interview questions focused on their feelings about school, relationships with teachers and peers, and their understandings of what constituted good and bad behavior. Each interview lasted 35–40 minutes.

We analyzed data using Roy D'Andrade's (2005) method for surfacing cultural cognitive structures by first abstracting interview data to gist propositions, then thematically coding the propositions based on our theoretical framework and connections to broader cultural narratives around race, behavior, and emotion. Prevalent themes in response to the research questions included self-concept, teacher disposition, and removal from the classroom.

FINDINGS

Self-Concept: "Everyone Hated Me"

One of our primary questions for the children was if they liked school, and what they did and did not like about school. In answering this initial question, Kody used striking, succinct and emotionally charged language. He remarked, "It's boring. There's nothing to do. My teacher just wasn't really fair." He later added, "Everyone hated me . . . kids bully me. They just wanted to fight me." Notably, Kody's mother, Mary, explained that he was bullied at school because he has red hair. Mary also noted that she had to leave work to pick him up from school so frequently that she pulled him from school entirely and now homeschools.

Heidi, Michael's mother, made a similar decision, switching Michael's school midyear, because she was unable to leave work and pick him up as frequently as she was being asked to. Michael described liking his new school because his teachers are "kind." He characterized the word "kind" by adding that if he "messes up, he can try again," saying:

> All my teachers, and other people—all the people at my school are really kind . . . and every time I mess something up, I can just try again, because my teachers aren't mean. And every time I get something right, I could clip up, or I can just leave it and just do a great job at school. Um, and also for my clip-up times, I got to pink, blue, and purple. . . . No, not blue, that's, not too high. Um, I got to purple, pink. . . .

"Clip up" and "clip down" are common phrases in early elementary classrooms (Brownell & Parks, 2022). They refer to the moment a teacher tells a child to move a clip, or clothespin, with their name on it up or down on a classroom behavior chart. Each color on the chart represents a category of behavior (including qualifiers such as "outstanding" at the top and "stop and think" and "contact home" at the bottom). The location of the child's clip is itself a reward or punishment. To clip up is an acknowledgment that a child demonstrated the teacher's desired behavior, and to clip down is to have the child acknowledge, in front of their class, that they did not perform desired behavior.

Since typically only a teacher can tell a student to clip up or down, the system is entirely dependent on the teacher's subjective expectations and interpretation of the child's behavior. Importantly, Michael based much of what he likes about school, as well as what constituted a good day or a bad day at school, on the fact that he could clip up and did not have to clip down. Put another way, *Michael's self-concept was based on his teacher's judgment and response to his behavior.* Therefore, the teacher's preferences for specific social norms were imposed on Michael, and he adopted the idea that the degree to which he performs these behaviors indicates "goodness" or "badness" (e.g., Broderick & Leonardo, 2016).

Clip charts mobilize both public reward and public shaming in the regulation of children's behavior (Brownell & Parks, 2022). By presenting to a classroom of children a *public ranking* of their peers—those whose clips are at the top are the "best," while those on other colors are, literally, placed below them—teachers encourage children to internalize this hierarchy. Clip charts are problematic at best and often harmful; they reinforce that those who can perform the teachers' expectations are inherently good, while those who do not are, literally, lower ranking and subject to the pseudo-moral exclusion of public shame.

Given teacher workforce demographics, these public rankings of child behavior construct a hierarchy of worth based on who is most able to perform white, middle-class norms of behavior. Complicatedly, though, this same system promoted Michael's sense of belonging, as long as he could remain on "high" colors. It is important to understand that Michael compared this experience to his previous school where he was regularly and routinely punished by exclusion. It is heartbreaking and enraging to know that the standard Michael was provided to understand his worth and belonging framed belonging as a competition for his teachers' favor, making belonging a scarce resource.

Michael's internalization of this logic was further evident in his reluctance to leave his former school, an environment where he was actively excluded. As Heidi, his mother, explained, "He did not wanna leave the other school . . . and even when I explained that to him he was like, 'Well, but I'm gonna miss my teacher and my classmates.' The same people who kept getting him in trouble." Michael's experience shows us his desire to belong, even in a place that excluded him. This demonstrates the dangerous pull and extreme pressure placed on him to want to succeed, and his hope to be accepted, even into an ultimately harmful environment.

Possibly relatedly, Andrew Johnson's answer to being asked about a good day at school was: "Friday, because it's the last day before the weekend."

Though this may signal that being at school doesn't bring Andrew Johnson as much joy as being away from school on the weekend, we did not press for more explanation.

Teacher Disposition

Andrew Johnson, Michael, and Kody all revealed the significance and effect of teacher disposition on the ways teachers interpret—and assign value to—to children's behavior. Describing his current teacher, Andrew Johnson said, "She has low tolerance for bad kids who interrupt her, and they often do that." He went on to explain,

> Well, some of them have no respect for the teacher [at my school]. And they normally give her trouble. Other kids—there's not a lot of them—but there are people who are doing the right thing. But we, I mean all of us, still get punished because it's not just one person.

Laura, Andrew Johnson's mother, contextualized his comments by saying,

> I think [the school] overcompensates for a lot. So, like, from what [Andrew Johnson shares] . . . there's a lot of kids with very big behaviors. And the class that he's currently in . . . it's very difficult to maintain order and control . . . she tries to be nice, but she has low frustration tolerance. Like, she yelled at him [laughs]. He was like, 'So . . . we don't yell at our house. We count to three and it is what it is.' And . . . he kinda melted down and that's when the behavior support got called because, you know, we can communicate. We can talk. There's ways.

First, that Andrew Johnson is a Black boy and told his white teacher that he and his Black family do not yell at their house runs counter to historical (mis)understandings and dominant cultural narratives of Black people as violent and boisterous (see Coomer, 2021, for discussion of how teachers construct understandings of children's behavior based on racialized notions of "violence"). Importantly, however, despite Andrew Johnson's response to his teacher's yelling, his teacher's behavior was maintained as acceptable and his actions did not actually matter. The teacher's (re)actions act as a governing structure to which his only choice is to react.

Relatedly, Andrew Johnson's conflation of "bad kids" with interrupting signals not only that the act of interrupting has been assigned a negative value but that its negative valuation extends to the child doing the interrupting. The reasoning follows: If interrupting is bad, and Child A interrupts, then Child A is bad. This is the message Andrew's teacher conveyed about the value of his peers—a message Andrew Johnson took up. The contrast he draws between the many "bad" kids who "have no respect for the teacher" and the few "good" kids offers insight into how a teacher's approach, use of, and disposition toward classroom behavioral systems signals to children the meaning attached to behavior, and by extension, children who exhibit those behaviors.

Consequently, being yelled at by his teacher had a profound emotional impact on Andrew Johnson, which he displayed through a "meltdown" (a phrase commonly referencing a child's crying, yelling, or other disruption), resulting in his removal from the classroom by "behavior support." Behavior support refers to both the person removing Andrew Johnson from the classroom and the actual removal from the classroom. Even though Laura and Andrew Johnson exhibited empathy for his teacher—explaining that kids in the class don't have respect for her and that she is overwhelmed—it is also clear that the teacher's approach had a negative impact on Andrew Johnson's behavior and affect in class. As Laura explained:

> [S]he's frustrated. She's overwhelmed and she feels like all the kids should just fall in line. But they're kids, right? . . . Communication means that. . . . Girl, like, be able to communicate with the child. You get a better result than yelling at him, right? Her yelling at him, that shut him down.

Notably, Andrew Johnson cried after this portion of the interview. Laura explained that talking about being yelled at hurt Andrew Johnson's feelings but that he will be "okay." Although Laura carefully attended to her son, it is striking that his recollection of his teacher yelling at him was so distressing for him that it still elicited tears. In this scenario, Andrew Johnson was removed from the classroom for his reaction to a teacher yelling at him. His teacher's behavior was presumed reasonable, yet his reaction was not.

Kody described his teacher as "unfair" and "giving [him] bad grades for no reason." Kody even went so far as to say his teacher "hated" him. Kody's mother, Mary, explained,

> His math teacher was very, very strict, and Kody's problem with math is he does really well in his head, but in lower grades, they want you to show work. So, he would get all the answers right on the test, but they would give him, like, a C for not having shown his work. So . . . he was doing it correctly, but not writing everything out like they wanted him to. . . . We had multiple meetings trying to, like, sort through what we could do differently or figure out to help. And she was just very, like, "This is how I run my classroom, and he either, like, conforms, or like, gets kicked out [laughs]."]

Mary understood Kody was supposed to show his work for his math grade, but also acknowledged that receiving low grades for correct work was confusing for him. Sadly, this kind of treatment signaled to Kody that he was not valued in the classroom, compounding his feelings of being "hated." Regarding his math teacher's disposition, Mary commented, "I think she would have been a great, like, fifth or sixth grade math teacher, but I don't think was in the right . . . in second grade, you're not gonna get kids just sitting here, doing worksheets easily. That's just not, like, gonna happen [laughs]."

In contrast, Michael described liking his current teacher, characterizing her with such words as "nice." He said:

> She's a really nice teacher, she gives out stickers if we're being good, and also she gives out stickers to the people that . . . can [achieve in the] math game if they like to, and put it on their sticker chart. And, um, also she is teaching me other ways to add, subtract and multiply.

Like the clip chart, a sticker chart is a reward system in which students can earn stickers they can later trade for an item or privilege. Once again, Michael based his evaluation of his current teacher on the degree to which he could be rewarded for performing desired behaviors in school. Importantly, in subsequent interview responses, Michael implicitly contrasted his current teachers with past teachers. When asked if he could describe a not-so-good day at school, he said:

> Not really at this school because, um, all my teachers, and other people, all the people at my school are really kind. So, um, so they are always . . . always kind, and every time I mess something up, I can just try again, because my teachers aren't mean. . . . My substitute that was here for [my teacher] . . . her husband had to get surgery. And that teacher . . . she's really kind . . . she always lets us clip up when we're being good, and every time we just need some practice, we don't have to clip up or down, but every time we're just doing the wrong thing, even though we know it's . . . not okay, then we're gonna have to clip down. But I haven't been clipping down since [substitute] got here. I have been clipping up instead of down.

Michael's responses signaled the impact a teacher's common behavioral practices (e.g., the clip chart) has on a child's self-concept. Although Michael did not explicitly state what his teacher did to demonstrate kindness, that he was able to clip up equated to a sense of belonging for him. This is problematic not only because of the reasons previously discussed, but also because it is reliant on Michael being in constant risk of exclusion. Furthermore, it subjected Michael to thinking that his teacher's surveillance and judgment were logical and indisputable.

Even so, empathy for teachers was common throughout the interviews. Like other participants, Michael's mother, Heidi, expressed empathy and understanding for Michael's previous school:

> I mean, some of it I think was semi-warranted, because Michael, when he feels that he's being treated unjustly, he gets really emotional and very upset, so he starts, you know, throwing things in the classroom. So that's what he got in trouble for. One time he got suspended for tapping the teacher on the shoulder because he wanted her attention. . . . I was like, "He's seven, you cannot expect the child not to tap the

> teacher on the shoulder." That, it to me is such a minor thing. Um, he got in trouble because he stood up for his sister. His sister's autistic, and, um, somebody gave her a hard time and he stood up for her and, um, I guess pushed a little boy away from her, and so he got suspended for that. Um, it's like, like things that are to me normal for the age, right? Um. . . . And it could have been resolved differently.

Heidi's explanation of Michael's behavior was significant, not only because she expressed understanding and empathy but because she framed Michael's behavior as "normal for the age." Heidi's use of the word "normal" broadens notions of "normal behavior" beyond compliance or even pleasantness. Without making a judgment on Michael's behavior as good, bad, desirable, or undesirable, she provided insight into Michael's sense-making and behavior.

Importantly, Andrew Johnson, Kody, and Michael, and their parents demonstrated some level of empathy or understanding for their teachers in ways that were not extended to them. Instead, children were problematized, resulting in their removal, suspension, or the parent's choice to pull them out of school entirely.

Removal From the Classroom as "Support"

Andrew Johnson and Kody both referred to their removal from class—or the removal of peers—as behavior support. Michael did not specifically mention behavior support or being removed from the classroom, but his mother, Heidi, referred to his repeated suspensions, starting in kindergarten. When asked what happens when a child misbehaves, Andrew Johnson responded, "Behavior support is called on them. And if it's really, really bad, they will take them to the office and call their parents." Although the term behavior support includes the word support (an implication of benevolence; Thorius, 2019), Andrew Johnson and Kody described the swift removal of children whose behaviors were deemed problematic by the teacher, including (as Andrew Johnson explained) interrupting.

Laura, Andrew Johnson's mom, explained that he had also behavior support called on him:

> But like, we've had some challenging days since we've been here . . . there were times a behavior support was called, and he had to walk out and go kind of like decompress and talk about it. Some of it was incidental, I think, like one time he didn't wanna eat breakfast. [Another time] he said the word hate, and he's like, "I didn't know I can't say 'hate.'" You cannot say hate at school (laughing). We learn.

Laura hinted at the arbitrariness of calling behavior support for saying the word hate. When asked if behavior support was helpful, Andrew Johnson said they are "pretty nice. They're trying to help you calm down." However, that Andrew

Johnson understood behavior support as someone helping him (and others) "calm down" perpetuated the idea that the child needs to adjust (calm down) and not the environment; thus, the teacher's actions remained "rational," and his response was "irrational."

Similarly, Mary (Kody's mother) explained what Kody meant when he said he was "kicked out of class":

> And what he means by getting kicked out is, like, when the teacher would get too frustrated or, like, a kid was, in their definition, acting up too much, they would make them go sit outside in the hallway. And then, um, they would flag, uh, like send a message . . . to have a support teacher come, like, pick them up from the hallway, and talk to them about what was going on.

Mary suggested that behavior "support" in Kody's school also involved removing children whose emotions teachers suspected of being the cause of disruption. Mary explained that when Kody was removed from the classroom by behavior support, he was often not allowed to return:

> Like sometimes I'd get called to come pick him up because, like, they couldn't sort through it or things like that. It's like, I'd have to leave work to, like, go get him. . . . And the bullying also, when those things would happen, sometimes they would call to have him picked up. 'Cause that was, like, one of the driving parts of pulling him, was that we were going home every day, you know, not every day, but a lot of days anyway.

Heidi shared a similar experience with having to pick Michael up from school. Heidi did not think it made sense to send a child home, particularly when the family experiences material consequences, such as not being able to work: "The suspension at that age, it just doesn't make sense. Like what is the punishment behind that? Like you get to go home and hang out with mom? Mom can't go to work? Well thanks, that's great."

Heidi offered that teachers can instead be cooperative and collaborative with parents, noting that sending a child home felt punitive to both the child *and* the family. She asserted that parents are, rightfully, defensive when they hear about their child's "bad behavior":

> I think . . . it's counterproductive to be punitive. I think every approach with a parent and a student should be collaborative, and seeking positive outcome, and it should be strength based . . . because every parent in the world is going to get defensive when all they hear about their child is about their bad behavior. Um, you know, so I think you get a lot more buy-in and, and cooperation from the parents and the students if things are kind of centered around positive impacts versus punishing the negative behaviors.

Similarly, both Mary and Laura shared that if they could give advice to schools on how to work with children like their sons, they would encourage them to be collaborative, flexible, and communicative. Mary shared,

> I would say, like, no homework . . . because I don't think kids need that busywork. They need the release and the freedom to, like, play and explore after school. Um, the project-based school Kody was in, though they wouldn't let him stand, they did have, like, lots of options for chairs, wobble chairs, the chairs with . . . rubber band things on the bottom for them to fidget with their feet. And, like, Kody some days would get to school early just so he could try to get to one of those types of chairs. So, like, obviously they definitely help. Or like, the fidgets that go on pencils or things like that. I think, like, trying to give kids those correct supports and, like, healthy fidget redirections is really important, rather than just being like, "You're disruptive, like, get out." (laughs)

Laura emphasized better communication with children and parents, saying that being able to communicate with the child is always preferable to yelling at them. Even though Laura said that behavior support helped Andrew Johnson "feel his feelings without crying," she implied that even that necessity is unfair. In her words, "We send him to school to learn, not to be broken."

CONCLUSION: A RELATIONAL, ECOLOGICAL FRAMEWORK FOR CHILDREN WHO EXPERIENCE EMOTIONAL AND BEHAVIORAL DIFFICULTIES IN SCHOOL

Mad studies promotes the reclaiming of lived experiences outside of prescribed, medicalized language, colonial values of hyper-independence and competition, and dominant discourses of mental health and illness. By exploring Andrew Johnson, Kody, and Michael's experiences through a mad studies lens, we gain insights regarding the affective impact not only of their own and their peers' behavior in the classroom but also their teachers' behavior. How each child understands their place in the classroom is informed by their teachers' emotional and behavioral response to them and how the child is made to feel that they belong or not. A mad studies approach surfaces the logic of, and disrupts the use of, public shaming and classroom removal to regulate children's emotional and behavioral expression. We disrupt the "naturalness" of teachers' responses to Andrew Johnson, Michael, and Kody's behaviors by centering the children's descriptions of themselves in school and their interpretations of their school experiences. Indeed, Andrew Johnson signaled how he understood "good" and "bad" kids in his class by how they either behaved or did not behave. Relatedly, we understood Kody's self-identification as a child who was "hated" by his class; a child who did not belong due to his behavior and was, supposedly justifiably, excluded based on the moral superiority of his peers.

It is unjust that children understand themselves through frames that rely on their teachers' subjectivities and are demonstrated through clip charts and exclusion. Andrew Johnson's tears when recalling being yelled at by his teacher signal a fear of being perceived as bad by his teacher and his peers, possibly being afraid of ending up like Kody, who had been frequently excluded from the classroom. Behavior systems inherently place kids in competition with each other for the (artificially scarce) resource of belonging. They are not safe for anybody. Alternatively, Michael, who is now consistently being affirmed as a good kid by the location of his clip on his classroom's clip chart, is happy and proud to describe his experiences at school, yet is still relying on the arbitrary, subjective, and unidimensional evaluations of his teacher.

Based on these findings, we forward a relational framework for understanding young children's emotions and behavior within classrooms. This framework shifts focus away from pathologizing children's behaviors and reflects how a teacher's emotions and behavior function in classrooms to name, assign value to, and ultimately control behavior.

1. ***Promoting Behavioral Practices That Affirm Children's Sense of Belonging:*** Behaviorist approaches to classroom management are not neutrally developed, applied, or interpreted by children. A relational, ecological approach attends to power dynamics between teacher and child and social hierarchies among children, and does not shun or publicly shame children to compel compliance. Instead, children are taught to encourage each other toward behavior that helps the collective classroom achieve shared goals.

   Hermeneutical injustice occurs when children, like Michael, are not offered any way to understand their emotional expressions and behavior beyond that of their teacher's preferences. In worst-case scenarios, children, like Kody, interpret that they are hated. Behaviorist approaches that are isolated from considering relational components of the classroom are reductive and harmful. Instead, approaches to classroom management should include the relational ecologies within the classroom, building the relational blueprints necessary for children to support each other in feeling as though they belong through guided conflict, restoration, and repair.
2. ***Focusing on Communal Goals, Collective Support, Community Wellbeing:*** Ultimately, children know when teachers like them and when they do not, and they grapple with possible reasons for their teachers' perceptions and subsequent actions. Going beyond relational pedagogies, teachers must acknowledge not only how their actions impact children's learning but also how their disposition toward children impacts affective networks within their classrooms. Mental disabilities are often relationally defined, socially mediated, and governed by white civility. Rather than assuming children's emotions

and behavior interrupt an adult teacher's agency, we can consider that children are agentically making meaning through the power of emotional expression and behavior. This lens reconstructs schools as places of relational development and implicates the teacher and child as mutually impactful on each other.

3. ***Conflict Resolution Through Repair:*** Finally, teachers can model conflict resolution between child and teacher without paternalistic determinations of belonging. Removing a child from the classroom, even under the name of support, ostracizes the child from the learning environment and affects their self-concept and view of school. Adopting an ideology in early childhood classrooms that there is *no moral ground for adult-mandated exclusion* on the basis of behavioral support allows room to consider the educational opportunities embedded in modeling how to engage in conflict, work through it, and restore relationships within the classroom community.

Looking forward, we believe teachers and teacher educators can root themselves in relational understandings of young children's emotions and behaviors, particularly young children with disabilities. In doing so, teachers can move away from controlling children's emotions and behaviors and instead, support children's sense of belonging and expressive freedom.

CHAPTER 3

Agency in the Inclusion Process of a Child With Multiple and Intersectional Disabilities

Alternative Means of Inclusion and Belonging

Bárbara Baptista de Oliveira and Ana Luisa Gediel

> They were very concerned about Sofia staying outside the classroom, very concerned. . . . Every time they tried to put her in the classroom, she cried a lot, excessively. We were even worried that she might become unwell due to how much she cried.
>
> —Alice

In the realm of inclusive education, the experiences of children with disabilities are often shaped by a complex interplay of factors, including societal norms, institutional practices, and agency (Davis, 1995). This complexity is further compounded when considering the intersectionality of ableism and racism (Annamma et al., 2013a). In this chapter, we delve into the educational journey of Sofia, a 7-year-old girl who is Black, Deaf, Autistic, diagnosed with Cornelia de Lange syndrome, and enrolled in a public school in the southwest of Minas Gerais state, Brazil. We discuss an ethnographic study of Sofia's schooling, which included participant observations and interviews with school staff. Through this study, we sought to uncover the intricate dynamics at play within inclusive education settings.

The excerpt presented at the outset of this chapter encapsulates a pivotal aspect of Sofia's educational journey: her agency. Extracted from an interview with her teacher, it underscores the struggle between Sofia's discomfort with staying in the classroom and the school's inclination to retain her within its confines. Within this dynamic, Sofia's agency emerged as a central theme, highlighting her inherent capacity to assert her preferences and needs within the educational environment. The school structure led Sofia to receive constant intervention for concentration, interaction, and socialization. She grappled with understanding and adhering to school rules and agreements, presenting a nuanced case for examining inclusive education.

To close the chapter, we explore the complexities inherent in inclusive education and advocate for practices that honor the agency and dignity of all children. Drawing on Foucauldian notions of disciplinary power (Foucault, 1975), which operates covertly by monitoring and regulating bodies to conform them to standardized and efficient forms, we examine its implications for inclusive education. Foucault's assertion that individuals who exercise disciplinary power are interchangeable underscores its systemic nature and pervasive influence on educational practices. By foregrounding Sofia's agency in the face of disciplinary control and the school's responses to her needs, we aim to shed light on the ways in which power dynamics shape the educational experiences of children with disabilities. We highlight not only the challenges posed by societal norms and disciplinary power but also the remarkable resilience and agency exhibited by children amid such constraints.

THEORETICAL FRAMEWORK

Disability and Power

In the 1990s, disability studies scholars began drawing on Foucault's critiques of institutional power and normalization in their analyses of how institutions manage lives (e.g., Allan, 1996; Davis, 1995). Foucault's concept of medicalization challenged the dominant medical model of disability, which viewed disability as an individual issue to be corrected. Foucault highlighted the exclusion and segregation of individuals with disabilities, revealing that "disability" can be leveraged to reinforce power and control over people's bodies. He showed how government legitimized regulatory practices based on injury and disability, with institutions labeling them as "abnormal" or law transgressors, justifying their exclusion through medical or ecclesiastical systems (Allen, 2002). Foucault's analysis exposed how modern power operates through regulatory mechanisms, influencing life through processes of qualification and measurement. Social norms, as instruments of power, stigmatize divergent experiences, including disability (Davis, 1995). Yet Foucault argued that power is not exchanged, given, or taken back, but rather is exercised and exists only in action. Power, in this sense, is productive, meaning it doesn't just repress but also produces and shapes social realities, subjectivities, and identities (Dudley-Marling & Dippo, 1995). Foucault's concept of disciplinary power (Foucault, 1975) operates covertly, monitoring and regulating bodies to shape them into standardized and efficient forms, thereby reinforcing discipline in society.

Inclusive education often reinforces, rather than challenges, ableism because of its focus on individualism—particularly "fixing" the individual—rather than tending to the collective (Baglieri et al., 2011). The school's structures influence the regulation of children's bodies, shaping them into standardized and normalized forms. Indeed, children are often treated as passive recipients of knowledge, where teachers "deposit" information into their minds without encouraging critical thinking or dialogue (Freire, 1987). Accordingly, school power dynamics enforce notions of normalcy.

Agency and Disability Justice

Ortner (2001) pointed to social agency as a power related to the "ability to act on their own behalf, influence other people and events, and maintain some kind of control in their own lives. Agency in this sense is relevant for both domination and resistance" (p. 77). However, when discussing agency and disability, this hyper-individualization may negatively impact oppressed groups and stall collaborative interdependence. For instance, a child with a learning disability may be placed in a general education classroom but receive only minimal accommodations. In such cases, teachers might expect the child to "work harder" to meet academic standards, prioritizing the individual's effort over necessary modifications to teaching practices, curricula, or assessment methods. This approach risks creating an isolating experience for the child, who may internalize their struggles as personal failures rather than recognizing struggle as a result of systemic barriers. In this context, hyper-individualization not only compromises the child's right to equitable education but also hinders the establishment of a genuinely inclusive school culture.

Campano et. al (2020) emphasized that when agency is seen from a collective perspective, involving cooperation among a group (e.g., children, teachers, school staff), we can challenge the existing order in education. Here, agency extends beyond individual empowerment to include collective action and community mobilization. Witnessing acts of agency can be empowering for individuals and communities to act in ways that enhance greater individual and community self-determination, ultimately fostering a more equitable and just society.

Disability justice activists further emphasize the importance of agency, bodily expression, interdependence, and resisting intersecting oppressions (e.g., racism, ableism), advocating for the recognition of diverse forms of communication, autonomy, and community organizing (Sins Invalid, 2019). They challenge ableist norms that impose a single standard of behavior or expression as well as notions of independence that discount the power of the collective. Following disability justice commitments, Zdeblick (2024) argued for "an alternative, interdependent conceptualization of agency as comprised of individual and group actions, mediated within sociocultural contexts and relationships, and undertaken to reshape power dynamics and bring imagined realities into existence" (p. 2). This call extends prior arguments for collective agency to assert that agency is not limited to conventional means of communication or interaction; rather, it includes diverse bodily expressions, gestures, and actions that reflect self-determination at both the individual and community level.

Finally, from a disability justice perspective, young disabled children are seen as whole, valuable beings in the present, rather than being measured by their ability to meet standardized expectations, "behave," or produce in the future (Beneke & Love, 2022). This perspective shifts the focus from requiring children to conform to narrow, ableist definitions of success and worth to honoring their unique identities, strengths, needs, and ways of being. Honoring young children's agency, particularly young children with disabilities, requires this shift. By dismantling systems that perpetuate oppressive norms, including individualism, and limited views of the child, we can advocate for an education system that values children's inherent worth and respects their agency regardless of ability or adherence to standard measures of performance.

SCHOOL CONTEXT AND METHODS

This study took place in a public elementary school in a small country city in southeast Brazil that offers inclusive[1] education. The school is situated in an economically vulnerable neighborhood, only a few minutes from the city center. At the time of the study, Sofia was enrolled in a classroom with 20 other 7-year-old children, the majority of whom came from economically vulnerable backgrounds and were either Black or of mixed race. The class included three children with specific diagnoses—a white boy with attention deficit hyperactivity disorder (ADHD), a Black girl with autism, and Sofia, the protagonist of this research, with multiple disabilities.

We generated qualitative data through participant observations and semi-structured interviews (Minayo, 2012). Participant observation was conducted across three months. We used cameras, pens, and a field notebook to observe and document actions involving Sofia. During this time, the researcher wrote 20 field notebook entries, and observations lasted 4 hours per day on average. This approach allowed for direct and extensive engagement, providing valuable insights into the context of the school and its inclusiveness.

We opted for semi-structured interviews due to the flexibility of generating new questions based on the collected data and the convenience of preformulated questions aligned with the study's objectives (Duarte, 2004). We interviewed professionals who had direct involvement with Sofia: two classroom teachers, two support teachers, the physical education teacher, the vice principal, and the coordinator (see Table 3.1). Each interview lasted approximately 40 minutes and was conducted individually. Interview topics included teacher education, inclusive practices, perception toward Sofia's education and inclusion, and perspectives on their practice and school organization. All interviews were recorded and transcribed for subsequent data analysis.

Content analysis was employed to describe the content of messages found within the analyzed data. Bardin (1977) asserted that content analysis enables the search for meaning in discourses by interpreting the explicit content expressed by participants. Content analysis consisted of three essential stages: pre-analysis, material exploration, and treatment of results and interpretation.

Table 3.1. Adult Participants for Interviews

Name	Teaching Period	Position	Education	Years of Teaching Experience
Alice	2022	Classroom teacher	Licensure degree in pedagogy	30 years
Beatriz	2023	Classroom teacher	Licensure degree in pedagogy	27 years
Emily	2022	Support teacher	Licensure degree in pedagogy and special education	3 years
Daniela	2023	Support teacher	Licensure degree in pedagogy and special education	3 years
Carol	2022/2023	Physical education teacher	Licensure degree in physical education	6 years
Gabriela	2022	Coordinator	Licensure degree in pedagogy and special education (in development)	23 years
Helena	2023	Vice principal	Licensure degree in pedagogy and Special Education	9 years

INSIDE OR OUTSIDE THE CLASSROOM? AGENCY IN THE SCHOOL STRUCTURE

This section describes how Sofia demonstrated agency in different school contexts while interacting with teachers and nondisabled peers. We highlight the importance of legitimizing freedom in early childhood and critique the standards of inclusive education that adhere to dominant rules of normalcy.

The Limits of Inclusion

One of the main tensions was the school's need for Sofia to stay in the classroom *versus* her desire to stay outside the classroom, as reflected in the first passage of a field note:

> The first thing I noticed when I arrived at the school was a student sitting at a table for six, while the rest of the cafeteria was empty. My mentor immediately pointed out, "That's her." The student wasn't alone; she was accompanied by a teacher.

During her first year in school, Sofia showed a notable resistance to staying inside the classroom. Once she spent more than 15 minutes in the classroom, she expressed the need to leave the room and walk around the schoolyard. If the teachers did not let her leave the class, she would demonstrate anxiety, crying out loud while hurting herself and making stimming movements. This led to changes in how teachers supported her, as Emily, Sofia's support teacher, explained in her interview:

> What's the point, you know, if it's supposed to be a pleasant and enjoyable environment, a place where she wants to stay, but if she's crying and having a meltdown, it's clear that she doesn't want to be there. So, I didn't insist too much. This was also a major challenge because the school, or rather, those who are outside, think that she should stay in the classroom. But all I wanted was for her to stay if she felt good and happy there, not crying.

Emily respected Sofia's comfort, giving her the option to stay outside of the classroom. In listening to Sofia's needs and adapting the environment to make education a comfortable place, Emily chose to turn against the idea of school primarily operating as a standardization tool. By acknowledging and responding to Sofia's unique needs, Emily engaged in a subtle act of resistance against the disciplinary mechanisms often embedded within the educational system (Campano et al., 2020). Emily's stance advocates for a critical consciousness as she actively grapples with the intricate interplay of social and political realities in Sofia's life.

Davis (1995) described the importance of resisting educational practices that contribute to cultural alienation, urging a shift toward an empowering pedagogy that encourages nuanced understandings of the multifaceted dimensions shaping individuals' societal engagement. In this case, agency was the power to resist educational practices based on the children' desire and the teacher's understanding and respect. Emily described how she reflected and acted from an inclusive perspective:

> It also involves accepting their limits and respecting that what may seem normal, like staying outside the classroom, for example, may be their way of expressing themselves. It's not about forcing them to conform to the school's routine; rather, it's about creating a routine that is tailored to the child's specific needs.

The notion that inclusion solely occurs within the confines of the classroom among other children is not universally applicable. For Sofia, remaining inside the classroom triggered anxiety and mood fluctuations, with her becoming overwhelmed frequently. Emily's decision to provide an alternative environment for Sofia challenged the notion that every child should have identical scholarly experiences. Emily understood inclusive education as accommodating children who diverge from the normalized ways of being and recognized that attempting to force a child into a standardized mold can, in fact, be inherently exclusionary.

Emily's approach acknowledged the need for flexibility and individualized support.

However, other teachers did not agree with Emily's flexibility. The classroom situation became a point of conflict between Emily and the coordinator *versus* teachers and principal. Gabriela, the coordinator, expressed her frustration:

> The issue . . . from the public, from the school community . . . [is] how they perceive Sofia. They have uninformed perspectives, we understand that. But often it's incomprehensible because her routine is very structured. Taking her out of that routine without knowing how this [Cornelia de Lange] syndrome affects her emotionally is very complex. So, I think we first need to understand this syndrome, what the relevant and irrelevant aspects are, what the consequences are of forcing her to do something, of maintaining a certain routine that she often disagrees with, and what the consequences of that would be. The fact that we have limited knowledge about this syndrome restricts our work, and this limitation creates misconceptions about her. It's like people think the teacher is letting her wander around, eat whenever she wants, and we know that's not the case.

Gabriela's interview reflects a lack of unity within the school community regarding the promotion of equity and highlighted misconceptions surrounding Sofia's disability, leading some school staff to mistakenly believe that the teacher permitted Sofia to wander and eat at will. Rather than collaboratively seek new solutions for Sofia's learning opportunities and physical presence in class, teachers tended to pass judgment on how specially trained professionals handled Sofia's education.

The dominant adherence to an inflexible and conventional model of education is inherently intertwined with the medical model of disability (Baglieri et al., 2011). This alignment poses a threat to inclusive education, manifesting in a notable absence of inclusivity. Instead of accommodating diverse needs, children with disabilities are expected to adhere to the behavioral standards set by those in power and enacted by their nondisabled peers. Drawing on Foucault's (1975) perspective on disciplinary power, the educational system perpetuates exclusionary practices to normalize disabled bodies and enforce conformity to societal standards.

Sofia's case reveals a power dynamic where normative expectations marginalize and pressure individuals with disabilities to conform (Freire, 1987). An alternative inspired by Foucault's critique would emphasize inclusion and empowerment by focusing on *individual needs,* rather than enforcing conformity (Davis, 1995), *and children's agency.* This could involve creating flexible curricula that adapts to different ways of learning and abilities, providing individualized support, and encouraging collaborative learning where children with disabilities actively participate and contribute. Teachers would act as facilitators rather than authoritative figures, fostering a classroom environment that values diversity and dialogue. Additionally, disciplinary structures would shift from controlling behavior to supporting autonomy and critical thinking, enabling all students to develop in ways that respect their unique identities and strengths and build on collective commitments.

The school conflict also reflects a power dynamic wherein institutional structures dictate conventional knowledge and skills disseminated to, and enacted by, educators. The journey toward inclusive education necessitates teachers, despite information gaps, embrace experimentation and flexibility (Collins & Ferri, 2016). The willingness to try different methods is critical for improving each child's learning experience. By fostering an environment that encourages innovation and adaptability, educators can significantly contribute to the creation of an inclusive educational landscape that values and accommodates the diversity of every student. In Sofia's case, for her agency to be respected, all teachers must be aligned, as a collective group that accepts the possibility of challenges to a nonstereotypical education—that is, they must enact collective agency to honor Sofia's individual agency.

Alice, the classroom teacher, weighed in on the issue during her interview also:

> They were very concerned about Sofia staying outside the classroom, very concerned. It was always because they didn't want her to miss out on interacting with her peers. She only stayed there with the support and the girl who helps her with eating. Sofia's life revolved around that. They were very worried about it because they knew it wasn't inclusion, no matter how much people tried, they couldn't make it work because she cried a lot. Every time they tried to put her in the classroom, she cried a lot, excessively. We were even worried that she might become unwell due to how much she cried. So, this year, they embraced the cause of making her feel comfortable in the classroom with her classmates.

As previously pointed out, Sofia had different teachers in her second year, which led to an intense focus on putting her inside the classroom. For this to be possible they restructured her routine. At 12:50, Sofia arrived at school; at 1:00 p.m., she had an early lunch; at 2:00 p.m., she had her first snack; at 3:00 p.m., she had her second snack and recess; and at 4:50 she left school. With this routine, Sofia had marked times to eat and to walk around the school. However, most days Sofia expressed resistance to staying inside the classroom as illustrated by this field note:

> *Sofia started crying a lot and insisting on leaving the classroom. But the teachers wouldn't let her leave, and her crying escalated with each attempt. It seemed like Sofia was having a crisis. She cried and hit herself, but the teachers didn't allow her to leave.*

The decision to keep Sofia in the classroom was driven by teachers' intense focus on shaping her behavior to align with the established norms of the other children. Again, we note here the conceptualization of inclusion as a process of fitting bodies into normalized expectations (Tremain, 2006). Despite her needs and desires, Sofia was obligated to align with the same behavior expectations as the other children. Sofia's case shows clearly how inclusive education is sometimes mistaken with training bodies to operate, as the power of institutions is organized to correct bodies and behaviors (Foucault, 1975).

Sofia's reluctance to enter the "inclusive" classroom serves as a poignant critique of the current state of inclusion, offering valuable insights of how children's agency can help adults understand their desires and needs:

- How might we recognize and value disabled children's agency as active participants in their educational journeys?
- How might we change classroom settings and supports in response to children's enactment of agency?
- How might we define inclusive education based on children's expressions, desires, and resistance rather than physical presence or conformity?

Sofia's Agency

Eventually, Sofia got used to staying in the classroom, and the crises decreased—but never stopped. However, even inside the classroom there was a clear mark of segregation. Sofia was always lying in the back of the class surrounded by her toys while her classmates did activities. To make the classroom more comfortable for Sofia, the school provided her with a carpet and mattress (see Figure 3.1). She also had a table and a chair to sit and eat in the back of the classroom (see Figure 3.2). Thus, even when Sofia was inside the classroom, she was not supported to actively participate.

As illustrated in Figure 3.1, Sofia exercised agency to show a lack of interest in classroom activities. However, she did have space, items that were meaningful to her, and comfortable seating. In contrast, Figure 3.2 shows how the classroom was organized, with chairs and tables placed in straight lines and little space for children to sit or move. This arrangement represents the hierarchy in conventional classrooms and the presence of disciplinary power. The need to normalize bodies and behavior through regulatory spaces is evident. We wonder if Sofia's education was actually being adapted for her needs or if she was just being forced to fit in a space expected for her age? Indeed, Sofia's lack of interest in classroom activities may be interpreted as resistance to a controlling space and expectations for conformity—rather than a behavior deficit. Despite this arrangement, Sofia did interact with her classmates.

In Sofia's physical education class (Figure 3.3), all her classmates were sitting on the ground playing a game to pass the ball. On this day, Sofia wanted to sit next to her teacher. This contrast with Figure 3.1 evidences her desire to participate in activities in open spaces, similar to her desire to leave the classroom and her desire for her separate space in the classroom, which offered much more room. The agency that she expressed was clear in her body communication (i.e., lying down inside the classroom versus sitting in the circle outside).

Figure 3.1. Sofia's Carpet and Mattress

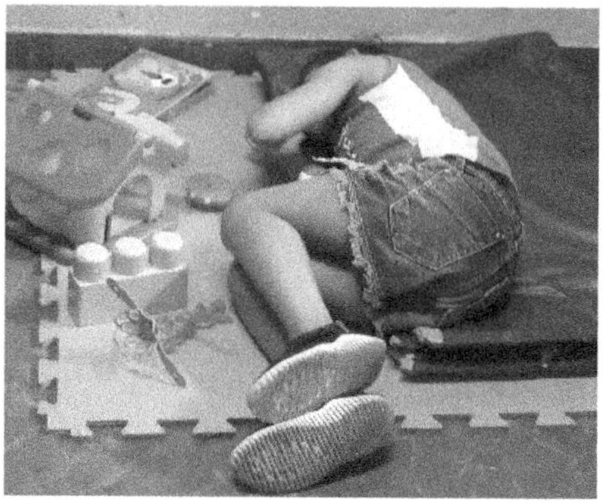

Source: Authors' gallery.

Figure 3.2. Sofia's Table and Chair

Source: Authors' gallery.

Figure 3.3. Physical Education Class

Source: Authors' gallery.

Sofia expressed her agency through her body and movement in many contexts and situations. When she did not want to participate in the class, she walked directly to the door or led someone by the hand and walked in a direction that she wanted to go. Sofia knew what she wanted and had preferences that made her comfortable. She demonstrated her desire to be with her classmates or not, depending on the activity and place.

She also expressed agency regarding food. If Sofia was hungry, she cried. This was observed several times around lunchtime, when she had not yet eaten. And when she was full, she rubbed her hand around her belly. Sofia took her bottle of water when she was thirsty. If she didn't have her bottle around, she put her hand in front of her mouth asking for water. Even though Sofia was not using oral language or standardized sign language to communicate, she presented clear and repeated expressions to describe what she wanted.

Sofia also demonstrated when she was happy in the school. She grunted to show she was calm and enjoying the moment. She made a "bee sound" ("zzzzzz") when she felt comfortable. She sometimes expressed a loud grunt with laughter or shook when she was happy and wanted to continue the same activity. Finally, Sofia would sometimes celebrate by coughing. Sofia clearly demonstrated her agency through body expressions regarding her desire to not stay inside the classroom when she was not feeling comfortable. Likewise, she used her body to show contentment and desire to continue activities.

Sofia exhibited clear control over her body and used nonverbal communication to express fundamental needs like hunger, thirst, and satiety. Her actions showed a strong sense of agency, which aligns with disability justice principles that respect and uplift diverse forms of autonomy. Her ability to indicate hunger by crying or showing satisfaction by rubbing her belly signifies that she had developed her own communicative strategies, which should be recognized and valued. Disability justice (Sins Invalid, 2019) organizers argued that everyone, especially disabled individuals, should have full control over their own bodies and how they use them to communicate or express themselves. Sofia's movements, gestures, and expressions demonstrate her ability to assert her needs and desires through her body. Finally, disability justice can guide pedagogical movements beyond ableist standards and intersecting oppressive ideologies in early childhood education. In this research, the same standards are applied to Sofia as to the other children, despite her fitting into multiple intersecting identities that demand a more nuanced and differentiated approach.

CONCLUSIONS

In this study, Sofia searched for inclusive spaces according to her needs. Her preference to stay outside the classroom contrasted the school's insistence on her presence inside with her peers. Our examination revealed that the school's efforts to adhere to what it perceived as inclusive education often resulted in exclusive practices, driven by a lack of understanding of true inclusion. At the same time, our observations enabled us to identify the many ways Sofia demonstrated her desires and enacted her agency. Even though Sofia expressed her agency with body actions, she did not receive a reasonable response from her teachers, breaking possibilities for confidence and trust. Although the teachers were aware of her physical movement, they did not know how, or were not able, to respond with her agency.

Drawing on disability justice principles (Sins Invalid, 2019), Beneke and Love (2022) pointed to the goal of rebuilding the rules of teaching and learning in early childhood. This approach means challenging the notions of normalcy and dominance in education. The process of building such collective consciousness is a challenge. Although schools are often physically organized to oppress, educators can make moves to attend to children's needs and desires. Sofia's case illustrates how children with disabilities exercise agency by asserting their voices and advocating for their needs within educational settings. By challenging assumptions about their capabilities and demanding access to appropriate accommodations and support services, disabled children assert their right to full participation in the educational process, thus challenging and transforming normative practices. However, this realization of inclusive ideals is often impeded by systemic barriers and entrenched norms, as evidenced by the teacher's actions in attempting to discipline Sofia's body.

It is crucial to acknowledge that teachers' actions stemmed from good intentions; however, they inadvertently perpetuated exclusion by obligating Sofia to remain in an uncomfortable space that did not meet her needs. This highlights the importance of teacher education, as educators themselves are subject to disciplinary power. Teacher training shapes understandings of how to educate children and introduces teachers to the expectations and standards that will guide their practice. Sofia's case reminds us that teacher education programs must prepare educators to be flexible and responsive toward children, endeavoring to fix the environment, not the child. Educators must be prepared to collaborate with others, engaging in collective agency that combats ableism and intersecting oppressions. Ultimately, educators must be prepared to view the child as an agentic being whose desires should be included in decision-making, regardless of how those desires are expressed.

Our analysis underscores the complexities of agency within the context of inclusive education, highlighting both its potential for empowerment and its limitations in the face of systemic barriers and entrenched norms. Moving forward, it is essential to continue interrogating and challenging these norms to create truly inclusive educational environments that honor the diverse needs and perspectives of all children. The inclusive education we advocate for stands in opposition to discriminatory practices and rejects the normalization of bodies through disciplinary power. To advance inclusive education, agency is a potent tool for resisting normative practices that perpetuate exclusion and marginalization.

Part II

ENACTING PEDAGOGICAL RESISTANCE IN EARLY LEARNING CONTEXTS

If we recognize the ways ableism structures everyday interactions in early educational settings—positioning some children as worthy while pathologizing others—how might we resist such dehumanization through our pedagogies? The chapters in this section explore ways early educators might pedagogically resist ableism.

In Chapter 4, Unadkat and 3rd-grade teacher Cuenca open the section by illustrating Cuenca's pedagogical resistance through a critical multiliteracies curriculum. They illustrate how this curriculum supported shifts in one neurodiverse child, Kit's, perceptions of himself and his sense of belonging. Next, in Chapter 5, Meyer, Tuffour-Mercedat, Barcay, Doherty, A.R.Shearer, and Stoffer discuss ways of pedagogically resisting how disability is often positioned as a problem to be fixed; they discuss ways of teaching about disability identity and history in early childhood curricula through a critical, asset-based lens. The section concludes with Christiansen's pedagogical narration within an Australian nature-based preschool in Chapter 6. She urges us to think about how outdoor education can position disabled young children as always already being in relation with people and place.

The chapters in this section offer hopeful possibilities of anti-ableist pedagogical strategies that early educators are already employing. In reading these chapters, we hope readers can see how early educators are moving beyond compliance and can begin to imagine additional ways early educators might practice pedagogical resistance in solidarity with multiply marginalized young children.

CHAPTER 4

Using a Critical Multiliteracies Curriculum to Foster Belonging for Young Children With Disabilities

Devanshi Unadkat and Caroline Cuenca

Kit, a 3rd-grade child, often sat by himself in the corner of the classroom, playing with blocks to gather his thoughts and regroup. Kit began 3rd grade expressing that he was "sad" some of his friends were not in the same classroom and perceived himself as "not good" at school. Kit's classroom teacher, who was seeking ways to help him feel more integrated with his peers, asked if he would like to help other children with troubleshooting Canva, a tool that was being used to reimagine the traditional literacy curriculum in the classroom. He enthusiastically agreed, and as the morning went on, Kit was summoned by child after child, assisting with font choices, adding elements, and color backgrounds. A feeling of pride and satisfaction was etched his Kit's face as he was dubbed "The Canva Expert" by one of his classmates. He expressed that he felt less negatively about himself than in prior years. Kit's feelings were shared by many of his peers, who expressed feeling like "part of the team" through what we refer to as a critical multiliteracies curriculum.

In this chapter, we trace shifts in Kit's perceptions of himself and his new sense of belonging. Amidst a culture of high-stakes standardized testing and accountability (Counsell & Wright, 2018; Diaz Soto & Tuinhof de Moed, 2011), we share Kit's and his classmates' experiences to argue for expansive literacy instruction rooted in multiliteracies and critical pedagogy (Cope & Kalantzis, 2009; Freire, 2014; New London Group, 1996). We illustrate how a *critical multiliteracies curriculum* can support belonging in early childhood classrooms (e.g., Comber & Woods, 2018; Sanchez & Ensor, 2020; Souto-Manning et al., 2021; Yuval-Davis, 2006), fostering children's abilities to reflect on their life worlds in meaningful ways and engage in meaning-making practices through the use of multimodal tools.

REFRAMING LITERACY

According to the National Early Literacy Panel (NELP, 2008; Lonigan & Shanahan, 2008), "early literacy skills" is a broad term that applies to children birth through age 5 and encompasses both precursor skills and conventional skills. *Precursor (or predictive or foundational or emergent) skills* are those skills seen as prerequisites for the development of conventional literacy skills and are moderately to largely predictive of the development of later conventional literacy skills (Lonigan & Shanahan, 2008; NELP, 2008). *Conventional literacy skills* are seen as more sophisticated and mature processes involved in reading, writing, and spelling instruction for elementary and secondary school students. From a traditional lens, the movement from precursor literacy skills to conventional literacy skills is what constitutes "literacy development" (Paratore et al., 2011; Yaden et al., 2000). This traditional conceptualization emphasizes cognitive processes implicated in the development of reading and writing print.

However, equating decoding and encoding print with literacy limits children's meaning-making potential, particularly disabled children. Specifically, we view disability as a social construct that is created by a mismatch between environmental context and a specific learner in that context, rather than because of a deficit within the learner (Collins & Ferri, 2016). Toward this end, we recognize that traditional literacy skills limit how children can express themselves (Beneke et al., 2024), creating an environment that causes a mismatch between children's myriad meaning-making practices and classroom environments. Through a sociocultural view of literacy (Scribner & Cole, 1981), we recognize that literacy is more than simply reading and writing a script. Rather, literacy is a "set of socially organized practices which make use of a symbol system and a technology for producing and disseminating it" (Scribner & Cole, 1981, p. 236).

Street (2003) emphasized literacy *as a social practice* rather than the acquisition of particular skills. From this lens, children engage in literacy as they apply knowledge for specific purposes in specific contexts; literacy practices involve multiple types of knowledge and multiple sets of skills (Gee, 1996; Scribner & Cole, 1981; Street, 1984). As increasingly complex technologies (e.g., paper and pen, ChatGPT) become more accessible at global scales, the number and complexity of corresponding literacy practices also simultaneously increases (Scribner & Cole, 1981). That is, older versions of literacy can be replaced with newer and more expansive versions of literacy practices (e.g., technology, media) in the context of changing global trends.

Turning to Paolo Freire's notion of critical literacies (1970; 2014), we view the ultimate goal of literacy as learning to read the word in order to better read and transform the world. From this perspective, literacy can provide children opportunities to develop critical consciousness as they engage in learning how to read words and the world. Such critical literacy practices can include the use of new technologies as children reshape literacy forms and functions through social practices that subvert older hegemonic forms of literacy.

Finally, we acknowledge the multiplicity of literacy practices and recognize the cultural and linguistic influences that shape meaning-making (see New London Group, 1996). Drawing on the premise that literacy, or its plural form, *literacies,* is a social practice that takes on distinct forms across contexts, literacy must not be confined to encounters between a reader and text, and must be recognized as a contested space with inevitable relation to questions of how literacy practices are shaped, recognized, controlled, generated, and distributed (e.g., Gee, 1996; Scribner & Cole, 1981; Street, 1984). Thus, we recognize that critical literacy practices are multiple and dynamic and use the term *critical multiliteracies*. This perspective allows us to recognize the multiple realities and practices that disabled children bring to classrooms (Beneke et al., 2024; Collins & Ferri, 2016).

CONCEPTUALIZING BELONGING

Comber and Woods (2018) highlighted that learning in classroom spaces is contingent on children feeling a sense of belonging and knowing how to relate to each other. Toward this end, they suggest alternatives to current accountability regimes (e.g., high-stakes testing, mandated curricula) by centering "social justice spaces where all children can learn to belong and then engage with belonging in diverse ways" (p. 264). Thus, an essential component of fostering belonging through literacy curriculum entails reenvisioning notions of disability as well as dismantling logics that perpetuate unitary ways of engaging with literacy (Beneke et al., 2024; Collins & Ferri, 2016).

We additionally contend that belonging takes place at multiple levels, in multiple forms, and can be discursive. Yuval-Davis (2006; 2011) highlighted three levels of belonging: The first involves one's intersecting markers of identity (e.g., age, gender, sexuality), the second accounts for one's ways of attaching or identifying with others (e.g., ways of signaling how one belongs or wants to belong), and the third entails ethical and political values regarding one's markers of identity as ascribed by society (e.g., who or what identities are privileged in a given context). This framework thus explains how one's intersecting identities might serve to privilege one in certain contexts and marginalize them in other contexts. Across these three levels of belonging, one's social location (i.e., their relative privilege in terms of social constructs or identity markers) "mediates their respective power and influence" (Halse, 2018, p. 8).

Belonging entails access to multiple resources in classrooms and societies (Comber & Woods, 2018). In this project, we bring conceptions of critical multiliteracies alongside frameworks of belonging within literacy curriculum, to center the multiple and intersecting identities of young children. We argue a critical multiliteracies curriculum allows children to access a wide range of literacy resources as they bring forth different aspects of their identities. Thus, by allowing young learners to engage in meaning-making practices that disrupt ableist notions of literacy and honor their multiple identities (including disability), young learners can access spaces that traditionally other them.

PROJECT CONTEXT

This work is part of the regular and ongoing curriculum in Cuenca's classroom, where Unadkat is positioned as a researcher. The authors are both early childhood teachers with an interest in promoting literacy practices that foster equity, inclusion, and belonging. This project explores and illustrates how a critical multiliteracies curriculum serves as a counternarrative to forms of ableism. Specifically, we ask, in what ways does a critical multiliteracies curriculum support children with disabilities in feeling a sense of belonging in an early elementary classroom?

We began collaborating on this project in spring 2023 by designing a series of literacy units that allowed children to engage in research, collaborate, critique and analyze information, and present their findings to peers through a number of modalities. Units centered on themes of identity, such as researching historical figures with marginalized identities (e.g., Ruth Bader Ginsburg, Martin Luther King), the history of various inventions (e.g., slime, Legos, Barbie), and so on. Children worked individually and in small groups on these 3-week endeavors. Through their work, children explored how individuals responded to barriers and challenges in their lives. They were also encouraged to consider what various inventions were used for, who these inventions were accessible to, and other elements of equity and distribution in their work.

Children engaged in one-on-one conversations with Unadkat and Cuenca to share more information about their goals, aspirations, successes, and things they would try differently or anew in subsequent units, as well as how they felt in the classroom in terms of belonging. In collaboration with Cuenca, children set their own goals and reflected on whether and how they met their goals within each unit. We documented their responses and qualitatively analyzed them using deductive and inductive codes along with their work and daily ethnographic field notes (Creswell, 2013; Maxwell, 2013; Miles et al., 2014).

FINDINGS

We illustrate how a critical multiliteracies curriculum fostered belonging within the classroom, as observed with one focal child, Kit, who understood his brain worked differently from his peers and identified as neurodiverse. While we talk about other children illustratively, the focus of this analysis is on Kit's learning and sense of belonging. Kit was a 3rd-grader who had been in school since transitional kindergarten. He was a creative and curious child who enjoyed reading, designing, learning, and building. During his first parent–teacher conference of the year, the primary goal for Kit collectively set by his parents and teacher (i.e., Cuenca) was to build social skills, including developing authentic relationships with peers, learning to set boundaries, and establishing confidence in decision-making. Kit also received a formal diagnosis of attention deficit hyperactivity disorder (ADHD) during the early part of the school year.

Shortly following Kit's ADHD diagnosis, Cuenca invited his mother to lead a lesson on ADHD. Kit's mother shared a short video about ADHD and read a story to the class. She then created a space for children to ask questions, which Kit answered, elaborating on situations that overwhelmed him, made him happy, and felt hard. Following this lesson, the children frequently checked in with Kit, asking him if he needed space or help, whereas previously when Kit chose to move to the back of the room or read by himself, his peers tended to follow him, not recognizing his need for a break. Explicit conversations about Kit's needs and his ADHD provided opportunities for the children to build a supportive community.

Kit's aspirations for perfectionism often prevented him from completing assignments due to overwhelming feelings of apprehension and anxiety. Ableist practices, such as the school's celebration of children who scored highest on standardized tests or finished assignments fastest, caused Kit to believe that he was "not good" at school. Traditional literacy practices further impeded his ability to feel successful and made him feel a lack of belonging. Some of Kit's anxiety was dispelled when he used various technology-based mediums in our curriculum, as he was less constrained when texts were easier to edit. He stated, "It makes me feel scared because sometimes I don't know what to write and I feel like I might mess up and when I use Canva, I know I can edit it." Thus, the reframed curriculum, which we describe later, allowed Kit to set his own goals and work toward them; the curriculum allowed him to feel agency and accomplishment.

When Kit was interviewed about how he was doing in school and whether he felt like he belonged, he exclaimed he was doing "very well" and that he liked coming to school because he enjoyed "learning new things and playing with [my] friends." Cuenca further engaged him in a conversation about the various tools he had used to pursue his literacy and reading interests, such as the use of Canva, moviemaking software, and Google Slides. Kit reflected that he loved using Canva because "it lets [my] creativity come true" by using "elements" and "pictures" to "show how my brain works." For example, after researching bobcats, he used images to demonstrate what he learned and superimposed himself on the green screen to further explain. He also used Canva to create a haiku poem on the topic of "rocks" and used many of the elements to enhance his poem. When learning about the weather, Kit googled the forecast and used the green screen to present the week's weather report. He forecasted, "puffer jacket and hot chocolate weather," and added those images in the background. Kit expressed he felt "less pressure" because it was easy to edit his work, and he didn't worry about making mistakes like he did using traditional text-based writing or literacy practices.

He was also able to leverage his skills and facility with technology to "help" his friends with their work. Kit reflected that in the past at times when he was (seen as) "not very good at stuff" at school, it made him feel like he did not belong. He felt like being "good" at using Canva allowed him to "belong" in the classroom. Most importantly, he was happy, excited, and proud of his learning.

The critical multiliteracies curriculum allowed for easy transfer of knowledge and provided Kit with ample opportunities to complete assignments with pride. In other words, using multiple kinds of symbol systems allowed him to express himself in ways that traditional print-based or traditional literacy curriculum and assessments would not have permitted him to do.

DISCUSSION

Kit's connections to his peers and classroom and his clearly articulated sense of belonging through the critical multiliteracies curriculum were shared by many of his peers. Like Kit, other children with disabilities often felt like they were "not good enough." With the expansive literacy curriculum, children were able to engage in meaning-making practices and participate in classroom (and school) spaces in ways that allowed them to feel confident, supported, and "good" about themselves.

In fact, Cuenca's students were regular contributors to the school newspaper since they had learned how to use Canva, a green screen software for movie editing, and other tools that allowed them to make short video announcements. This positioned all children as active and agentive contributors to a central part of the school's messaging and, importantly, created a space for all children in the classroom to participate where previously those who were deemed "not proficient" readers by hegemonic standards were left out. Overall, this work elucidates how a critical multiliteracies curriculum subverts traditionally oppressive early literacy curriculum in three important and overlapping ways that we highlight below.

Recognizing Learning Differences

Prior to the lesson on ADHD by Kit's mom, many of the children were under the impression that ADHD simply meant that an individual was "hyper." On learning about ADHD, the children discussed how it uniquely affected Kit and how learning looks different for everyone. Misconceptions that children who "finish first" or "read fast" were better than the rest were quickly dismantled. Consequently, all children took steps toward self-acceptance about individual growth, learning, and differences.

Explicit conversations about learning differences thus created a space for children themselves to dismantle technocratic and ableist discourses within school culture (Baglieri et al., 2011; Beneke & Love, 2022; Diaz Soto &

Tuinhof de Moed, 2011; Halse, 2018; Souto-Manning et al., 2021). In this way, children, particularly those who were traditionally othered in school and classroom spaces, engaged in meaning-making practices that honored their multiple identities, created access, and cultivated feelings of belonging.

Centering Multiply Marginalized Identities

As illustrated through Kit's story and the surrounding explicit classroom conversations, much of the curriculum allowed children to consider notions of othering and belonging through reflections on practices in their classroom, school, and beyond. It was apparent that the children, including Kit and others with disabilities, had come to equate test scores and academic performance with achievement. Toward this end, the expanded literacy curriculum centered on researching famous historical figures with multiply marginalized identities, whose successes or fame allowed children to rethink their conceptions of achievement.

These projects supported children to engage in reflections on systemic factors that marginalize some and privilege others, including considering identity markers such as race, class, gender, disability, immigration status, and sexuality. In this way, children explicitly made connections to identity markers that mediate power and privilege and recognized influences that might contribute to othering and belonging in various spaces, including school (Comber & Woods, 2018; Halse, 2018; Yuval-Davis, 2011).

Making Real-World Connections

Conversations about individual differences and multiply marginalized identities through studying historical figures, inventions, and other local and global events allowed children to make meaningful real-world connections. As children became cognizant and articulated individual strengths, differences, and systemic markers of identity that privilege or marginalize others, they used design elements and made multimodal choices to express their ideas. For example, one child used rainbow colors in his presentation on astronaut Sally Ride "since she was gay," while another added a slide that said "LGBTQ ally" to her presentation of pop icon Taylor Swift. Using multimodal elements and digital tools allowed children to make decisions and meaningfully share messaging about real-world issues in ways that highlighted their creativity. Thus, the critical multiliteracies curriculum allowed children to engage in a form of reading the world in ways that leveraged their creativity, strengths, and interests (Freire, 1970).

CONCLUSION

As he engaged in learning, Kit became increasingly aware of his talents using various digital tools. He highlighted his strengths as he shared his process with peers. This instilled a sense of pride that ultimately led to feelings of belonging. Kit's peers felt similar feelings of belonging and pride through their own learning in the critical multiliteracies curriculum. This approach permitted them to become agents of their own learning. They found joy in literacy practices that were rooted in collaborating about font choices, color choices, and images that creatively highlighted learning targets. Normally reticent children were eager to get started on projects and "couldn't wait" to use Canva.

A critical multiliteracies curriculum thus has the potential to foster belonging and subvert traditionally hegemonic learning spaces that privilege standardized test scores. We hope that this work elucidates how early educators might work toward dismantling dominant schooling ideologies, as they emphasize and recognize literacy practices in their multiple forms. We also recognize that future work can engage children in enacting change beyond the classroom and hope that future iterations of this curriculum will create spaces for young children to more fully engage in transformative praxis beyond school.

CHAPTER 5

Creating and Holding Space to Celebrate Disability History and Disabled Communities in Early Childhood Classrooms

Kathryn M. Meyer, Rosie Tuffour-Mercedat, Elizabeth A. Barcay, Brianna Doherty, A.R.Shearer, and Jasmin Stoffer

> I want to say unequivocally that disabled people are everywhere. . . . No matter what community you're working with, you are working with disabled people.
>
> —Mia Mingus (2017)

Disability is a natural form of human diversity, intersecting with every other identity marker, yet school-based curricula often fail to meaningfully center disability as an identity with a rich, ongoing history (Mueller, 2021; Mueller & Beneke, 2022; Thompson, 2020). Instead, schools implicitly reproduce a narrative that disability is something to be fixed, cured, or even ashamed of, which both others and harms disabled students, educators, and families (Artiles, 2011; Baglieri et al., 2011; Hehir, 2002).

We are educators who believe transformation occurs when school-based workers resist the dominant urge to erase disability in pre-K–12 classrooms. Meyer is a white, disabled teacher educator and researcher; Tuffour-Mercedat is a Ghanaian American woman and educator; and Barcay, Doherty, Shearer, and Stoffer are all disabled educators. In this chapter, we explore how early elementary educators can cultivate and sustain pedagogies that affirm, celebrate, and honor disability histories and communities in their classrooms.

ABLEISM, INTERSECTING SYSTEMS OF OPPRESSION, AND "NORMALCY" IN PRE-K-12 SCHOOLING

Disability activists and critical scholars have long called for schools to reject positioning disability as something shameful, wrong, or in need of fixing. They assert that schools should reframe disability as an identity to be claimed and its histories as an essential part of understanding past, present, and future justice movements (e.g., Arvey & Rosenberg, 2020; Mueller, 2021; Mueller & Beneke, 2022; Thompson, 2020). These histories cannot be divorced from the children we teach and the families with whom we work. Educators, children, and families enter schools with assets and lived experiences, which are connected to their multiple communities and identities. How their assets, lived experiences, and needs are realized, affirmed, and met in school, however, is shaped by how their identities are positioned within existing systems of power, privilege, and oppression (Crenshaw, 1989). Disabled children—particularly those marginalized based on their race, ethnicity, gender, sexuality, class, and/or language—often navigate ableist school systems that were not designed or maintained with them in mind (Annamma et al., 2013a).

Ableism is baked into U.S. schooling and intersects with other oppressions (e.g., racism, cisheterosexism, xenophobia; Annamma et al., 2013a). While it is no longer legally permissible to exclude disabled students from public education (IDEA, 2004), many children still experience segregation and serious stigma, harm, and injustice (Annamma et al., 2013a). For example, disabled children of color are suspended, expelled, and placed in segregated classrooms at significantly higher rates than their white disabled peers (Cooc, 2022; Cruz et al., 2021; Hehir et al., 2014). Massachusetts—the birthplace of public *and* special education—continues to allow disabled children, teenagers, and adults to be violently tortured with aversive shock devices at the Judge Rotenberg Center (Neumeier & Brown, 2020). Even when children are included in their neighborhood schools and taught in classrooms with nondisabled peers, they are often pressured to acquiesce to nondisabled white Eurocentric norms and expectations (e.g., Boveda et al., 2019).

When school systems position disability as a singular identity and problem to be fixed, they hinder the development of positive disabled identity (Mueller, 2019) while erasing the ways disability intersects with other identities (Sins Invalid, 2019). Identity is not static; it can be formed and claimed by an individual, as well as shaped by one's experiences in broader society (Forber-Pratt et al., 2017; Mueller, 2019). Many disabled people have spoken about developing an asset-based understanding of disability identity after rejecting mainstream, ableist messages about disability (Wong, 2020). To counter implicit messages that might perpetuate deficit-driven messages about disability, and to honor the wisdom and value disabled people bring to our world, we now turn to pedagogies that center disability as a worthy part of someone's full identity.

COUNTER PEDAGOGIES: TEACHING ABOUT DISABILITY FROM A CRITICAL, ASSET-BASED LENS

Since disabled people have always existed, the history of people with disabilities can be found in every era and movement. Many disability activists, scholars, and educators have written about making this history more visible and accessible in mainstream society. Vilissa Thompson (2020) shared the importance of teaching Black history without erasing people's disabled identities—for example, teaching about Harriet Tubman's full identity as a Black disabled woman and centering the contributions of multiply marginalized people in disability and civil rights movements (Schalk, 2022; Thompson, 2020). Additionally, educators can connect the past and present to show how disability history is still unfolding (Mueller & Beneke, 2022). For example, disabled people are playing key roles in climate justice movements, practicing mutual aid during disabling environmental disasters (Nishida, 2024).

Scholars have also encouraged educators to center the meaningful past and present histories, contributions, and strengths of disabled and multiply marginalized people. We organize our teaching of disability history through DisCrit Classroom Ecology—a pedagogical framework rooted in critical, intersectional, and culturally relevant praxis that centers the strengths, gifts, and lived experiences of multiply marginalized learners (Annamma & Morrison, 2018). DisCrit Classroom Ecology is anchored in resistance and three constructs:

1. **DisCrit Curriculum** ensures instructional content and materials include meaningful discussion and examination of the histories of disabled people of color and their communities.
2. **DisCrit Pedagogy** empowers educators to animate methods and practices that celebrate the assets and lived experiences multiply marginalized children *already* bring to their classroom, while honoring the diverse ways learning can be engaged with, represented, and expressed.
3. **DisCrit Solidarity** centers teacher–learner relationships rooted in "care, respect, and love, rather than hyperfocusing on behavior and management" (Annamma et al., 2023), rejecting oppressive discipline systems that rely on compliance and punishment.

Together, the work of disabled activists, educators, and critical scholars serves as guideposts for our teaching that strives to affirm, celebrate, and support disabled and multiply marginalized children.

ANIMATING DISABILITY IDENTITY, DISABILITY HISTORIES, AND COLLECTIVE CARE IN OUR PRACTICE

Meyer and Tuffour-Mercedat have spent the last three school years teaching young children about disability history, positive conceptions of disability, and the importance of dismantling ableism and facilitating access for all bodies and minds. After our first year, Meyer developed the Disabled Educators Curriculum Collective (DECC; Barcay, Doherty, A,R.Shearer, and Stoffer). DECC was created to center the wisdom and lived experiences of disabled people when developing curricula. We met monthly to reflect on our curricula, methods, and materials, interrogating whether they are accessible, meaningful, and responsive to children. First, we share how we developed a deep understanding of community, accessibility, and disability identity with young children. Next, we discuss how we engaged children in learning about past and present disability histories.

DisCrit Solidarity

Building a Deep Understanding of Community. We began by expanding children's conceptions of community—encouraging them to see beyond geographic borders and to think about shared parts of their identity (see Figure 5.1).

We invited children to tell, show, draw, and/or write about their communities. As we listened to and affirmed their responses, they were positioned as the experts of their own lives. Making space for them to identify multiple ways of being in a community (e.g., race/ethnicity, nationality, disability, hobbies/interests), we did not impose identities or communities on them. We embraced whatever they were willing to share with us.

We centered disabled and multiply marginalized young learners when developing our instruction, believing that when provided the time to explore who they are—both as individuals and as community members—they might see themselves reflected in the histories we share in our practice. We also asserted that children should be given time, space, and support to develop a robust understanding of their identities and communities (Locke et al., 2022). Both extant research and the lived experiences of many disabled and multiply marginalized

Figure 5.1. Expanding Conceptions of Community

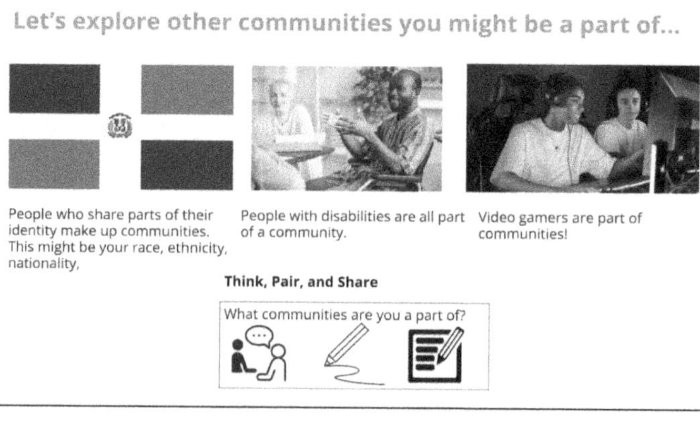

people demonstrate how history is whitewashed and sanitized in schools, such that children who do not hold dominant identity markers often do not see themselves reflected in curriculum (Muhammad, 2023). Defining communities to explicitly include diverse sociocultural identities allowed us to contextualize honoring and meeting accessibility needs as both individual and community endeavors. Making connections to the concepts of interdependency and community care (Sins Invalid, 2019), we reminded children communities of learners work together to learn more about themselves and the world (Ladson-Billings, 1995), and that access is a natural part of being in community.

Accessibility, Disability, and Ableism. We reject the notion that to be a "good" learner or community member, one must be fully independent and without any access needs. Therefore, we normalized checking in with ourselves and each other. Since this practice might not be privileged in prior learning spaces, we modeled by starting with our needs. Meyer shared that she needs a comfortable chair to sit in because the carpet is not supportive for her body. Children were then invited to identify what they need to feel safe, cared for, and ready to learn. Using hand signals (i.e., thumbs up/down/to the side), children showed if they had what they needed. Striving to be flexible and open to what children were expressing, we practiced transparency with them about our abilities to meet their needs. We explained that some access needs can be more easily met, such as providing water, breaks, and fidget tools. Other needs, like opportunities to immediately access family or community members outside school, might not be possible for us to meet. We validated and affirmed their needs while naming the complexities of being in a community where there might be barriers to access (e.g., "Let me see if I can meet the important need you are sharing with us"). We aimed to explicitly embrace body and mind variability and reject a one-size-fits-all model that expects disabled and multiply marginalized children to suppress their needs or hide aspects of themselves to conform to nondisabled, dominant norms.

As children practiced checking in with their bodies and brains, we connected accessibility to disability and ableism using *We Move Together* (Fritsch et al., 2021b), a picture book rooted in disability justice and positive conceptions of disability identity and culture (Fritsch et al., 2021b). While reading, we encouraged children to think about what it means to learn and live in an accessible community where disabled people are valued and supported. To meet this aim, we developed accessible definitions for *disability*, *ableism*, and *accessibility* (see Table 5.1; Beneke et al., 2022; Fritsch et al., 2021a; Laureano et al., n.d.).

Our definition of disability is multifaceted, drawing on many disabled and multiply marginalized people's realities. First, it is grounded in the social model of disability, which positions body and mind variability as a natural part of the world, and our ableist society—not disabled people—as the problem. Using accessible language, we asserted that disability is socially constructed and maintained by dominant society's narrow conceptions of how they believe bodies and brains should move, sense, or exist (Lewis, 2022). We leaned into difficult

Table 5.1. Accessible Definitions for Key Concepts

Concept	Accessible Definition	Connections to *We Move Together*	Prompts to Support Critical Thinking (adapted from Fritsch et al., 2021a)
Disability	A word used to describe when a body or brain moves, senses, or exists in a way that is different from what powerful people in our world expect. Disabled people are often unfairly treated because their bodies and brains are wrongly seen as less valuable, normal, and worthy. This is called ableism (Fritsch et al., 2021a). Disability is not a problem or a bad word. It's a natural and important part of human diversity. No one is the same, and difference makes our world a better place.	Read the opening page showing a group of multiracial, gender-diverse, disabled, and nondisabled children. The children are using a variety of modes and tools to move, including scooters, wheelchairs, crutches, bicycles, legs/feet.	How are kids moving? Are they moving in the same way? Do you see kids moving in ways that you like to move? Does anything surprise you from this picture?
Ableism	When "people think that some people are better or worse than others because of their bodies and brains" (Beneke et al., 2022, p. 1251). When people think it is better to walk than use a wheelchair. Ableism is when there is no ramp for wheelchair users (Beneke et al., 2022; Hehir, 2002). "Creates barriers or obstacles for disabled people, making it hard to meet friends, learn at school, find a place to live, get a job, participate in community events, or even go for ice cream!" (Fritsch et al., 2021a, p. 8).	Read the part when a character using a power wheelchair is not able to access an ice cream parlor.	What is going on in this scene? What is the problem? How do you think we can fix the problem?

Concept	Accessible Definition	Connections to *We Move Together*	Prompts to Support Critical Thinking (adapted from Fritsch et al., 2021a)
Accessibility	"Making changes to our rules, buildings . . . [communities, and] . . . behaviors to make sure everyone feels welcome and is included" (Fritsch et al., 2021a, p. 8).	Read the part where a diverse community of adults and children come together to build ramps.	What is happening here? What do you think they are making?

conversations about oppression, harm, and stigma, foregrounding how social constructions of disability are not neutral and can often result in injustice. Drawing from a long lineage of critical pedagogy and our lived experiences, we know that disabled and multiply marginalized children come to schools with rich strengths and home and community practices (Annamma & Morrison, 2018). Yet these strengths are not always privileged in mainstream society; many children with disabilities already know what it feels like to be marginalized. We view our definition as a form of solidarity with children who are already impacted by ableism. This solidarity extends to the final part of our definition: Disability is not the problem, nor is it a bad word. In fact, it is a natural and important part of human diversity.

We know that our curriculum does not exist in a static vacuum and is mediated by our own social positionings, sociopolitical contexts, and pedagogies (Wertsch, 1998). Therefore, we recognize the facilitators and benefits of having a disabled educator (Meyer) teach this content. Although no disabled educator will approach teaching in the same way, I (Meyer) grounded my practice in honesty and transparency about my lived experiences as a disabled child, learner, and now adult. My experiences of ableism in education afford me a nuanced understanding of the dangers of positioning disability as a tragedy and something to pity. Therefore, we approached this work with both/and in mind: Disabled people and communities can be celebrated *and* we can have authentic conversations with kids about ableism and injustice.

Teaching Past and Present Disability Histories

Next, we taught disability histories, particularly histories of multiply marginalized disabled people, as ongoing and connected to disability rights, disability justice, and other movements (e.g., racial justice). We used DisCrit Curriculum and Pedagogy as practical frameworks for our practice and as organizational tools (Annamma & Morrison, 2018).

DisCrit Curriculum. We centered the contributions of multiply marginalized people with disabilities (Mueller & Beneke, 2022). Prioritizing disabled people of color is essential for several reasons. Disabled people of color have made, and continue to make, significant contributions toward a more just world (e.g., Piepzna-Samarasinha, 2022; Schalk, 2022). These contributions, however, are often overshadowed by mainstream narratives privileging whiteness. The disability rights movement is often associated with the accomplishments of white disabled people (Sins Invalid, 2019). Not only does omitting other narratives shortchange all children with an incomplete history, but it can alienate multiply marginalized children from disability communities of which they might be a part. We prioritized telling disability stories that amplified the lived experiences of people of color, women, and people with other marginalized identities.

Centering Black Disabled People and Communities in Disability History. We began by teaching about Johnnie Lacy, a leader of the independent living movement; Brad Lomax, a key figure during the 504 Sit-In; and the Black Panthers as a group committed to racial justice and disability rights (Schalk, 2022; Thompson, 2020).

We started with a discussion about how Lacy experienced both racism and ableism:

> *Johnnie Lacy went to school in Louisiana in the 1930s and 1940s. The law required that Black and white people be separated. Johnnie went to school with other Black children, and white children went to school with other white children. Black children went to schools that were older and often got books and materials that were old, ripped, or broken. What do you think about that? Let's show, tell, or draw what we think.*
>
> *Johnnie also experienced a lot of ableism. When she went to college, the people in charge would not provide ramps (Lacy, 1998). What do you think about this? What do you think the people in charge should have done? Let's show, tell, or draw what we think.*

Connecting Lacy's schooling experiences to broader resistance to ableism and racism, we invited children to explore how the school could be more accessible to disabled people. We also shared how Lacy led an independent-living movement that provided disabled people with support and opportunities to be fully included in their community. Recognizing that mainstream society, including schools, privileges completing tasks without help (Piepzna-Samarasinha, 2018; Sins Invalid, 2019), we purposefully defined independence as "people's right to choose for themselves how they live and how they get help."

When teaching about the 504 Sit-In, we taught children about Brad Lomax's work within disability rights and racial justice movements, intentionally centering the contributions of a Black disabled leader (Schalk, 2022). More specifically, we spoke with children about how Lomax's coalition building between the 504 Sit-In activists and the Black Panthers was key to the action's success:

> *There were over 100 people living in an office building during the sit-in. What do you think people might need to safely live in a building that is not their home?*
>
> *That's right! Food, water, and beds! Brad was also a member of the Black Panther Party. One of the many important things this group of Black activists did was provide free meals to Black communities. Do you know what else they did? They brought hot meals and other necessities to the protestors. Many people say that without Brad Lomax, the sit-in couldn't have happened. The food they received kept people fed, safe, and healthy.*

Building Links to the Present and Taking Action

Centering Disabled Teachers and Learners. To connect our instruction to children's lives in school, we focused on the experiences of people with disabilities as learners *and* as teachers. We disrupted narrow conceptions of what is considered "normal," troubling binaries that position disabled people as students and never as educators (Mueller, 2021). To animate this, we unpacked Judy Heumann's experiences as both a learner and an educator, offering children opportunities to explore how ableism shaped her schooling. Using videos and quotes from Heumann, we explained that she was excluded from her neighborhood school until she was in 4th grade because she used a wheelchair (Heumann, 2020). Then, after completing college and passing the exams to become a teacher, she was not allowed to become a teacher—again because she used a wheelchair and was considered a fire hazard (Microsoft, 2020). Children discussed whether this was fair and what schools could have done to make sure she could move around the building and stay safe during an emergency. We also created space for children to consider why it's important to have disabled teachers.

Positioning Disability History as Ongoing. We then shared work from disabled creators who educate outside of traditional schools. For example, we used Plank's (2018) video essay with Emily Ladau to illustrate how the United States remains inaccessible for many disabled people. Showing children the barriers Ladau encountered as she met Plank for coffee allowed us to disrupt the notion that disability rights and justice had been fully realized with the passage of laws. It also allowed us to focus on demanding change with children, illustrating how disability rights and justice movements are ongoing. Our class discussions about Ladau, and many other disabled people's experiences, led to schoolwide petitions to government leaders demanding improved access. Through shared writing, children co-constructed a letter that included asking for more ramps and sensory supports.

DisCrit Pedagogy

Our curriculum seeks to affirm children's knowledge, lived experiences, and support needs. We honored the multiple ways children can engage in instruction and express what they know and have learned (Fritzgerald, 2020; Waitoller & Thorius, 2016). We also represented content in varied ways to privilege disabled and multiply marginalized people's lived experiences (Annamma & Morrison, 2018).

Using Multimedia to Center Disabled Voices, Perspectives, and Lived Experiences. We intentionally relied on multimedia created by disabled people, highlighting how disabled people have always resisted ableism and worked toward building a more just world. For example, we showed children excerpts from an NBC News video (2016) of Alice Wong sharing her life story and experiences as a disabled person. Firsthand accounts helped us position those with disabilities as agentic people who lead complex, full lives (Wong, 2020).

We also aimed to build disabled children's connections to community and identity through curricular representation. Privileging works written by disabled authors, we read a variety of books that meaningfully animate the joys, realities, and challenges of navigating our world as a young person with a disability. For example, we used both *Sam's Super Seats* (Brown, 2022) and *A Day With No Words* (Hammond, 2023) to share stories that celebrate the multiple identities and lived experiences of children of color with disabilities, while disrupting notions that disabilities and access needs should be hidden. *Sam's Super Seats* allowed us to explore Black disabled joy and everyone's right to rest while countering dominant notions of disability as a single marker of identity. *A Day With No Words* rejects narrow conceptions of language and communication and positions Autistic identity as a natural part of human diversity. Together, these stories dispel harmful falsehoods that disability is tragic and something to fix or cure. Both texts push the bounds of how disability is represented in children's literature, providing stories that can be shared with disabled and multiply marginalized children as a practice of solidarity: we see you and we value all of you.

Honoring Multiple Ways of Being, Knowing, and Expressing. We provided varied ways for children to demonstrate their knowledge. Because speaking is only one of many ways to communicate, we incorporated "turn and share" opportunities rather than "turn and talk." With universal access to dry-erase boards, children were invited to respond by showing, telling, drawing, and/or writing. With support from a visual board (see Figure 5.2), children shared via writing and other means of communicating (e.g., pointing).

We have found that "turn and share" empowers all children to communicate their knowledge, ideas, and/or questions. As educators, it also allowed us to slow down instruction in meaningful and supportive ways, helping us to engage deeply with children and build connections across responses.

Colleagues have asked us how we respond to children's wonderings and balance competing perspectives and needs. We lean on the belief that every child is the expert of themselves (Fritzgerald, 2020). If we believe there are multiple

Figure 5.2. Visual Board Example

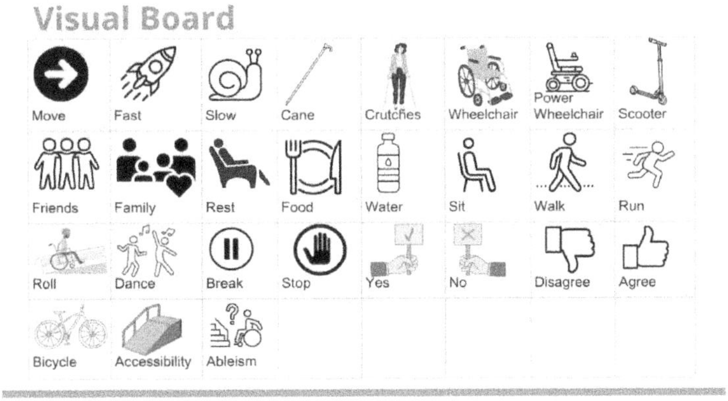

ways of knowing, we must also be prepared for responses and perspectives that widely vary. Therefore, we strive to honor children's perspectives while also facilitating learning and growth (Ladson-Billings, 1995).

We do not "correct" children when they talk about themselves; if they are exploring disability and wondering if they have a disability, we do not impose or gatekeep identities. We affirm connections children make to their own experiences and explain that they get to decide who they are; it's OK to wonder and explore. Simultaneously, we encourage them to interrogate understandings of disability as a deficit. For example, while reading about a book character using a mobility device (e.g., wheelchair, crutches), we responded to children's conceptions that perpetuated ableist tropes, such as assuming you use a wheelchair because your legs are broken or you need a cane because you are old. Instead, we drew on prior curricular examples that resisted these stereotypes and prompted children to return to the text:

> *I am wondering about all of the people we have learned about who use wheelchairs and canes for many different reasons. It's important that we don't make guesses about someone else's body and brain. Let's go back to our text and see if the author shared this with us.*

By balancing children's curiosity alongside gentle pushes to resist deficit-based assumptions about disabled people, we aimed to support their cultural consciousness.

ONGOING WONDERINGS AND OUR CALL FOR COLLECTIVE ACTION

We view our teaching about disability and disability histories as a form of deep solidarity with multiply marginalized disabled children who have often not seen their lived experiences and full identities represented in school (Mueller, 2021). We also grapple with ongoing wonderings and institutional barriers that we believe must be attended to as we build a more just educational system.

One limitation of our teaching is that it has been limited to one day per week as an "add-on" to core instruction. Teachers, particularly ones serving a high proportion of multiply marginalized children, are more likely to feel pressure to acquiesce to the very norms we are trying to trouble (e.g., high-stakes testing, standardized Eurocentric curricula; Au, 2007). We wonder: How do we empower educators to take on more expansive approaches to curriculum and pedagogy when high-stakes tests privilege a "one size fits all" approach to learning and assessment? Similarly, we recognize how our methods trouble behavior management systems that focus on compliance (e.g., silent, still body; Beneke et al., 2022). How do we empower teachers to reimagine what a classroom can look, sound, and feel like so that it does not reify oppressive norms?

While we do not have easy answers, we believe the work starts with building a collective of committed educators and educational leaders. We urge leaders to invest in pedagogy and curricula that center and celebrate multiply marginalized children's whole selves. We believe this work must be funded, and studied, at the classroom level with ample, protected time for planning and collaboration. For example, school districts can implement co-teaching models where educators use teacher inquiry cycles to explore disability history and curricular integration (Cochran-Smith & Lytle, 2015). We also urge districts to meaningfully reflect on their commitment to recruiting, hiring, retaining, and supporting disabled teachers, especially those with multiple marginalized identities (Loeppky, 2021). To be clear, we do not believe that disabled educators should be hired to teach about disability; rather, the labor of teaching about disability must be on all educators. However, disabled teachers bring valuable lived experiences and assets to school communities, and they can serve as powerful mirrors and windows to the future for disabled children.

CHAPTER 6

Beyond the Developmental Benefits of Early Childhood Outdoor Learning

Thinking *With* Materials and Place in Bush Kindergarten

Ame Christiansen

"One hand or two?"

Juliet looks up tentatively. She hesitates, glancing down as Darebin Creek speeds its way through a narrow concrete gap. Being with the parklands this morning involves crossing Darebin Creek at an unpredictable yet familiar spot. Undecided, Juliet lingers on the eastern edge. Water bubbles and churns. Rushing and gushing, it draws our collective attention. Children and teachers chatter calmly, reading place (the creek, rocks, slippery ledges, and water) with curiosity. Andy maintains the pause, watching Juliet's face. His movement is slow, his voice low and calm. All eyes wander, with wondering and indecision.

Andy stands astride the gap and holds out an outstretched palm. Juliet and Andy each drop their gaze on it. He smiles and, maintaining shared attention, silently opens his other palm in offering. He doesn't repeat the question but softly gestures it again, lifting one hand and then the other ("one hand or two?").

Glancing at the water and taking his outstretched hands, Juliet quietly confirms, "two." She pulls their hands down and jumps up, legs and water leaping, steadily springing across the meter-wide gap. Landing on the other ledge, she turns—called back to the water again—and then bounds off up the rock steps. Andy turns back to the bouncing line of eager 4-year-olds asking quietly with arms outstretched, "One hand or two?"

In this chapter, I share small, situated moments from pedagogical encounters during my doctoral research in an Australian "bush" (outdoor) kindergarten (Christiansen, 2022). As a late-diagnosed Autistic woman and settler with Irish and Scandinavian ancestry, I explore the complex relations of teachers, place, children, materials, and the more-than-human. As an uninvited guest on the unceded lands of the Wurundjeri Woi-wurrung people, Traditional Owners

Figure 6.1. Concrete Crossing Darebin Creek

Source: Author's gallery.

of Naarm (Melbourne), I conceptualize bush kindergartens not as romantic or neutral spaces but as pedagogical contact zones (Hamm & Boucher, 2017)—conceptual spaces where different ways of knowing "meet, clash and grapple" (Pratt, 1998, p. 173). Based on an extended time period with children, teachers, and place in 2019, I activate pedagogical narration as a process of thinking with theory (Jackson & Mazzei, 2017) and writing as a method of inquiry (St. Pierre, 2007). In doing so, I think beyond minimum compliance with inclusion policy and regulations that celebrate the developmental benefits of bush kindergarten for normative child development. Instead, I story critical and relational conceptualizations of disability and inclusivity in early childhood.

WHAT IS BUSH KINDERGARTEN?

In Australia, bush kindergarten is an increasingly popular means of exploring and strengthening children's relations with local places—beaches, creeks, bush reserves, and managed parklands (Hughes et al., 2022). This research took place at the first bush kindergarten, "Bush Kinder," which was established by the director and committee of Westgarth Kindergarten in 2012. Distinct from specific site-based learning by and with Indigenous people, which has occurred in Australia for over 60,000 years (Thorpe & Zerella, 2023; Turner et al., 2023), bush kindergartens represent practice settings in which young children and their teachers routinely access local places as part of their everyday early childhood programs (Christiansen et al., 2018). They involve teachers taking children beyond the physical boundaries and regulated spaces of early childhood facilities. There are now hundreds of bush kindergartens (and similar outdoor early childhood programs) across Australia. In the lead-up to the state government election in 2022, the incumbent government pledged $3.6M to support expansion of bush kindergarten programs, funding an additional 150 services each year until 2027. This funding initiative reinforced the developmental benefits of bush kindergartens, suggesting that:

> Increasing the amount of time children spend outdoors and in natural environments can improve: children's wellbeing, physical development, fine and gross motor skills, core strength, coordination, balance, eyesight and physical endurance; encourage children to build deeper understandings of science, technology, engineering and math (STEM); support children to make decisions and judgements that challenge and safely explore established boundaries; improve children's connections to nature, which can encourage their knowledge and commitment to environmental sustainability into adulthood. (Victorian Government, 2023, para 4)

This initiative was supported by a large and growing international and local evidence base that outlines the benefits of outdoor learning for normative child development (e.g., Gill, 2014; Li et al., 2019; Mygind et al., 2019; Speldewinde, 2022). Less research has considered the lived experiences of children with disabilities in bush kindergarten programs, despite their relatively high participation (Kids in Nature Network, 2018).

The program explored in this chapter was developed over a decade ago by a teaching team and volunteer committee eager to connect children with nature in meaningful ways. By privileging unstructured, child-led, and risky play, the teachers suggested bush kinder "leveled the playing field" as it attuned families and teachers to broader ways of thinking about and responding to diverse ways of playing and learning. This led teachers and families to recontextualize risk-taking, physicality, and neurodivergent attunement to materials as legitimate ways of playing and learning rather than areas of deficit that needed to be fixed.

While each Australian bush kindergarten program is different, in general, young children and their teachers in these programs spend extended periods of time (usually one-half or full day per week) being with place (walking, watching, wondering, noticing, playing, touching, making, and exploring). They tend to be "all weather" programs that intentionally create opportunities for unstructured play and children's own assessments of risk. Teachers privilege children's agency by promoting play-based learning that integrates child-led and adult-guided pedagogies as well as direct instruction and intentional teaching.

POLICY, FUNDING, AND THE REGULATORY CONTEXT FOR "INCLUSION" IN BUSH KINDERGARTEN

The regulatory and legislative framework for "inclusion" in Australian early childhood settings (including but not limited to bush kindergartens) is complex. As part of the state-based and universally funded preschool education system for 3- and 4-year-old children in Victoria, bush kindergartens are fully regulated under the National Law and National Quality Standard (Australian Children's Education and Care Quality Authority [ACECQA], 2017). Bush kindergartens are integrated services and form part of universally accessible kindergarten programs for 3- and 4-year-old children. While families have historically paid fees to access kindergarten programs, kindergarten is currently free for all families (State Government of Victoria, 2024).

Bush kindergartens are led by university-qualified early childhood teachers and educators with certificate or diploma-level qualifications (Quality Assessment and Regulation Division [QARD], 2023). They are legally mandated to include all learners under national and state legislation. Compliance with quality processes is "assured" through self-assessment and Quality Improvement Planning, as well as "Assessment and Ratings" visits by the state's regulatory authority (ACECQA, 2017). Teachers and early childhood service providers must ensure that one of two approved curriculum frameworks inform the curriculum plan.

Bush kindergarten programs can be supported by equity-based Kindergarten Inclusion Support (KIS) funding, which is available via an application process, to "enhance the kindergarten's capacity to support the access and participation of children with a disability or developmental delay and high support needs" (Victoria State Government Department of Education, 2024). However, the bush kindergarten involved in this research did not have KIS funding for any of the children with a diagnosed disability who were enrolled that year.

The approved national curriculum framework, the EYLF 2.0 is premised on inclusive theories and "Practice Principles," which include "Respect for Diversity" and "Equity, Inclusion and High Expectations." Educators must also make reasonable adjustments to support participation and remove barriers to learning. While the 2016 version of the Victorian Early Years Learning and Development Framework is currently under review, a recent update of the EYLF has seen greater emphasis placed on relational and culturally responsive pedagogies but little context for how these relate to disabled children and families.

WHAT IS PEDAGOGICAL NARRATION?

Pedagogical narration (Pacini-Ketchabaw et al., 2015) is a critical and flexible analytic research practice. More than visual and textual observations of individual child development or reflections on what has happened in early educational encounters, pedagogical narration leverages multimodal and multisensory "listening" to make visible the complex ways that children, place, and things mutually render one another capable from one moment to the next. It repositions teachers and researchers as activist-practitioners who can bring collective awareness to children's strengths and capacities as well as oppressions, silences, and erasures.

Pedagogical narration can also uncover tensions that are always present in early childhood contexts—including the deficit-based ways disabled children are often positioned. The stories and narratives we create and tell in educational contexts (about children, about place, about past and present, about pedagogies and power) always render reality thinkable in some ways and not others. As Haraway (2016) reminds us, it matters which stories we use in our efforts to tell other stories. Indeed, if the stories we tell about disability or inclusion position children (or families, or teachers) in deficit ways, then it is very hard to tell a story of inclusivity attuned to mutual belonging and capability.

Storying, or representing, disability through pedagogical narration invites teachers and researchers to resist the erasure of lived experiences of disability in the literature concerned with young children and nature programs (Christiansen, 2022) and the presence of ongoing Indigenous relations with the lands with which outdoor learning is taking place (Nxumalo, 2019; Styres, 2019). In this chapter, I put this methodological orientation to work while drawing on critical perspectives (Pacini-Ketchabaw et al., 2015) and Indigenous ways of knowing (Kwaymullina, 2018; Martin, 2016; Styres, 2019). In doing so, I attend to multiplicity—challenging the centrality of white, settler, developmental, middle-class and ableist norms in early educational theory and practice.

RELATIONAL APPROACHES TO (RE)STORYING DISABILITY: CENTERING FREEDOM AND BELONGING

Dominant discourses in research concerned with disability in Australian early childhood contexts tend to emphasize what children cannot do through developmental approaches. By pathologizing difference, these approaches locate problems within children and try to fix or intervene based on their diagnoses, disability labels, or other markers of marginalization. In so doing, dominant approaches to early education and research ignore the relational, social, political and ethical realities of disability and inclusivity.

Critical disabilities studies scholars trouble and reconceptualize developmental and interventionist approaches, foregrounding an affirmative approach to difference and an image of the child as capable. They also promote an understanding of disability and ability as conceptually co-constituted (Goodley, 2014), attending to complex, relational understandings of disability (Cologon & Thomas, 2014). Critical and relational approaches to disability advocate for the removal of barriers to doing and being and open a critical space for nondisabled people to see themselves as mutually implicated in processes of disablement (Mackenzie et al., 2016).

The image of the child as capable is central to restorying disability in early childhood education. Reconceptualizing *all* children as capable requires that we begin from a position in which the role of the adult is defined "not as a transmitter [of knowledge], but as a creator of relationships—relationships not only between people, but also between things, between thoughts, with the environment" (Malaguzzi, 1996, p. 56). Conceptualizing inclusivity through critical, relational, and capability-focused approaches to disability and difference means traditional binaries, like teacher and child, humans and place, nature and culture, exist "in-relationship" and cannot be separated.

Moving from the idea of "being in relationship" to "being in relation with" (Haraway, 2016), we can recognize how children's *ways of being* and ways of knowing are inseparable. That is, one *knows* about the world through *being*. After all, we are not able to experience the world outside of ourselves. Knowing and being come not from being separate from the world or standing outside and observing it, but from our direct relation with the world—being in and of it (Barad, 2007). Thus, people, place, materials, and things are entangled and enmeshed in a state of imminent being and becoming.

Such conceptualizations of "being in relation with" are not new; they draw on Indigenous ways of knowing and being with the world—the oldest continuous ways of knowing and being on the planet (Smith, 2012). Thus, in considering relational approaches to storying disability, I not only draw from Euro-Western theories but return to the work of Indigenous scholars (Cumpston et al., 2022; Kwaymullina, 2020; Martin, 2016; Wall Kimmerer, 2021). In doing so, I seek to learn with and from Indigenous and non-Indigenous scholarship while acknowledging that all bush kindergartens in Australia take place in relation with lands already damaged by ongoing settler colonialism (Kwaymullina, 2020).

From a critical, relational lens, those with whom a child is always already in relation—both human (peers, teachers, parents, siblings) and more than human (places and things)—are simultaneously implicated in processes of disablement and enablement. Adopting a critical, relational approach to disability does not mean erasing individual difference or disabled identities, nor discarding the human. Instead, it requires shedding limited models of "inclusion" in which some people automatically belong (e.g., by virtue of their whiteness, ability, or class) while others "need to be included" (Taylor & Giugni, 2012). A critical, relational approach to disability attends to a broader, intersectional sense of "inclusivity" as mutual belonging, making visible the multiple ways that disabled and multiply marginalized children experience belonging and freedom through relations with others and their worlds.

Reconceptualizing disability and inclusivity opens space to resist dominant notions of normalcy and developmentalism and attunes us to a more-than-human sociality—in which "nature" (places, animals, materials, things) becomes more than simply a neutral backdrop. In the following section, I expand on the pedagogical encounter with which I opened the chapter, making visible how pedagogical narration can be put to work as a method of inquiry for activist-practitioner research.

PEDAGOGICAL NARRATION: REMOVING BARRIERS TO BEING AND DOING

Restorying Ability: Being in Relation With People

Reread the opening encounter at the start of this chapter. In writing/narrating the above encounter in this way, I center an image in which the child and teacher are in relation with one another and with place. I do not begin with a list of Juliet's developmental delays or diagnosis. I don't list strengths, capacities, or challenges that may position her as disabled or in deficit. Juliet is not *figured* through her verbal speech/interests/choices or other identity markers; instead, her experiences are amplified by attending to the multimodal and multisensory ways of being and doing she employs in relation with people and place (e.g., facial gaze and expression, fine and gross motor movements and orientations, gestures, responses, pauses, silences, and indecision). Storying the encounter in this way makes visible how being in relation with an attuned teacher in physically and sensorially challenging educational contexts can create possibilities, not only for Juliet's participation on her own terms (through agency, freedom, choice, and power in decision-making), but also in the teacher's orientation to differentiation and assistance that is child-led.

"*One hand or two?*" is a common refrain heard from Bush Kinder educators. In our interview, Andy tells me that he learned it by watching other educators. The phrase is not used as an instrumental practice of "what works" but instead is recognized as an intentionally enabling pedagogy (or way of doing) that opens a space for respectfully centering children's capacities to communicate on their own terms. Whether children take one hand, two hands, or no hands doesn't depend on their "ability" in an enduring way but is in relation with people and place on a more fluid, temporal, and physical level—which may change depending on the amount of rain in recent days, the speed of flowing water, the slipperiness of the rocks, the amount of moss, the time of day, the season or year. Andy told me:

> *I learned that from my colleagues here, watching the way they approach that space, and how they treated the children's abilities. It seemed appropriate, it feels respectful, it offers the same opportunity to each child regardless of ability. . . . I can't recall a child refusing the opportunity to jump over that section. I think that's largely because they're given the opportunity to choose how they'll do it.*

Storying disability by attending to relations with people and place in this way provides an alternative narrative to dominant intervention-focused regimes in early childhood education. It attends to Juliet's abilities and challenges but, importantly, makes visible the multiple, inclusive, and strategic moments of political and ethical decision-making being negotiated in this moment "in relation with" people and place.

My research found that Bush Kinder educators tended to emphasize the importance of relationships and time. How Andy *responded* to the political (questions of power) and ethical (questions of rights and justice) in this moment of decision-making (how to provide support) is multimodal, multisensory, and relationally and temporally attuned. Andy demonstrated his capacity to respond in this very short "everyday moment" through a range of slow, enabling, and inclusive pedagogies. He created predictability through rhythm and routine. He used limited option questions and followed questions with extended pauses for processing time. He followed Juliet's focus while listening multimodally (through visual, tactile, auditory senses). He brought shared attention back to the task and used facial gaze to offer support rather than demanding eye contact. He asked multimodal questions by reinforcing verbal prompts with gestures (silently raising one hand then two instead of repeating the question verbally). Using a low, calm voice, he countered the rush and anxiety created by the flowing water, mediating a known point of challenge for Juliet (physical stability, coordination, and balance) by positioning himself across the "concrete gap" (see Figure 6.1) to provide physical support and strength as well as emotional reassurance. Each of these slow, intentional ways of being and doing in relation with Juliet provided additional assistance that reduced physical, sensory, and attitudinal barriers to being and doing—supporting Juliet to participate on her own terms.

However, if we leave the narration there, this continues to be a romanticized vision of children's relations with place. I have focused on relationships between teacher and child, highlighting the teacher's pedagogical intentions and engagements. However, we can also attend to the vibrant influence of place (e.g., the creek), materials (e.g., rocks, water), and the co-presence of Indigenous relations (Murphy 2019; Murphy & Kennedy, 2016; Styres, 2019; Taylor & Giugni, 2012).

Rethinking Agency: Being in Relation With Place

Nxumalo (2019) warned against upholding the benefits of nature kindergarten for normative child development in ways that reinscribe settler colonialisms and non-Indigenous claims to colonized places. In outdoor programs, "nature" is often figured uncritically and incorrectly (Fletcher et al., 2021) as pure, wild, or a natural site for nurturing child development and environmental stewardship (Nxumalo, 2019). Without reference to past, present, and enduring Indigenous and colonial relations, outdoor programs, like all educational settings, are limited in their capacity for enacting just educational futures (Kwaymullina, 2018). Thinking *with* materials and place can make visible ongoing colonial relations with stolen lands (Kwaymullina, 2020) and can provoke educators to consider how people, materials, and place are enmeshed—how we live entangled, complex, and problematic lives (Pacini-Ketchabaw et al., 2015).

Bush Kinder teachers and children storied place and continuous Indigenous relations with the parklands in everyday moments, foregrounding the parklands as Wurundjeri Woi-wurrung Country. The teachers reiterated that their ways of relating with Wurundjeri Woi-wurrung Country included formal and informal everyday practices—from acknowledging Traditional Owners through formal Acknowledgements of Country and conversations with elders, to everyday slow pedagogies like walking and attuning to the creek and parklands as Country. Each teacher shared how being with the parklands supported their capacity to learn from and better understand First Nations expertise. For example, they learned about and through the local Wurundjeri Seasons, which are more complex and locally situated than dominant European conceptions of seasonal change (Darebin Creek Management Committee [DCMC], 2025). The teachers reinforced with children that Wurundjeri Woi-wurrung people have been educating children on Country here forever, taking care to not appropriate those relations or spiritual connections, but instead prioritize Indigenous perspectives.

Families, children, and teachers at this Bush Kinder are predominantly non-Indigenous and the local area is socioeconomically affluent, hinting at larger "on-going settler colonialisms" (Nxumalo, 2019, p. iii) and the inherent friction that all Australian education takes place on unceded lands with which Indigenous people are always spiritually connected. Further, revisiting the above narration from the perspective of this being Country makes visible my own complicity in ongoing systems of colonization (Kwaymullina, 2018; Smith, 2012).

The "concrete gap" over Darebin Creek where this pedagogical encounter takes place is part of a pathway with public signage called the Darebin Spiritual Healing Trail. The Creek Management Committee described the signage as "gifted by Aboriginal and Torres Strait Islander community as a gesture of reconciliation" (DCMC, n.d., p.3). The DCMC further suggest it was conceived by the "Darebin Aboriginal Reconciliation Working Party with the approval of members of the traditional custodians of the land and with the support of members of the local Aboriginal community" (DCMC, n.d., p. 10) to teach non-Indigenous Australians about the Wurundjeri Woi-wurrung creator spirit (Bunjil) and enduring Wirundjeri connections with the land, trees, animals, skies, and waterways of the parklands.

While teachers and children did not follow the self-guided walk or signage while I was there, their connections with Darebin Creek traverse the trail. The teachers were aware of the trail as a means of engaging with and learning from ongoing Wurundjeri Woi-wurrung connections. The specific crossing point at which this pedagogical encounter took place, the concrete "gap" (Figure 6.1), is the fourth point of reflection on the trail. The guide suggests it "symbolizes possibilities and the need to take one step at a time to overcome big obstacles" (p. 8). The gap is a "fish ladder" and encourages parklands visitors to consider how relations with people and place (e.g., waterways, rocks, animals) act as ladders and offer support when one faces challenges. While this may only be a very small understanding of its larger significance, it is one offered for non-Indigenous people to begin to learn from. For Bush Kinder children and teachers, the concrete gap was indeed a physical barrier. The practice of "one hand or two" created a physical scaffold or ladder of support at this particular point in the parklands, as teachers worked relationally with people and place informed by those whose native lands they are visiting.

However, the concrete gap was also a physical barrier for native fish that migrate up and down the river from saltwater to freshwater, including the Common Galaxis and Short Fin Eel (Melbourne Water, 2024). In 2022, long after my time with the Bush Kinder community, Melbourne Water installed a "rock ramp fishway" replacing the concrete gap with large boulders. The boulders allow water to cascade through the structure, forming eddies and low steps for fish heading up the river. Melbourne Water reports that the rock ramp fishway has increased the presence of the target species upstream, supporting fish migration and habitat connectivity. At the same time the fishway has, according to local news outlets, reportedly reduced accessibility for people crossing Darebin Creek in periods of high water (ABC Radio Melbourne, 2022). I wonder now about how Bush Kinder teachers and children are adapting with this reconfiguration? How are they negotiating new moments of ethical and political decision-making together with Darebin Creek?

THINKING BEYOND BENEFITS

Adopting a critical, relational model of disability and an image of the child as capable, this chapter has positioned disabled children as always already in relation with people and place. I argue that those interested in activist-practitioner research can mobilize and learn from critical, relational perspectives to disrupt normative regimes in early childhood and support the ethical co-creation of more just educational futures. Pedagogical narration can further support resistance to ableist norms in educational research, theory, and practice. I have engaged here with pedagogical narration as a research practice; however, it is also an approach to pedagogical documentation and professional learning available to early childhood educators everywhere. I do not seek to offer specific universal strategies for practice, although there is much that a reader may learn from the ways the teachers at Bush Kinder position themselves in relation with children and place. The ways of being in relation explored in this chapter—slow, strengths-based, and rights-oriented, enabling pedagogies attuned to the politics and ethics of people *and* place—may be useful for those seeking to resist deficit discourses about children with disabilities and disrupt human-centered, apolitical, and ahistorical "benefits" and "stewardship" narratives in early childhood outdoor learning.

Part III

PRIORITIZING FAMILIES' PERSPECTIVES AND STORIES

In this section, chapters illuminate racialized families' experiences in early childhood education and challenge how compliance with dominant views of family–professional partnerships can also perpetuate ableism. That is, they illustrate how institutionally determined goals and processes for parent involvement—normed on white, Eurocentric, middle-class practices—can lead to devaluing the caretaking *abilities* of racialized families.

The section begins with Chapter 7 by Hancock and Morgan, in which they show how Black and multiracial families intentionally resist covert assimilationist purposes embedded within interactions with Early Head Start home visitors and strategically repositioned themselves as capable. They offer important strategies for professionals to honor families' resistance in the context of home visiting and educational decision-making. Then, in Chapter 8, Park highlights how Latina multilingual mothers created pedagogies of relationality and interdependence for their young children with disabilities as they navigated remote education during the early days of the COVID-19 pandemic. The mothers' stories position them as pedagogues in their own right, teaching us how struggle and interdependence are interconnected and at the heart of our work with young children. Begaye-Tewa, Ruiz, and Begay conclude the section by uplifting Indigenous families' stories and experiences in early childhood special education in Chapter 9. Rooted in Indigenous knowledge systems, they offer a framework for elevating families' stories and perspectives regarding disability and childhood, ones grounded in culture and tradition.

Each of these chapters squarely center the wisdom and knowledges of racialized families who have young children with disabilities, whose caregiving abilities are frequently devalued or overlooked within traditional models of family–professional partnerships. By prioritizing the perspectives and stories of families who have been marginalized by expectations of compliance, the authors also offer practical strategies for pushing back on and strengthening current conceptions of partnerships with families of young children with disabilities.

CHAPTER 7

Honoring Family Resistance to Foster Shared Decision-Making

Christine L. Hancock and Chelsea W. Morgan

Early childhood programs often conceptualize family engagement in ways that center institutional priorities, such as attendance at school-based events and assistance upholding classroom behavioral expectations (Ishimaru, 2019; Love et al., 2021a). Despite purported messages about partnership, underneath these visions for family engagement are presumptions that educational institutions and professionals know best what children need, and that families should demonstrate engagement by listening to and following their recommendations (Hong, 2019). Moreover, educator beliefs about what children need—and how families should be engaged in response to those needs—are influenced by white, nondisabled norms, constraining opportunities and expectations for those outside of the norms (Beneke & Love, 2022; Park, 2024). Yet multiply marginalized families routinely resist these strictures, drawing on community and cultural assets to strategically advocate on behalf of their children (e.g., Gillborn et al., 2016; Harry & Ocasio-Stoutenburg, 2020). As Santamaría Graff and Vazquez (2014) explained, "Resistance is an act against expectations and norms of what it is to be a parent and to be involved" (p. 82).

Marginalized and multiply marginalized families must contend with two interrelated and limiting perspectives of resistance when they do not engage in normative ways. First, professionals tend to frame resistance as a deficit. Second, professionals often miss opportunities to acknowledge how resistance responds to oppressive systems and norms, particularly racism and ableism. To reckon with how expectations about family engagement can further marginalize families of color, many scholars have called for professionals to reject deficit-based views of resistance and recognize various forms of family advocacy (Alvarez, 2020; Love et al., 2021a; Park, 2024; Santamaría Graff & Vazquez, 2014).

Narrow family engagement expectations can contribute to deficit-based views of children and families marginalized based on myriad factors (e.g., race, ability, language, class; Beneke et al., 2021; Ishimaru, 2019; Love et al., 2021a). Families may be blamed for perceived deficits of their children (e.g., Baquedano-López et al., 2013; Posey-Maddox, 2017). Further, professionals often perceive family resistance as indicating a lack of knowledge or skills to engage in the "right" ways.

Park (2024) found that educators positioned immigrant families of children with disabilities as either helpless or defiant and in denial, either way rationalizing professional control over decision-making. These deficit-based views obscure how normative expectations play a role in constructing resistance, even when families attempt to participate in expected ways. For example, when Black families, and particularly Black fathers, attend school events, engage with their child's teacher, or visit their child's classroom, they are more likely to be interpreted as aggressive and interfering with educators' practice (e.g., Gillborn et al., 2016; Posey-Maddox, 2017).

Professionals often neglect to acknowledge resistance as an integral way marginalized and multiply marginalized communities survive, reject, and counteract oppression (Annamma et al., 2013a; Yosso, 2005). Researchers have identified meaningful resistance enacted by families of color, detailing its transformative potential. In particular, Black and immigrant families have rejected deficit positioning of themselves and their children, instead asserting their competence and value (Alvarez, 2020; Beneke et al., 2021; Love et al., 2021a; Park, 2024). For example, Black parents reframed perceived problems with their daughters' behaviors as problems with school expectations and actions to shift school priorities from discipline to provision of supports (Love et al., 2021a). Families have also engaged in resistance by equipping children with knowledge and skills not prioritized in schools, including sustaining bilingualism and rejecting singular constructions of identity (e.g., Mexican or American; Alvarez, 2020), and teaching children how to process and respond to racism and ableism (Love et al., 2021a). When professionals have promoted decisions that do not honor children or their support needs (e.g., restrictive placements, medication), families have strategically subverted expectations to carry out recommendations (Park, 2024).

FAMILY RESISTANCE IN THE CONTEXT OF HOME VISIT DECISION-MAKING

Home visiting with families of infants and toddlers identified with or considered to be "at risk" for disabilities is often perceived as inherently collaborative, given its emphasis on family–professional relationships and mutual activities (e.g., joint planning). However, home visiting is not exempt from dominant views of family engagement. Instead, these expectations are bound up in the ways home visit practitioners (HVs) and families interact, particularly as they engage in decision-making about how to support child development and family well-being (e.g., developing individualized child or family goals, determining how to refine caregiving practices).

Professionals can learn from and alongside families through home visits. Yet scholars have detailed how home visiting has historically served assimilationist purposes, particularly when HVs teach families who are immigrants or experiencing poverty how to adopt normative caregiving practices (e.g., specific approaches to hygiene, speaking only English at home) presumed to support child and family development (Baquedano-López et al., 2013; Szech, 2023). While HVs may be less explicitly didactic within current approaches to decision-making, when they offer advice to families they position families as recipients of HV expertise (e.g., Hancock & Cheatham, 2024; Lea, 2006; Paulick et al., 2022). In essence, assimilationist purposes have become more covert but remain embedded within interactions.

Across home visit models, family participation is often conceptualized as enrollment, attendance, or retainment, contributing to views that engagement is primarily about family presence and follow-through on institutional priorities, such as responsiveness to HVs' curriculum or requests (e.g., Kleinman et al., 2023). As in other contexts, practitioners may frame family resistance during home visits from a deficit perspective, such as labeling families as disengaged or noncompliant (e.g., when families attend to household tasks rather than interacting with the HV and child, cancel home visits, or decline HV recommendations; Baker et al., 2020; Park, 2024). Such decontextualized views of family resistance do not consider power dynamics and interpret families' actions as indicative of denial, defiance, or lack of understanding (Park, 2024). Meanwhile, HVs are often positioned as experts who set and control visit agendas with marginalized families, dominating decision-making (e.g., Hancock & Cheatham, 2024; Lea, 2006; Park & Paulick, 2024; Paulick et al., 2022). Thus, resistance in the form of families actively disengaging may be the primary means through which families can shape how decision-making unfolds.

Resistance in Real Time During Home Visits: A Discursive Perspective

While family resistance takes many forms, power dynamics and resistance are enacted through discourse (i.e., language in social interaction; Gee, 2014) during interactions like decision-making. Following Gee (2014), discourse involves not only details about language use such as word choice or volume, but also speakers' actions (e.g., offering advice, proposing ideas) and the identities they construct (e.g., engaged parent, collaborative partner). These discourse features do not exist in isolation; how one speaker engages in discourse (including actions taken and identities constructed) shapes the context for how the next speaker responds, which shapes the subsequent turn, and so on (Gee, 2014). Throughout this turn-taking process, families can strategically enact resistance, in terms of both *what* they say and *how* they say it.

Discourse features (see Table 7.1) can be documented through detailed transcription (Bolden & Hepburn, 2018) and investigated through discourse analysis (e.g., Gee, 2014). For example, when a HV asks a narrow, detail-oriented question, an expectation is implicitly set for the parent to respond by providing requested information. In doing so, the HV is positioned as an assessor and the parent an informant. Offering other information—even if the question was

Table 7.1. Discourse Features, Relation to Family Resistance, and Transcription Conventions

Discourse Feature	Relation to Family Resistance	Code	Code Explanation
Overlap	Establish or extend a turn without waiting for HV, reconfiguring turn-taking	Katie: cause //he is,// Meher: //yeah//	Simultaneous talk enclosed in double slashes
Latching	Establish or extend a turn without waiting for HV, reconfiguring turn-taking	Katie: encouraging him to talk= Meher: =yeah	No gap between speaking turns
Lengthening	Indicate hesitation or emphasis, demonstrating preference or priority	o:h	Elongation of syllable
Intonation	Signal intent to continue speaking or extend a turn, holding the floor	,	Low-rising intonation (e.g., continuation)
	Frame comments as definitive, highlighting expertise	.	Falling intonation (e.g., conclusion)
	Request response from HV, shifting expected pattern	?	Rising intonation (e.g., question)
Silence	Decline to respond to certain topics or questions, reshaping agenda	(1.3)	Silence measured in seconds
Laughter	Soften comment, demonstrate solidarity or bravery	-	Laughter tokens - = "ha"; -- = "haha"
Actions and context	Redirect engagement, such as by turning attention to child	((description))	Contextual descriptions and information (e.g., parent leaves room to help child)

Note. Builds from Bolden and Hepburn (2018). HV = home visit practitioner

not particularly relevant to current family priorities—requires that the parent negotiate conversational expectations (e.g., answering the request and then redirecting the topic; Hancock & Cheatham, 2024). The strategic discursive moves families engage in may be identified through turn-taking patterns (e.g., what typically happens after a HV asks a question, what happens if a HV's question is not answered). Families might also signal hesitation. Within transcripts, hesitation can be coded as *lengthening,* wherein a vocalized sound is prolonged (e.g., "hmmm" represented as "hm:") or *silence,* wherein gaps between or within turns are timed (Bolden & Hepburn, 2018).

Additionally, families may disrupt expected turn-taking patterns. HVs typically control home visit agendas and set discussion topics, adhering to institutional priorities and accountability requirements (e.g., completing official paperwork; Hancock & Cheatham, 2024; Paulick et al., 2022). These turn-taking patterns position HVs as experts responsible for driving home visits, while families are positioned as respondents (Paulick et al., 2022). Rather than letting HVs hold the floor and determine the decision-making flow, families may interject to establish their own turns. These moves may be represented in transcripts through codes indicating *overlap*, when two speakers simultaneous talk, or *latching,* when a speaker rushes to complete or begin a new turn (Bolden & Hepburn, 2018). In short, families may use a range of discursive strategies to enact resistance as they respond to entrenched power hierarchies and position themselves and their children as capable in the face of narrow expectations about both caregiving and child development.

Recognizing and Responding to Family Resistance

While researchers have uncovered many details of how marginalized families resist and shape decision-making, more study is needed to understand how families discursively enact resistance and position themselves as knowledgeable and competent through their moment-to-moment interactions with HVs. In this chapter, we build on the work of scholars who have reframed marginalized families' resistance as purposeful and transformative (e.g., Alvarez, 2020; Beneke et al., 2021; Love et al., 2021a; Park, 2024; Santamaría Graff & Vazquez, 2014), offering insight into nuanced ways families discursively resisted normative expectations about child development and family caregiving strategies. We embed transcript excerpts from a study investigating decision-making during home visits to offer real-life examples of family resistance.

CONCEPTUAL FRAMEWORK

Our work is framed by critical family and community engagement (critical FCE; Hong et al., 2022) and disability critical race theory (DisCrit; Annamma et al., 2013a, 2018). Hong et al. (2022) coined *critical FCE* to describe a growing body of scholarship that applies tenets of critical race theory to the context of partnerships. Critical FCE seeks to interrogate power dynamics among educational institutions, educators, and families with the recognition that these relationships are not separate from systems of oppression such as ableism and racism. Critical FCE rejects deficit-based notions of families and highlights family assets and contributions to their children's lives and education (Hong et al., 2022). Scholarship that reframes deficit-based interpretations of family resistance aligns with critical FCE in its attention to how power and systems of oppression shape expectations about appropriate family engagement (e.g., Hong, 2019; Ishimaru, 2019; Santamaría Graff & Vazquez, 2014).

Building from critical race theory and disability studies, DisCrit offers an intersectional framework to examine how ableism and racism intertwine to uphold notions of normalcy within institutional processes such as family-HV decision-making (Annamma et al., 2013a; 2018). DisCrit provides a lens to consider how ideologies are reproduced and enacted through expectations for family engagement and in specific interactions with families (Gillborn et al., 2016; Harry & Ocasio-Stoutenburg, 2020). We focus here on two DisCrit tenets. First, DisCrit reveals how ability/disability and race are social constructions with material consequences, including how educators may rationalize discriminatory practices (Annamma et al., 2013a; 2018). For instance, when Black and immigrant families advocate for broader conceptions of their children's assets or reject deficit-based framing of their children's abilities (Love et al., 2021a; Park, 2024), professionals may frame such engagement as unreasonable or the result of "denial," justifying further control over decision-making (Beneke & Love, 2022; Park, 2024). Secondly, DisCrit honors varied forms of resistance (Annamma et al., 2013a; 2018), encouraging recognition of ways that multiply marginalized families interrupt and resist deficit positioning of themselves and their children (Love et al., 2021a). For example, Gillborn et al. (2016) detailed how Black middle-class families drew on economic, social, and cultural resources to advocate for their children in response to educators' deficit-based perceptions of Blackness and disability.

Together, critical FCE and DisCrit offered insight into how family–professional power dynamics and resistance are enacted during home visits. Along with discourse analysis, these frameworks afforded moment-to-moment exploration of how HVs reproduced normative expectations regarding caregiving and child development through their talk, and how families subtly and strategically pushed back against these expectations.

UNCOVERING FAMILY RESISTANCE TO NARROW EXPECTATIONS

In the following transcripts, we highlight moments when families discursively drew on expertise and turn-taking as they resisted narrow expectations about themselves and their children. Transcripts present four caregivers from three different families: (a) Kadejah, (b) Meher, and (c) Andrew and Megyn. The families were all enrolled in Early Head Start (EHS), a federally funded U.S. program for families of infants and toddlers whose incomes meet federal poverty guidelines. At the time of the study, this meant that the families had a maximum annual income of $25,100 for a family of four. The families participated in two different EHS programs that provided services through weekly home visits in one midwestern state. Caregivers identified as Black (Kadejah, Meher), multiracial (white and Black; Andrew), and white (Megyn). Meher and her family were refugees from Sudan who had been in the United States for two years and were bilingual Arabic and English speakers. The other families' primary language was English. The HVs in the transcripts (Katie, Sheila) both identified as white women and spoke English as their primary language.

EHS describes its services as "designed to promote the development of the children, and to enable their parents to fulfill their roles as parents and to move toward self-sufficiency" (Office of Head Start, 2022). This goal was reflected in the home visits. For example, during one visit, a HV brought cardboard tubes and multicolored pom-poms, encouraging a mother and her son to playfully identify colors and explore cause-and-effect by rolling the pom-poms through the tubes. Throughout home visits, families and HVs engaged in various decisions about child development, from updating child goals to determining how to apply strategies from parent–child activities outside of visits. The presented transcripts illustrate how families enacted resistance during decision-making. See Table 7.1 for transcription conventions.

Kadejah

The following excerpt presents Kadejah (mother) and Katie (HV) discussing 39-month-old Kamilah's language development. Earlier in the visit, the pair discussed how Kamilah was generally silent outside of the home, including familiar contexts like church, resulting in other family members expressing concerns. Yet at home, Kamilah frequently initiated and extended conversations with her mother. Kadejah was not concerned, and Katie validated this. In Figure 7.1, Kadejah highlighted her expertise about Kamilah. She described her daughter's playful confidence with speech at home, using interjections to establish and extend turns. When Katie attempted to translate Kadejah's observations into a recommendation, Kadejah's responses turned minimal. She then leveraged a change of subject to recenter the conversation on progress.

In this interaction, Kadejah demonstrated her expertise and created another opportunity to discuss Kamilah's competence (line 1); and she described how Kamilah's increasing speech had led to playful teasing from her older brothers (lines 1, 5). When Katie suggested that Kadejah "start watching what [she's] saying" (lines 9–10), Kadejah used laughter and interjections to gently dismiss the need to monitor her language (lines 11, 13, 14). Katie adjusted her recommendation, instead encouraging Kadejah to "warn" other family members about their language (line 15), which Kadejah deflected (lines 16, 17). Katie began additional turns that seemed designed to share additional recommendations (lines 18, 20) but stopped as Kadejah used interjections and overlapping talk to establish her turn and share more (lines 19, 21–23, 25, 27). Katie validated Kadejah's observations and added her own interpretation (lines 23–24, 26, 29–30).

Figure 7.1. Kadejah (Mother) Resists Katie's (HV) Recommendations

1	Kadejah:	that's what they've been calling her this week, the echo.
2	Katie:	oh cause she's just
3	Kadejah:	---
4	Katie:	//repeating what you're saying//
5	Kadejah:	//I didn't even notice she was// doing it till they started calling her the echo
6	Katie:	//so//
7	Kadejah:	//she// repeats
8	Kadejah:	literally //everything//
9	Katie:	//I was gonna say you gotta start watching//
10	Katie:	what you're saying if she's //repeating//
11	Kadejah:	//I// it ain't me that's bad ---
12	Katie:	//well I didn't think so but//
13	Kadejah:	//------//
14	Kadejah:	it ain't me.
15	Katie:	you gotta warn all //them.//
16	Kadejah:	//-//
17	Kadejah:	//it ain't me.//
18	Katie:	//gonna say//
19	Kadejah:	//she, I'm like//
20	Katie:	//if she starts// acting
21	Kadejah:	I'll be like get y'all butt in here and get this kitchen cleaned up.
22		she, get the kitchen cleaned up. I'm like
23	Katie:	----- she's letting everybody know she's here, even more than she //
24		usually does//
25	Kadejah:	//right now// and Malik will be like okay, //echo.//
26	Katie:	//yeah//
27	Kadejah:	or Cole will be like, echo we don't need you right now.
28		//I'm like don't call my daughter no -echo//
29	Katie:	//-----//
30	Katie:	- she is the echo.
31		(1.5)
32	Kadejah:	so that's what she been doing this week too, - echo everything.
33	Katie:	gonna say you gotta have her, echo and then do whatever it
34		//is-, like// help out
35	Kadejah:	//mm hm//
36		((Kamilah returns from attempting to wash her hands and needs
37		help. Kadejah goes with her into the bathroom, and the two talk
38		together. Katie writes notes on paperwork . . .))
39	Kadejah:	((returning from bathroom)) yeah then she was like, mama this
40		fish is deli- no she said chicken. this chicken is delicious. I said
41		that is fish. ((as Kamilah)) it's still delicious.

After a longer pause (line 31), Kadejah seemed to initiate a closing of this topic by restating her initial observation (line 32). Katie provided an additional recommendation (lines 33–34), suggesting that Kadejah could use the "echoes" as an activity to further other aspects of Kamilah's development (e.g., following directions, connecting vocabulary to concrete actions). Kadejah briefly acknowledged this but did not commit to enacting Katie's recommendation (line 35). When mother and daughter returned from washing Kamilah's hands, Kadejah used the pause as a change of topic and introduced another detailed observation of Kamilah's language skills.

Throughout, Kadejah demonstrated her deep expertise about Kamilah's communication, highlighting Kamilah's competencies and how her home offered a rich language environment. With interjections and laughter, Kadejah gently pushed back on Katie's suggestion to monitor her or other family members' language and subtly resisted the recommendation to use "echoing" as a planned opportunity for learning. Without explicitly rejecting Katie's idea, Kadejah re-centered conversation on the progress she observed through naturally occurring conversations.

Andrew and Megyn

While preparing for a family activity of creating a feelings book with collaged images from magazines, Sheila (HV) discussed how the book could support Andrew (father) and Megyn's (mother) communication with 15-month-old Maddox. Figure 7.2 illustrates how Andrew and Megyn drew on expertise and silence to resist Sheila's recommendations about teaching Maddox sign language. While the conversation took place, Andrew fed Maddox and Megyn identified photos for the feelings book.

Sheila began by asking about teaching Maddox sign language. Though she raised the issue as a question, it presumed that the family intended to do so (line 1), which Andrew questioned (line 2). As Sheila began to provide additional information (line 3), Andrew interjected, drawing on his knowledge of his son's visual and motor skills to suggest that sign language would not be a relevant skill at this time (line 4). Sheila began to counter this, and everyone began to simultaneously speak (lines 5–7). After a pause to recalibrate turn-taking (Bolden & Hepburn, 2018), Sheila modeled signs for "eat" and "more," suggesting that those could be taught to Maddox (lines 9–10). Megan minimally agreed (line 11). Sheila acknowledged Andrew's prior comment and restated the possibility of teaching sign language, "even though" Maddox was not yet pointing (line 13). Sheila used general statements about child development to bolster her recommendation, pointing out that children much younger than 15-month-old Maddox "can do" a variety of signs (line 19). Andrew returned his attention to feeding Maddox and did not talk any further on the topic (lines 16, 18).

Figure 7.2. Andrew (Father) and Megyn (Mother) Resist Sheila's (HV) Recommendations

Sheila:	have you taught him any: sign language yet?
Andrew:	sign language?
Sheila:	mm hm. oh yeah, //babies-//
Andrew:	//he still// can't point yet.
Sheila:	o:h, //ye:s://
Andrew:	//yeah won't//
Megyn:	//((unintelligible))//
	(1.2)
Sheila:	s:o:. (2) EAT. ((models sign)) so maybe teach him eat. and more.
	((models sign))
Megyn:	kay.
	(0.5)
Sheila:	babies? (1.1) even though he's not pointing yet?
	(0.9)
	((Maddox fusses))
Andrew:	((to Maddox)) c'mon //boy.//
Sheila:	//babies// at (0.6)
Andrew:	((to Maddox)) r:::
Sheila:	nine months of age, ten months of age can do more. ((models sign))
	(1.1) thank you. ((models sign)) (1.1) eat. ((models sign)) (0.8) so:.
	um, so maybe some of those might be some of the things that you
	might start teaching him?
	(0.8)
	((Sheila returns to describing activity of making a feelings book))

After restating specific signs that the family could implement (lines 19–22), Sheila rephrased her recommendation more tentatively, using rising intonation and conditional language (might, maybe; lines 21–22). While this seemingly offered the family more agency, their desire to use sign language was never confirmed, and other options were not discussed (e.g., learning more about sign language before deciding, using alternative ways to support Maddox's communication). Neither caregiver responded, drawing on silence to resist the proposed strategy. The conversation ultimately continued as Sheila introduced a new discussion topic.

As demonstrated through Figure 7.2, Andrew and Megyn enacted several strategies to resist Sheila's presumptive recommendations. Faced with narrow expectations about their caregiving and no opportunities to discuss alternatives, Andrew and Megyn primarily enacted silence. Rather than positioning himself as an engaged father by agreeing to Sheila's recommendations, Andrew leveraged his expertise about Maddox's current skills and engaged with his son, demonstrating other ways in which he cared for and supported Maddox.

Meher

In the following transcript, Meher (mother) drew on her expertise of her 19-month-old son Tabish to resist expectations for program engagement, as well as to counter recommendations from Katie (HV) about Tabish's expressive language. Earlier in the conversation, Katie initiated a review of Tabish's current child development goals with Meher. They determined that one goal was met (following directions) and another would continue (Tabish sleeping in his own bed). With one goal completed, there was an opportunity to create a replacement goal, which Meher declined (Figure 7.3). While Katie accepted this, she offered her own priority: language development. Meher described Tabish as already engaging in related skills. Although Tabish was simultaneously learning Arabic and English in his bilingual household, Katie did not address this aspect of his language development.

Katie began discussion about identifying a new goal with a yes-no question (lines 1–2). After a pause, Katie added onto her description, perhaps to clarify (line 3). Katie's use of a yes-no question created an opportunity for Meher to select how she wanted to engage with this program requirement, and Meher declined to set a new goal (line 6). However, this may not have been what Katie intended: She qualified Meher's statement (line 7), leaving the possibility open to create another goal. This would align with institutional priorities, as the general expectation was for each child to have two goals. Meher explained her rationale for declining to set a goal by leveraging her knowledge of typical development and referencing Tabish's skills in relation to his age (line 10). While Katie described Tabish's strengths (lines 11, 13), she avoided explicitly agreeing with Meher's interpretation of age-appropriate development, creating an opening for future recommendations.

Katie then introduced a new priority for Tabish, saying, "I think the big thing right now is encouraging him to talk" (line 18). Meher resisted this priority by continuing to highlight her knowledge of her son, quickly adding that Tabish had already "started" to talk (line 21). When Katie acknowledged Tabish's skills, Meher used overlapping talk to signal agreement and emphasize Katie's comments (lines 23, 25, 32). When Katie qualified Meher's statement (line 24), attempting to distinguish between their interpretations (i.e., encouraging a child to talk was different than spontaneous speech), Meher countered by reminding Katie of a previous discussion (line 26) and then specified that Tabish was not speaking discernable words but using sounds in patterns similar to speech (line 28). Katie restated Meher's description (line 31), and Meher agreed (line 32). Although her phrasing was vague, Katie indicated Tabish's skills were different then her original recommendation (line 33). Meher then interacted with Tabish, pointing out his communication attempts and providing additional justification for her resistance (lines 34–36). Katie acknowledged Meher's observations by engaging with Tabish (line 37). Although Meher framed Tabish's

Figure 7.3. Meher (Mother) Resists Katie's (HV) Recommendations

1	Katie:	is there anything else with the bed one that y- or anything at all that you want to add for him?
3		(1.6)
4	Katie:	for working on
5		(3)
6	Meher:	no. not really.
7	Katie:	not right now, //okay//
8	Meher:	//yeah?//
9	Katie:	//sounds good.//
10	Meher:	//because I// think (0.7) um (1.5) Tabish in his age he's doing fine.
11	Katie:	mm hm, yeah he does a very good job.
12	Meher:	yeah.
13	Katie:	he is very social,
14	Meher:	yeah.
15		((. . . Katie looks through folder for paperwork; Meher interacts with Tabish and his sisters))
17	Katie:	((to self)) here's what I was looking for
18	Katie:	I think the big thing right now is encouraging him to talk=
19	Meher:	=yeah=
20	Katie:	=to -
21	Meher:	and he started.
22	Katie:	cause //he is,//
23	Meher:	//yeah//
24	Katie:	yes he's starting to //say// words here and there
25	Meher:	//yeah//
26	Meher:	and I told you that day he said like a full sentence.
27	Katie:	yes, I think you did.
28	Meher:	yeah, but it's not, it's not like a word but (0.6) the, like I don't know mm hm.
29	Katie:	yeah
30	Meher:	like this
31	Katie:	mm hm. you can tell that he's like saying //things with his inflection// but it's
32	Meher:	//yeah. yeah, yeah//
33	Katie:	but it's not really like, it's more just
34	Meher:	((to Tabish)) what. more?
35	Meher:	I think he's saying more.
36	Meher:	((to Tabish)) come.
37	Katie:	((to Tabish)) more?
38		(1.1)
29	Meher:	((to Tabish)) more.
40	Katie:	he's like I know you're talking //about me over// there. he's like I'm listening.
41	Meher:	//yeah//

communication as a request (line 35), Katie described it as receptive language (line 40). Thus, both parties used observation of Tabish to further their claims.

As Figure 7.3 illustrates, Meher used a variety of strategies to resist narrow expectations about her engagement and her son's expressive language. She leveraged predominant framings of typical development to decline setting another goal. Though Katie accepted this, she continued to present her own priority for Tabish's development without acknowledging the complexities and assets of his bilingual context. Meher countered framing of her son's skills as lacking, asserting her expertise as she shared detailed prior observations and pointed out his communication in the moment. While Katie did not explicitly dismiss Meher's observations, she framed them as beyond the scope of her recommendation.

BUILDING SOLIDARITY BY HONORING FAMILY RESISTANCE

In this study, families of color experiencing poverty used several discursive strategies to resist narrow framings of their engagement and their children's capabilities. Drawing on caregiving expertise and disrupting turn-taking patterns, families subverted expectations to add or change caregiving practices to support their children, instead highlighting the value of their ongoing engagement. Building from these findings, we offer three recommendations for HVs and other professionals to honor family resistance: (1) recognize resistance as an asset, (2) treat resistance as a source of feedback, and (3) broaden expectations for family engagement and child development.

Recognize Resistance as an Asset

Following DisCrit, resistance reflects essential knowledge and skills of families of color and multiply marginalized families as they reject and counteract racism, ableism, and other forms of oppression. By reframing family resistance as an asset rather than a deficit, professionals can create new opportunities to learn from families (Santamaría Graff & Vazquez, 2014). For example, when Katie attempted to take control of decision-making and use her own expertise to translate Kadejah's observations into recommendations, Kadejah resisted (Figure 7.1). Instead, Katie might have stepped back to learn more about how Kadejah already supported her daughter's language skills, affirming Kadejah's expertise.

To cultivate home-visiting practices that recognize family resistance as an asset, HVs can reimagine decision-making processes by structuring conversations with intentional and varied opportunities for families to share expertise. Rather than HVs controlling discussion topics (e.g., Hancock & Cheatham, 2024; Paulick et al., 2022), families might set the agenda by sharing photos, videos, or verbal descriptions of recent moments with their child. Decision-making could then center on caregiver choices to continue or refine already-established practices (e.g., Keilty et al., 2022), shifting away from HVs providing recommendations that families incorporate new or different approaches. In the moment, HVs might facilitate decision-making through questions that center families' expertise and agency, such as: Tell me more about how/why you decided to try that. Were you happy with how it went? Why? Is that something you want to keep doing? By positioning themselves as learners and families as experts, HVs can build more solidarity with families.

Treat Resistance as a Source of Feedback

Despite the value of resistance, HVs can dismiss family resistance as inappropriate or undesirable when "appropriate" family engagement is framed as practices upholding whiteness and dominant notions of ability. As a result, family resistance becomes treated as a problem to be managed, with the end goal being family agreement with HVs. To illustrate, HVs often responded to resistance by providing families more information, as Sheila did when she countered Andrew's objection by modeling various signs and describing how children younger than his son could sign (Figure 7.2). This type of response frames family resistance as the result of a lack of knowledge or understanding, rather than a valid response (e.g., Park, 2024).

To counteract this tendency and build solidarity with families, HVs can adopt practices that treat family resistance as a source of feedback. HVs might consider how to extend decision-making across visits, leaving families with more time to process how various possibilities fit (or not) with family context. As demonstrated through transcripts, HVs were often quick to recommend new strategies for families to expand their repertoires, resulting in family resistance. Instead, HVs might slow down and create opportunities for families to learn more, explore alternatives, or seek feedback. During home visits, HVs can be attuned to family silence and interjections, and be willing to address them. For example, rather than responding to family silence by offering more information, HVs might first confirm that families are interested in the strategy being discussed, or that the strategy addresses a current family priority.

Broaden Expectations for Family Engagement and Child Development

As illustrated through the transcripts, family resistance is often a necessary response to narrow expectations that HVs and educational institutions impose on marginalized families and children. These expectations uphold norms of whiteness, ability, and monolingualism as universal and frame family participation in decision-making about their child as agreement with HVs' recommended strategies to foster particular aspects of child development, such as Tabish's verbal English communication (Figure 7.3). As a result, resistance such as Meher's could be treated as denial. While Katie did not directly discount Meher's choice to decline a goal, she set the stage for future discussions that would uphold program expectations for engagement and address her perception of Tabish's communication.

To honor the roots of family resistance, HVs can subvert and counteract narrow expectations for family engagement and child development. HVs might broaden their expectations by first reflecting on the choices families are typically encouraged to make during home visits and identifying new decision-making opportunities. When given the option to set an additional goal for Tabish, Meher chose not to do so and instead highlighted his strengths (Figure 7.3). HVs might consider creating opportunities for families to set their own parameters for how they want to engage. HVs can also broaden expectations for child development when discussing priorities for children. In particular, HVs can interrogate who benefits when professionals artificially separate development into different domains and prioritize skills associated with white, monolingual, and nondisabled ways of being (e.g., complex communication in spoken English as a desired end point; Beneke & Love, 2022).

CONCLUSION

Rather than an obstacle to decision-making, family resistance can be a source of growth, strength, and opportunity. When HVs honor family resistance during decision-making, they can enact solidarity with families and foster shared decisions that center family expertise, priorities, and ways of being. While we have focused on the potential for HVs to act in solidarity with caregivers, it is also essential for all adults—particularly those who are nondisabled—to consider how and when their decision-making is truly in solidarity with marginalized and multiply marginalized children. In doing so, HVs and families can collaboratively design services that cultivate freedom and belonging for young children.

Pedagogies of Relationality and Interdependence

Latina Mothers[1] Reinventing Education for Their Young Children With Disabilities During COVID-19

Jie Y. Park

Con eso creo que se pueden entender las dos personas y eso es lo que ella a hecho. Me a dado su tiempo y me a escuchado y cuando la clases aveces se terminan yo le pregunto "mira que pasa esto, dígame esto, explíqueme. . . ." Ella siempre tiene un tiempo para explicarme las cosas y creo que es cuando hay tiempo se puede dialogar de todas las cosas y eso tiene que ver mucho con la relación que se crea—cuando hay tiempo (y) dedicación eso creo que es muy importante.	I think, with that, two people can understand each other and that is what she [teacher] has done with me. She has given me her time and she has listened to me and when the classes sometimes finish I ask her "Look what happens here, tell me this, explain. . . ." She always has time to explain things to me and I think that where there is time you can create a dialogue about everything and that has a lot of impact with the relationship that you form—when there is time (and) dedication, I think that is very important.

I begin with this statement from a Latina mother who describes her relationship with her child's teacher during the COVID-19 pandemic. She highlights the importance of relational practices associated with listening, investing time, and being in dialogue. In this chapter, I center Latina mothers' perspectives and show how they invented a pedagogical approach for educating their young children with disabilities during COVID-19. Drawing on disability critical race theory and mothering as pedagogy, I illuminate how Latina mothers' pedagogies are rooted in relationality (Godínez & Baquedano-López, 2022) and interdependence (Beneke et al., 2023). Their pedagogies countered the school district's policies and practices, which were based on white and ableist notions of learning, development, and participation.

THEORETICAL FRAMEWORKS: DISABILITY CRITICAL RACE THEORY AND LATINA MOTHERS AS PEDAGOGUES

Disability Critical Race Theory (DisCrit)

DisCrit highlights the ways in which "racism and ableism interdependently uphold notions of normalcy" (Love & Beneke, 2021, p. 31). Race and ability are mutually constitutive, meaning "development" and "ability" are racialized constructs, shaped by sociopolitical and ideological forces (Annamma et al., 2013a). White children are typically seen and educated as "able," "normal," or "developmentally on track" because developmental standards are grounded in whiteness (Love & Beneke, 2021). Black children, Indigenous children, and other children of Color,[2] on the other hand, who are judged against whiteness, are more often seen and educated as "disabled," "in need of intervention/remediation," or "developmentally delayed." DisCrit reveals the racist and ableist mechanisms (often presented as race neutral or "scientific") that sort Black children, Indigenous children, and other children of Color into remedial spaces and see their minds, bodies, and languages through deficit perspectives.

To share a personal example, my partner and I were told that our 5-year old—who is multiracial and lives in a translanguaging household (i.e., we fluidly move between multiple languages; Garcia et al., 2017)—might need "remediation" pending results from an early language assessment. While presented as a screening process to help young multilingual children, this practice upholds dominant raciolinguistic ideologies (i.e., an ideology that frames Black children, Indigenous children, and children of Color as linguistically deficient) and pathologizes multilingual children and families (Flores & Rosa, 2015).

In this chapter, I apply several DisCrit tenets. First, I utilize the tenet that states, "DisCrit values multidimensional identities and troubles singular notions of identity such as race or dis/ability (sic) or class or gender or sexuality, and so on" (Annamma et al., 2018, p. 56). DisCrit attends to intersectionality (Collins, 2019; Crenshaw, 1989) and the recognition that multiple forms of oppressions converge (e.g., racism, classism, linguicism, patriarchy) for disabled people of Color, necessitating an *integrated* analysis and practice of struggle (Combahee River Collective, 1981).

Second, the construction of disabilities often occurs through invisible processes and discourses (Annamma et al., 2018; Love & Beneke, 2021). This means that a focus on individual actors (e.g., teacher) minimizes how ableism and racism are baked into systems that uphold white supremacy, or the "comprehensive condition whereby the interests and perceptions of white subjects are continually placed centre stage and assumed as 'normal'" (Gillborn, 2006, p. 318). DisCrit is both a critical theory of inequality and a theory of change that centers "micro-level responses to macro-level oppression" (Love & Beneke, 2021, p. 40). The Latina mothers in this chapter invented "micro-level responses" through pedagogies of interdependence and relationality.

Latina Mothers as Pedagogues

To frame Latina mothers' pedagogical responses, I also draw on *mujerismo*—a critical feminist perspective that is Latina oriented. Mujerismo, or Latina womanism, recognizes Latina women's everyday experiences as sources of knowledge (Dyrness, 2008; Galván, 2005; Nygreen et al., 2016; Villenas et al., 2006). It positions Latina mothers as pedagogues who are intimately involved in teaching and learning—as both participants and designers (Dyrness, 2008; Gonzales et al., 2023; Nuñez & García-Mateus, 2021). Mujerismo addresses the gender(ed) dimensions of pedagogy as well as motherhood. As an example of pedagogy in mothering, Guzmán (2012) documented Latina mothers who educated their daughters about surviving white supremacy and patriarchy through *testimonios*. The mothers simultaneously taught and learned from their daughters, not for personal gain but for collective uplift.

More recently, Godínez and Baquedano-López (2022) highlighted "mothers' energies and knowledge in constructing teaching and learning opportunities in socially, linguistically, and politically restrictive contexts" (p. 190). They found that Mexicana *campesinas* (farmworkers) engaged in a praxis of relationality and coalition-building in an agricultural context mired in exploitation (Godínez & Baquedano-López, 2022). Studying an intergenerational storytelling workshop, Gonzales and colleagues (2023) characterized Latina mothers as critical literacy pedagogues who create multimodal and translingual compositions that fostered intergenerational learning, challenged deficit constructions of immigrant families, and redesigned school-based curricula. This small but rich body of work suggests that Latina mothers' meaning-making and meaning-sharing practices can be understood through critical literacies—reading and writing the word and world (Freire & Macedo, 2005) in ways that hold both critique and hope.

Latina mothers possess particular knowledge that guides their mothering. As such, mothers-as-pedagogues challenge traditional ways of knowing (i.e., positivist, Eurocentric) and narrow notions of pedagogy and space (Godínez & Baquedano-López, 2022). While mujerismo is often associated with the private, intimate, and everyday spaces of women's lives such as the home or church (Villenas et al., 2006), mothers' pedagogies can be transnational, enacted in open or liminal spaces (Godínez & Baquedano-López, 2022). Grounded in mujerismo are also concepts like *la facultad* (knowing through experience and intuition), *pesadora* (creative thinkers), and *convivir* (praxis of living together) (Villenas et al., 2006). The last concept, convivir, is particularly salient to this chapter and its focus on Latina mothers' pedagogy of relationality and interdependence.

Pedagogies created by mothers with and for their young children with disabilities have not received much attention, even in DisCrit studies (see Annamma et al., 2018). Furthermore, while there has been some research on Latine parents with young children during COVID-19, much of it focuses on the degree and type of parent involvement in home–school activities designed by classroom teachers (Soltero-González & Gilanders, 2022). The research presented in this chapter addresses both areas—Latina mothers educating their young children with disabilities and Latina mothers as pedagogical designers during COVID-19.

METHODOLOGY AND PARTICIPANTS

In spring 2020, most U.S. public schools shifted to remote learning due to the COVID-19 pandemic. The school district that I write about in this chapter delivered Chromebooks and Wi-Fi hotspots to families and created a website for parents and caregivers with training videos for web-based platforms (e.g., Google Classroom). These measures, however, often left out families with young children (ages 0–5). That prompted my research colleagues and I to partner with a cross-sector coalition for families with young children. Formed 20 years ago, the coalition is made up of early educators, health and human service providers, parent groups, and higher education institutions. The coalition enlisted our research team to understand the early education and care experiences of families with young children during the pandemic. The research team was made up of myself and three colleagues (Laurie, Deisy, and Gurutze[3]). Deisy and Gurutze identify as Latina. At the time of the study, Deisy was an undergraduate in education studies and community development. Gurutze is a mother of three children. I am a 1.5-generation Asian American cis-het woman with two young children.

We were committed to using justice-driven and inclusive research methodologies (Annamma et al., 2018; Love & Beneke, 2021), which reject race-neutral frameworks and attend to counternarratives of resistance and agency. Qualitative research methodologies encompass methods and orientations to how knowledge is generated in and through relational practices (Okazawa-Rey, 2015). Drawing on critical feminist perspectives (Collins, 1990; hooks, 2014), we recognized that women of Color navigate their material reality and carry unique understandings through an intersectional standpoint. Relationally we centered dialogue, which asks participants, including the researcher, to listen to understand. Dialogue also offered opportunities for everyone to become more reflective and reflexive. Therefore, we structured focus groups as spaces of dialogue, counter-storytelling, and collaborative theory building. We presumed that through dialogue and counter storytelling we would be aligned with and extend theories of DisCrit and mothers of Color as pedagogues.

Deisy recruited 22 participants—all of whom identified as female Latina mothers living in a large New England city. In an initial questionnaire, mothers indicated they had one to four children, with at least one child under the age of 5. Sixteen reported using both Spanish and English at home. For this chapter, I focus on the five mothers who indicated they had a child with a disability who was receiving some form of early intervention service. Three mothers noted intervention services were for delayed speech or language, while two said it was for autism. In the city where the research took place, over 21% of the residents were born outside of the United States, and approximately 40% speak a language other than English at home. A heterogeneous group, Latine are the city's largest minoritized population, with the largest percentage living in poverty.

Deisy and Gurtuze, native Spanish speakers, facilitated five hour-long focus groups. When scheduling the focus groups, Deisy asked whether participants preferred English or Spanish. Based on mothers' preferences, Deisy and Gurtuze facilitated all focus groups in Spanish. Deisy then transcribed the audio files in their entirety and provided English translations. We analyzed the data in English, but the interactions between the women were far richer than is captured by the English translations (see Emmerich, 2023). To preserve the power and complexity of what the mothers shared, I present their quotes in Spanish and then provide an English translation.

After reading and annotating the transcripts, and guided by DisCrit and mujerismo, I identified instances where Latina mothers expressed their understandings and impacts of, and responses to, disability. This led to analytically constructing the mothers' cultural models of disability. Cultural models are a set of assumptions that "define for us the way things are and should be" (Reese & Gallimore, 2000, p. 106). This analytic move generated nuanced understandings of how mothers resisted normalcy and accepted differences as natural yet political. I also identified moments where mothers shared observations about their children as learners (i.e., children's strengths and perceived and/or documented needs); beliefs about teaching and learning (i.e., learning happens through . . . what helps my child learn is . . .); and home-based activities (i.e., what they actually did with their child in the home). I began to see how the mothers understood that their children learned better through relationship-building and play. I returned to the literature and my theoretical framework to construct two themes that show how Latina mothers critically read disability and their children's schooling as texts (i.e., mothers' critical literacies), and developed their own pedagogies to foster their children's learning.

LATINA MOTHERS' PEDAGOGY

Here, I present two themes: (1) mothers' critical literacies and capacities to question constructs of normalcy and disability, as well as a system that sorted and controlled young bodies; and (2) how mothers consequently invented a pedagogy rooted in relationality and interdependence.

Mothers' Critical Literacies of Education

A concept from Paulo Freire, critical literacy refers to how people read the word and the world, and come to see that social realities and ideologies are constructed through language (Luke, 2012). The Latina mothers exercised critical literacies—"reading" their child's educational setting with criticality and advocating for educational activities that leverage differences instead of pathologizing them (Beneke et al., 2022). Carla, whose daughter has autism, noted that the school and teachers sorted children based on normality. She shared:

En mi caso, no puedo hablar de todos, pero en mi caso como que mezclan todos mas o menos a lo que se llaman niños normales y para mi todo la normalidad es dependiendo de como uno lo vea—este por lo menos la mía se frustra y Ami me frustra verla así/	In my case, I cannot speak for everyone, but in my case it is like they mix everyone more or less what they would call normal kids and for me, normality depends on how one sees it. Mine gets very frustrated and I get frustrated seeing her like that.

Carla was careful not to generalize children's education and experiences, but she criticized the common practice of sorting and grouping children by perceived ability. Carla understood that normalcy is a sociopolitical construct (i.e., "normalidad es dependiendo de como uno lo vea"). She also noted that her daughter, even at an early age, resisted the sorting and grouping, suggesting the perceptiveness of young children.

Carla's comment prompted another mother in the same focus group to respond:

Ya. Me imagino, me imagino. Yo digo siempre que la normalidad no existe y que cada uno nacimos de una manera, quien define lo normal?	Yea. I can imagine, I can imagine. I always say that normality does not exist and that all of us are born a certain way, who defines normal?

This mother did not have a child with a disability. However, she challenged the concept of normalcy, asking who gets to define who is normal and what counts as normal. In her statement, "All of us are born a certain way," she recognized that difference is a natural part of life. In a different focus group, a mother whose son was receiving speech therapy for his expressive language, noted, "Yo soy fiel creyente que no todos los niños aprenden de la misma manera." *I am a firm believer that not all kids learn the same.* While rejecting the concept of normalcy and understanding differences as natural, the five mothers sought intervention services for their child, not because they believed their child was deficient but because they understood that their child could be further marginalized by the school system if they challenged a diagnosis or refused intervention services (Lalvani, 2014).

In addition to challenging the school's emphasis on "normal" behavior or development, the mothers critiqued the overcontrolling and surveilling of young bodies. They identified cases where their child could not move, eat, or even greet friends on Google Classroom. Sandra described her young son's challenges with the restrictive environment.

El siempre me esta preguntando—okay "Cuando se acaba esto? Cuando tengo algún merienda—algún break?"	He's always asking—okay "when is this over? When do I have a snack break—any break?"

Lalvani (2014) described the dominant belief that professionals' knowledge matters more than parents' insights. Instead of unquestionably accepting the teachers as professionals who know best, the mothers pushed back, offering approaches to teaching and learning that differed from the teachers'.

Pero los nenes aveces tratan de como hablarse entre ellos y las maestras llevan eso tan estricto que no los dejan aveces como ni—por ejemplo aquí el nene es bien apegado a una nena de su salon y cuando la ve el se emociona y quiere saludarla y no se lo permiten porque tiene que empezar rápido. . . . No no les permite en ese . . . eso cinco minutos.	But sometimes the kids tried to talk among themselves and the teachers have been so strict and sometimes they don't even let them like—for example my child is very attached to a girl in his classroom and sometimes when he sees her he gets excited and wants to say hi to her and the teacher doesn't permit it because she has to start quickly. . . . They don't permit them those five minutes.

While acknowledging the teacher's schedule, this mother saw relationships as the foundation to engagement and learning. Instead of distracting from learning, friendships and the associated excitement are central to learning and thriving.

From Critical Literacies to Pedagogy

With their critical literacies, Latina mothers "read" their child, the classroom, and the school as texts, asking: How is my child experiencing the classroom? How is my child positioned by the teacher, school, and district? Their critical literacy also informed the mother's pedagogies. One of the mothers in the first focus group shared:

Hubo una preparación que esto estaba claro, fue algo imprevisto, algo que no sabia que iba a pasar, pero ni siquiera una orientación que nos dieron primero a los padres para ayudar a los niños, usted entiende? Para explicarnos cuál es la mejor manera, la mas fácil para ayudarlos, como ayudarnos hacer su tarea, como—nosotros tuvimos que apunchar y adivinar demasiado y fue algo frustrante, la verdad que sí.	There was no preparation to ensure that things were clear. It was improvised, something that we didn't know was going to happen, but there wasn't even an orientation first for us parents to help our children, you get me? To explain is what is the best way, the easiest way to help them, like help them with homework, like—we had to stick it out and figure so much out and that was very frustrating, it really was.

In her statement, she criticized the school district and city agencies responsible for Head Start for their inadequate support of parents. She also underscored that mothers did not just observe their children's educational experiences from afar. Instead, they "figured so much out" in ways of supporting their children's education. They invented their own pedagogies. The mothers, as social change agents, were "not interested in simply reporting how evil institutions are; [and believed] critique needs an action plan" (Porter et al., 2000, p. 613).

For their action plan, the mothers invented a pedagogy of relationality and interdependence. A mother whose son was receiving language intervention services said:

Al principio era un poquito estresante porque- al principio el estaba medio—que se distraía mucho—un poco desenfocado—entonces a eso también se le agrega que el esta recibiendo terapia de lenguaje—ósea que para su edad tiene cierta dificultad para expresar algo—entonces eso lo hacia sentir como mas frustración cuando el quería preguntar algo pero no lo entienden muchas veces—entonces, fue un proceso al principio el—yo también cojia clases.	At first it was a bit stressful because—and at first he was a bit—he would be distracted often—a bit unfocused—so to that you add the fact that he's receiving language therapy—like for his age he has difficulty in expressing something—so this has made him feel frustrated when he wants to ask something but they often can't understand him—so that was, it was a process at first. I would also take classes.

The mother's practice was to sit next to her young child in his virtual class. She was not the only one who described how mothers engaged in joint, goal-directed activities characterized by togetherness. Another mother stated:

Cuando dicen que bailes yo me paro y bailo, dicen aplaude y yo me paro y aplaudo, si la maestra dice sapo yo también brinco yo me vuelo muchacho igual que el nene y la nene y cojo clase como dice la otra mamá coje clases igualito.	When they [teachers] say dance, I get up and dance. When they say clap, I get up and clap. If the teacher says frog I'll jump. I become a child with them and I take class with them like others have mentioned—I take class the same.

Their pedagogy was relational, with the child and mother intimately involved in teaching and learning from each other. The mothers not only positioned themselves as a student taking the class but created a learning space within and against the "official" Google Classroom. As such, they navigated a complicated position. They had to be within the structure of the class but also invent an alternative way for their child to learn. Recognizing that their child might learn differently, and recruiting what they know about their child's interests (e.g., the importance of relationships), the mothers invented a pedagogy of togetherness. They treated their children as co-learners and co-designers, involving them in many decision-making processes. One mother described negotiating different roles with her daughter during class time. The mothers' pedagogy, therefore, broke down not only the home/school separation but also the parent/child separation (Love et al., 2021a), empowering the young child and parent to codirect the content and practices associated with learning.

While highlighting the creativity, resourcefulness, and intentionality of individual mothers, I do not want to gloss over their struggles or misrepresent their work at home as individualistic. In addition to togetherness, the mothers' pedagogy stemmed from (and created) interdependence, with mothers receiving support, not only from the child but from partners, family members, friends, paraeducators, and teachers. Interdependence assumes that "each of us relies on one another and no one moves through the world without support" (Beneke et al., 2023, p. 365). One of the mothers whose child received speech therapy said:

<table><tr><td>No se que paso de que todo estaba en el mode de off, porque incluso ni la nena lloro, los nenes no se levantaron, mi pareja ayer tenia libre no se levanto, los nenes perdieron la clase de—la terapia del habla, perdieron la clase de head start [. . .] somos tan agotada todos los días y a todo eso este—es el ser todas las profesiones, limpiar la casa, lavar, regar, cocinar, los nenes, ser esposa, ser compañera, educadora.</td><td>I don't know what happened that I was like in "off mode" because even the baby didn't cry, the boy said to wake up, my partner wasn't working and he also didn't wake up, the boys miss class and speech therapy, [. . .] we are exhausted every day and having to be—having to be all of these professions, cleaning the house, washing, hanging up clothes, cooking, being a mom, being a wife, being a partner, an educator.</td></tr></table>

Struggle is often pathologized, but struggle is and has always been part of creating more socially just worlds (Beneke et al., 2023). Pathologizing struggle, therefore, upholds whiteness as well as ableism. In the above statement, the mother named some of her struggles and what and who support her in educating her young child. While support is important for everyone, the mothers rejected superficial forms of support—for example, "support" given by the school district that did not account for racism, xenophobia, linguistic discrimination, poverty, and the stressors of COVID-19. In contrast to superficial or paternalistic support, the mothers identified relationships of interdependence and reciprocity with spouses, friends, teachers, and therapists. Describing her relationship with her son's language therapist, the same mother said:

<table><tr><td>Como por ejemplo la terapeuta del habla. Ella—yo tengo su numero que por lo menos—cualquier inquietud le puedo textiar—Ella también me dice la</td><td>Like for example his language therapist. She—I have her number at least—whatever concern I can text her—she also tells me what time therapy is, what</td></tr></table>

hora de la terapia, a que hora el niño tiene que tiene que conectarse. Si hay una alguna eventualidad que no también me lo avisa. Entonces en esa parte como que lo importante es mantener la comunicación de ambas parte—no al momento que niño valla a recibir el servicio—sino que—como que no hay improviso.	time the child has—has to connect online. If anything happens, she lets me know. In terms of that—it is very important to maintain communications on both sides, not only at the moment the child is going to receive a service—so that—like so that there doesn't have to be any improvisation.

In her role as educator, the mother depended on the language therapist, but the language therapist also depended on her—communication involved both sides. The mother described contributing to their child's language therapy by signing the child on to Zoom, tidying the room for the Zoom appointment, and making therapy a part of the child's routine. The concept of interdependence, as described by the mothers, debunks the myth of meritocracy, which portrays teaching and learning as matters of individual hard work (Beneke et al., 2023). It also challenges the individualism and perfectionism that are part of white supremacy culture (Okun & Jones, 2000). Perfectionism makes people believe that struggling is shameful, and individualism makes people believe that they alone are responsible for solving problems. The Latina mothers' pedagogy—characterized by relationality and interdependence—suggests that struggle and support are part of powerful teaching and learning. Moreover, Latina mothers, through their pedagogies, resisted how ableism and racism positioned them and their child as "bad." One mother described how the school threatened to call the Department of Child and Family Services because she was unable to log her child on Google Classroom every morning. Other mothers shared how English-only practices in the school did not account for their children's and family's language resources and described their Spanish as a limitation ("la limitación del idioma"). Mothers named these practices as inappropriate and resisted them through their pedagogies.

DISCUSSION

While we are beginning to understand how Latina immigrant mothers navigated remote learning and caregiving during COVID-19 (see Bruhn, 2023), few studies focus on the mothers' actual pedagogical practices or the "pedagogies of the home" (Garcia & Delgado Bernal, 2021). This is even more the case with mothers of Color who have children with disabilities (for exceptions, see Cioè-Peña et al., 2024; Torres, 2024; White-Johnson, 2024). The Latina mothers in this chapter invented pedagogies characterized by relationality and interdependence. They did not just comply with school mandates, policies, and curricula. Instead, understanding their child's interests and ways of knowing as well as sociopolitical constructions of disability, they created joint, goal-directed activities in which mothers and young children learned together. They created a world for and with their young children, drawing on the strength of family members, friends, teachers, paraeducators, intervention specialists, social workers, and health care providers. In doing so, they debunked the myth of educators as autonomous individuals who have to problem-solve alone. Instead, mothers-as-educators were both supported and enabled by others, even as they supported and enabled others, including school-based educators and paraeducators, family members, and children.

Study findings also add to existing arguments that constructions of "normalcy/normalness" and "good/goodness" uphold whiteness and ableism (Lalvani, 2014; Love et al., 2021a). Indeed, "goodness is often conferred on a student based on racial position—not earned through behavior or disposition—thereby reinforcing white supremacy" (Annamma et al. 2018, p. 60). The link between white supremacy and goodness extends to mothers and mothering. Latina mothers in this study described school expectations and policies that positioned them as "bad" mothers. They understood that they were being positioned as bad mothers and that being a bad mother had consequences for their child. Yet, through their pedagogical moves, the Latina mothers argued that all children are good and affirmed disability as a natural variance that educators should be responsive to. The mothers positioned their own children as "good," not because they exhibited the characteristics associated with whiteness (e.g., good grades, dominant developmental expectations), but because of their children's care for other children, their patience, and their excitement at discovery. The Latina mothers also affirmed each other as good in the focus groups, recognizing each other's struggles and creative resistance.

This chapter contributes understandings of Latina mothers as pedagogues of young children with disabilities and complicates the positioning of Latina mothers as reluctant or inadequate educators of their children (Bruhn, 2023). It also challenges the status quo of early childhood special education (ECSE) research that privileges white, monolingual female teachers', families', and researchers' perspectives. If multilingual Latine parents are included in ECSE research, they are described through deficit-based language steeped in dominant raciolinguistic ideologies (Martínez-Álvarez, 2019; Soto-Boykin et al., 2021). This chapter reflects one approach to methodologically centering multilingualism and theorizing it as an asset (for meaning-making, navigation, communication, and social change). Finally, this chapter "validates mothering in academic research" (Godínez & Baquedano-López, 2022, p.186), with theories, analytical tools, and methodologies that recognize mothering as not only essential labor (Garbes, 2022), but a critical praxis with sociocultural and political dimensions. Struggle and interdependence are central to the work of social justice educators (Beneke et al., 2023), and this chapter shows how struggle and interdependence are generative concepts for understanding parents of Color as educators of their children with disabilities.

CHAPTER 9

Weaving Familial Stories

A Conceptual Early Childhood Special Education Framework of Decolonial Praxis

Rae L. Begaye-Tewa, Elizabeth A. Ruiz, and Nicole S. Begay

> Zachery is Diné; he is Dzíł ááh áí táách'ííni born for Kinyaa'áanii. He prefers to be called Zac. He enjoys playing video games, watching sports, and keeping track of player statistics. He enjoys attending Phoenix Suns games, WWE events, and music concerts. He has met Shaq and Cody Rhodes (his favorite wrestler). Four-year-old Zac is vastly creative, full of energy, and loves wrestling. He reenacts elaborate fights he watches with his WWE figurines. Other times, he becomes a wrestler, taking over the living room and suplexing his favorite stuffed giraffe. Pillows are the imaginary chairs he uses to defeat his opponents.
>
> Nihich'i' Ha'dzii': Kodóó Hane' Nihí Dahałnédó[1]

Indigenous families hold each child's story with an understanding of their past and present. As cultural creators and knowers, families are often conscious of best practices to address their children's strengths and needs. Familial stories contain hope, strength, heartbreak, uncertainty, and dreams for an optimistic future. Narratives (i.e., stories) of children provide a holistic view that is vital to early childhood educators and the child's well-being. Thus, we begin with a story to implore the reader to deeply listen to and elevate the familial stories of Indigenous and Native people[2] in their practice.

Stories are recognized not only as systems of knowledge but also as tools to learn collaboratively. As Tachine (2018) explained, "Stories provide a space to learn from and unite with others" (p. 65). As such, we offer Weaving Familial Stories (WFS) as a conceptual, decolonial framework of practice that centers Indigenous familial voices and their stories to support children holistically within early childhood education and beyond. Through WFS, we posit that practitioners can elevate familial stories and create more holistic, asset-based supports for children.

As a mother who was also a special education teacher, I fought for early intervention services since Zac was 9 months old. I was concerned that he was not meeting his developmental milestones. Zac received early intervention services in our home for three years until he transitioned into the public school system where he received services such as speech therapy, occupational therapy, physical therapy, and academic support. It was an adjustment to entrust my son to other professionals outside our home. In educational settings, Zac was not the same child we saw at home. He was viewed through a deficit lens where educators and service providers focused on skills he lacked. Standard checklists monitored Zac's progress, noting his lack of gross motor activities with red marks. Conferences centered around his present level of performance filled with disheartening conversations around his physical limitations rather than his abilities.

SITUATING DISABILITY IN SOCIETY AND NATIVE AMERICAN CULTURE

Disability is socially constructed, situated within a society made up of obstacles faced by those who are classified as impaired (Cologon & Thomas, 2014). These labels can be oppressive and are frequently imposed by nondisabled people, hindering the participation of people with disabilities in society (Oliver, 1990; 1996). Disability can also be seen as the result of social oppression (Thomas, 1999; 2004). Thomas (2004) noted that disability signifies socially imposed "restrictions of activity that result from the exercise of the power to exclude" (p. 29). Cultural and social contexts can influence how a person is identified—or identifies with—a disability.

Native American tribes exhibit significant diversity in their linguistic, traditional, cultural, and social frameworks among themselves. The personal stories provided in this chapter pertain to the conceptualization of disability and culture based on the lived experiences of one Navajo (Diné) family in the Southwest region of the United States. Additionally, we recognize that the definition and concept of *disability*, specifically in Indigenous communities, may be in contradiction with their native tongue.

In the Diné language, the term disability is absent. The Diné language is descriptive; therefore, when someone is introduced, they may be described through a medical model lens pointing out impairments, whether the disability is apparent or not. However, a Diné person with a disability does not carry the term or description beyond formal introductions. Most Diné elders focus on seeing the person for their ability, rather than their disability. For example, Lee (2024) described how an elder Diné did not accept the term disability in describing their grandson and instead referenced how everyone deserved to be treated equally and had a role or purpose in life, such as participating in cultural ceremonies. Picton and Tufue-Dolgoy (2019) described how disability perspectives are "sometimes felt as collisions of agendas" and posit how "the collisions have implications for the social, political, economic, cultural, and individual identities of people with disabilities" (p. 189). These collisions or contradictory translations and an awareness of cultural differences are crucial aspects to consider when engaging with Native and Indigenous individuals (Kalyanpur & Harry, 2012).

> *Zac's father, Renaldon, and I had two perspectives on his transition into K-12 schooling. I was focused on Zac's academic abilities and support services to ensure his individualized education program (IEP) was implemented appropriately. My husband was more concerned about how Zac fit in with his peers and if someone would open doors for him when he was in his walker. Renaldon would tell me that all the IEP stuff was for me and not his priority. He trusted my knowledge and expertise when dealing with the school, IEPs, and providers. I ensured the IEP addressed all of Zac's academic needs and appropriate accommodations while Renaldon focused on Zac's social needs by taking Zac to school, interacting with his teachers, participating in peer activities, and attending therapy.*

INDIGENOUS FAMILIES IN EARLY CHILDHOOD SPECIAL EDUCATION

There is a dearth of literature on Native families' stories and experiences in early childhood special education (ECSE). Yet, across the United States, American Indian and Alaska Native children are disproportionately identified with a disability and receive special education services (Faircloth, 2006; Zhang et al., 2014). Native American children account for <1% of the pre-K–12 school population yet represent 19% of those who receive special education services under IDEA Part B for the 2022–23 school year (NCES, 2024). In addition to confronting ableism, ECSE policies and practices must contend with other oppressions (e.g., racism and classism; Ferri & Bacon, 2011) that negatively affect families and children from marginalized communities (Trainor, 2010). Normative practices in educational contexts continue to center whiteness as the "unnamed norm that students are measured against. The concept of normal creates a binary in which students of color are marginalized based on differences from the desired" (Love et al., 2021b, p.183). Because whiteness is centered, families of color are frequently and falsely positioned as in denial, uninformed, confrontational, or uninvolved simply because their ways of support do not meet normative expectations (Love et al., 2021b; Powell & Keeney-Parks, 2021). Further, children from marginalized communities experience inequitable access to educational experiences (Boveda et al., 2019). Black, Indigenous, and other youth of color with disabilities are more likely to be placed in segregated educational settings (Cooc, 2022; Skiba et al., 2006), to be categorized in special education categories that are subjective (e.g., emotional disturbance; Bal et al., 2019; learning disability; Shifrer, 2018), and to be subjected to exclusionary discipline (Welsh & Little, 2018). Considerations of the cultural values, beliefs, or languages of families and children of color, particularly Native families, within ECSE are often sparse, if not entirely absent (Artiles, 2011; 2019; Blanchett et al., 2009).

Since my advocacy started from a deficit perspective, all conversations with specialists, doctors, and educators focused on what my son couldn't do, his unmet milestones, and his delays. Much of my energy went to securing the services Zac needed and making sure he was receiving them. I was researching programs, therapies, and other resources to help him progress and be on par with his peers. I often subjected Zac to more work outside of school since I had access to current information and research concerning best practices in special education. I allowed my experiences as a special education professional to overshadow my instincts and capabilities as a mother; I had become one of Zac's teachers, which put a lot of strain on my family, especially with Zac. One day, while struggling through homework, our frustration peaked, and we both cried. I decided then that I would be just Zac's mom. This shift in perspective allowed me to focus my energy toward the school, pushing them to see Zac for who he is and what he can do.

POSITIONALITY

We come to this work as two Diné asdzáás (women) and one white woman; we are all nondisabled parents, educators, students, advocates, and special education team members simultaneously conscious of those realities outside our own. Our experiences are represented through multifaceted lenses as two asdzáás who worked within our own tribal community or another tribe. As one of the asdzáás, Nicole is a parent of a child with a disability, navigating special education from early intervention services to the transition into public school, which has solidified their commitment to continue their family advocacy work.

As we conceptualize the decolonization of ECSE (i.e., the return of material resources to Indigenous families and the proliferation of Indigenous knowledges and ways of being), we also explore and, at times, interrogate our own experiences, beliefs, and understandings that have shaped who we are and how we approach this work. Our experiences, both similar and different, led us to reframe how we communicate and serve families and children in ECSE. There is a need to acknowledge familial voices and create space where families can share lived experiences to shape special education practices.

As authors, we aim to interrogate and expand our own views of disabilities, reframing how family engagement is developed for marginalized children in ECSE. We are educators with a combined 35+ years of teaching experience, and we recognize how children's and families' complex, intersectional social and cultural realities shape their encounters within a system rooted in white, colonial normative practices (Sabzalian, 2019).

Since Zac was young, our family made a group effort to care for him. Zac's grandparents were equally involved. As a family, we knew how to work with him and how he functioned at home. As Zac transitioned to early intervention and preschool, we as a family shared concerns and questions about how others would care for Zac. Zac's preschool teachers weren't prepared to have a student like him in their classroom early on. The teachers often relied on our input as Zac's caretakers, advocates, and knowledge experts. Dialogue at meetings strengthened cultural differences among Zac's early intervention and special education teams, including pertinent narratives from extended family members.

DECOLONIZING EARLY CHILDHOOD AND EDUCATIONAL SPACES

Challenging colonialism (i.e., the displacement and control of Indigenous families) is at the crux of our scholarship. As more diverse knowledge systems, including Indigenous knowledge systems, are being recognized in higher education and being utilized in more scholarly works, scholars are confronting the dominant Western canon in their research methodologies and field of study, though these efforts are still limited (e.g., Boveda & Bhattacharya, 2019; Patel, 2016; Smith, 2012). More research must confront complacency and elicit new practices, procedures, and policies. Picton and Tufue-Dolgoy (2019) posited that "this decolonizing perspective, when interwoven with disability, is an opportunity for critical knowledge and experiences of Indigenous disability to be voiced by Indigenous people with disabilities" (p. 190).

To decolonize ECSE spaces, it is imperative to disrupt how Native families are frequently dismissed throughout their children's education, particularly when they have children with disabilities. Standard practices often position Indigenous families as recipients of information rather than knowledgeable and valuable resources with insights into their children's strengths. Our main goal is to combat colonization with all the possibilities for families encountering unsettling situations "in settler colonial places and spaces" (Nxumalo, 2019, p. 7) within education. To address decolonization in special education, the WFS seeks to reframe how Indigenous families are involved in ECSE, defining the problems Indigenous families face and identifying solutions based on their stories. As theorized in Tachine's (2018) use of the story rug, "Stories are a legitimate tool for relating with others, sharing knowledge across generations, analyzing life circumstances, and seeking solutions for the future" (p. 65). Storywork in ECSE settings allows practitioners and families to create relationships, share knowledge, analyze the child's strengths and needs, and find solutions to support the family and child. Through storywork, families provide the thread that weaves the overall design and tapestry created for the child.

STORIES AS FRAMEWORK

Drawing from Kirkness and Barnhardt's (1991) research, Indigenous storywork foregrounds *respect, relevance, reciprocity,* and *responsibility*. Jo-ann Archibald, also known as Q'um Xiiem, from the Stó:lō Nation of Canada, adapted and extended Kirkness and Barnhardt's principles in working with elders from Coast Salish and Stó:lō communities to include *holism, interrelatedness,* and *synergy* in storytelling for educational purposes. Archibald (2008) shared that if and when these seven principles are used, stories can "take on their own life" and "become the teacher" (p. ix) to drive practice.

WFS FRAMEWORK OF PRACTICE

Within ECSE, we incorporate Archibald's (2008) seven principles so that families can share their lived experiences (stories) to shape practices. Engaging in authentic storywork with families in ECSE requires that all seven storywork principles be present throughout the process: respect, reverence, responsibility, reciprocity, synergy, holism, and interrelatedness. The WFS (Table 9.1) provides ways to incorporate each of the principles with families with several components (e.g., respect and reverence; reciprocity and synergy) combined as their meaning is symbiotic.

Respect and Reverence

Archibald (2008) discussed respect in terms of cultural responsibility. Cultural storytellers are given respect from listeners in caring for the narratives and communicating an enhanced meaning. While reverence is usually understood within a spiritual context, here it relates to a respect for life—both physical and spiritual. In ECSE, to proceed with respect and reverence means that the opinions, perspectives, and stories of others are held with regard. The stories families share should be utilized to uplift and serve the child.

To engage with Indigenous families from a place of respect and reverence, practitioners must first employ a critical consciousness to understand the families they serve (Garcia, 2019). That is, ECSE providers must situate themselves in communities' social and historical contexts. Many Indigenous families' schooling experiences are rooted in histories of survivance, forced colonial education, and Indigenous boarding schools that attempted to eradicate their culture, language, and ways of being (e.g., Garcia, 2019; Romero & Yellowhorse, 2021; Sabzalian, 2019; Windchief & Joseph, 2015). For example, the state of Arizona was home to the second-largest population of Indigenous boarding schools in the United States (Newland, 2022). Most Diné people, both past and present, have had some experience or connection with forced colonial schooling and have fought to keep their language and culture (Lomawaima & McCarty, 2006). We share this because Native American children and families currently receiving ECSE services bring wisdom from personal experiences and/or proximity to

Table 9.1. WFS Framework Overview

Storywork Principle	Definition (Archibald, 2008)	ECSE Context	Practitioner Implementation	Examples
Respect **Reverence**	*Viewed as cultural responsibility; cultural storytellers are respected through the care of their narratives* *Respect for life—both physical and spiritual*	Hold the opinions, perspectives, and stories of families and children in high regard. Familial narratives center and support the child from an asset-based perspective	(1) Employ a critical consciousness to understand local communities alongside their historical schooling experiences and survivance stories (2) Show care for stories inclusive of the child's familial background and culture (3) Use shared narratives to enhance understanding of the child for their benefit (4) Avoid deficit-centered discussions about a child's ability when speaking with families (5) Exhibit mindfulness in allowing families to express what is valuable to them	(1) Strengthen your knowledge of Indigenous education through Indigenous authors (e.g., Sabzalian, K., Romero, M. E., Garcia, J., Bang, M., Joseph, D. H., Faircloth, S., Lomawaima, K. T., McCarty, T. L.) (2) Initiate meaningful conversations to include child interests and life outside of school (3) Utilize other means of narrative building such as child interest surveys, inventories, and interviews completed by the child and their families (4) Center discussions on what the child *can do* (5) Provide space for families to share their values explicitly, understanding that your personal values may not align
Responsibility	*The duty in caring for the narrative once trust has been established and permission shared*	To handle the stories of families with accuracy, care, and confidentiality	(1) Create an environment that is based on trust in order to create the space needed for families to share their stories	(1) Understand trust is established through action; hold multiple spaces to engage with families outside of the annual meeting

(continued)

Table 9.1. *(continued)*

Storywork Principle	Definition (Archibald, 2008)	ECSE Context	Practitioner Implementation	Examples
			(2) Communicate explicit permissions as to what narratives may be recorded, documented, or shared (3) Keep information confidential (4) Communicate and/or restate narratives that are representative of the original	(2) Receive family permission prior to placing their stories in writing with an understanding that some stories are not meant for all (3) Take care in sharing information specifically among individuals on the IFSP/IEP team; familial stories are not a point of gossip (4) Invite families to review and provide feedback on any documentation or communication to ensure accuracy
Reciprocity Synergy	*The intended result of respect and responsibility also referred to as balance* *Synergistic actions produce an alliance or unity through interaction with the narrative, storyteller(s) and listeners*	Reciprocal and synergistic interactions balance relationships among team members to create an alliance. Power dynamics are moderated and family knowledge and input are treated with equal value	(1) Establish culturally appropriate norms (2) Be specific in conversations about what disability means to the family (3) Invite family members to present their narrative first (4) Engage in active listening (5) Communicate consensus; do not assume agreement (6) Employ conflict resolution strategies that are culturally relevant as needed	(1) Collaboratively establish meeting norms that center families, recognizing that all Indigenous people do not represent a monolith 2) Disability in special education versus disability in various cultural communities may have different meanings (e.g., read Beth Harry's work on cultural reciprocity) (3) Spend time in introductions and allow opportunities for families to lead meetings (4) Take the time to listen first, pause, and seek clarity before providing input

Storywork Principle	Definition (Archibald, 2008)	ECSE Context	Practitioner Implementation	Examples
				(5) Seek verbal agreement rather than interpreting silence as consensus; offer time outside of meetings to review documents before finalizing (6) Hold space for families to communicate their child's abilities and needs through multiple meetings as needed; seek to understand rather than to be viewed as "right"
Holism	*Human formation as a whole is based on the connection of its parts*	Consideration of all of the intricate facets of the child and how each component may be interrelated and impact the whole child; viewing the child beyond the lens of special education diagnosis	(1) Be cognizant of seeing the whole child (2) Consider all information shared about the child beyond academics or behavior	(1) Encourage stories that center the child's strengths and interests outside of formal settings to discover what may be unknown yet interrelated (2) Include information provided by families regarding the child that is also reflective of their abilities and interests outside of school
Interrelatedness	*Connection between the intellectual, spiritual, emotional, and physical realms that form a person as a whole*		(3) Allow opportunities for collaboration and communication outside of formal meetings (4) Focus on asset-based connections	(3) Connect with families in other environments such as community events (4) Create goals and objectives that also reflect the child's interests and skills, regardless of whether it is related to their academics, behavior, or transition

forced colonial education, and that often influences the ways they educate their children and engage with the ECSE system.

Once practitioners understand families' sociohistorical contexts and experiences, they can move forward with practices that embody respect and reverence. This may involve integrating children's and families' Indigenous perspectives (e.g., stories that reflect their values and traditions) and meaningful community engagement into practice, such as (1) showing care for stories inclusive of the student's familial background, culture, and history; (2) using shared narratives to enhance understanding of the child for their benefit; (3) demonstrating sensitivity to or avoiding deficit perceptions; and (4) exhibiting mindfulness by giving families time to think, pause, and share what is valuable to them before responding. For instance, Zac's early intervention and special education teams included pertinent narratives from extended family members during meetings—reflecting the value Indigenous families place on relationships beyond the "nuclear family"—while acknowledging the complexity involved in his care, enabling a comprehensive understanding of his strengths, tendencies, and preferences.

Responsibility

In the context of storywork, responsibility refers to one's duties in caring for the narrative once trust has been established and permission shared (Archibald, 2008). Within ECSE, teams handle families' stories with accuracy, care, and confidentiality. Taking responsibility may involve fostering an environment where all stakeholders actively participate in the learning process and community.

ECSE practices that can foster responsibility include (1) creating an environment that centers trust for families to share their stories; (2) communicating explicit permissions as to what narratives may be recorded or shared; (3) keeping information confidential; and (4) communicating narratives to others ways that are representative of original tellings. With Zac's story, this meant the narratives shared by his parents and extended family members stayed within the team and remained confidential. Team members can explicitly communicate what narratives may be documented with the child's and family's permission. This commitment allows team members to consider power dynamics and enable families to share their stories, especially the family's disability perspectives. Holding families' stories responsibly, in many ways, eschews the ECSE field's emphasis on documentation—instead, emphasizing the need to build trust and follow families' lead.

Reciprocity and Synergy

Reciprocity is a product of respect and responsibility, also called *balance* (Archibald, 2008). Synergy further produces an alliance or unity among people who interact with narratives, listen, and regard one another with respect

(Archibald, 2008). Reciprocal and synergistic interactions within ECSE strengthen collaboration and benefit families. Thus, power dynamics can be moderated, and the knowledge of the family and child is elevated.

Incorporating reciprocity and synergy in ECSE can enhance the learning environment and nurture meaningful relationships. Practitioners and families may exercise reciprocity and synergy through the following: (1) establishing culturally appropriate norms; (2) understanding how disability may be defined or viewed by families; (3) inviting family members to present their narrative first; (4) engaging in active listening; (5) communicating consensus, not assuming agreement; and (6) employing conflict resolution strategies that are culturally relevant, as needed. Collaboration between the family and team members allows everyone to acknowledge and incorporate stories respectfully. For example, Zac's family members shared their narratives with the ECSE team, but the meetings would have been strengthened through specific dialogue regarding cultural differences among team members.

Holism and Interrelatedness

Holism is the human interrelatedness among intellectual, spiritual, emotional, and physical realms that form the person as a whole (Archibald, 2008). In ECSE, it is essential to consider the child's intricate facets and how other social realms are interrelated. Special education and early intervention practices, by design, tend to fragment children into categories defined by what the child cannot do (e.g., developmental domains). Instead, ECSE teams should create an environment that holistically addresses assets through critical care. The WFS provides the space for stories to create a holistic view of the child, bridging gaps that individual family service plans (IFSP) may lack.

Practitioners should recognize the interconnectedness of all aspects of a child's development—cognitive, social, emotional, and cultural well-being. Holism and interrelatedness in practice may incorporate any of the following: (1) being cognizant of seeing the whole child, not just their perceived deficits; (2) considering all information shared about the child (beyond academics or behavior) that reflects the child's life; (3) allowing opportunities for collaboration and communication outside of formal meetings; and (4) focusing on asset-based connections. The collaborative endeavors of the early intervention team enabled Zac to have a significant presence within his family and community without being defined solely by his impairment. The IFSP and IEPs did not aim to rectify or eliminate Zac's impairment but rather provided him with the means to enhance and fortify his strengths.

In sum, the WFS utilizes storywork to engage with family-centered narratives through respect, reverence, responsibility, reciprocity, synergy, holism, and interrelatedness. The framework offers pathways to strengthen family–team partnerships while respecting and grounding the work within Indigenous culture.

Zac has an exciting future. He is dictating his aspirations. I now know how to hear and guide him through his thoughts. Rather than concentrating on his limits, we are focused on making his goals a reality. Zac wants to be a basketball coach in the Special Olympics and is interested in working as a sales associate or game tester in the video game industry with a wife and two children to complete his dream. My hope is for people to see Zac as a whole person.

IMAGINED FUTURES

The WFS provides a framework of action that can empower ECSE practitioners to elevate and honor the stories of Indigenous families. It fosters collaboration among families, educators, and specialists to create supportive and safe environments. WFS can also be adapted to different contexts or populations within ECSE as it provides structure and promotes inclusive environments. Storywork centers families' culture and knowledge, and consequently helps develop IFSPs and IEPs that center the child from an asset-based lens. ECSE practitioners and service providers must come to this work humbly understanding that their methods and ideas may not serve the child. Instead of adopting prescribed ECSE narratives, families must be given the space to share their perspectives on disability grounded by their culture and traditions. We can elevate family narratives like Zac's story through storywork with imagined futures that transform colonial understandings of disability. Ałtso Nihéch'i' Ha'dzii: Ahxéhee'.[3]

Part IV

ENGAGING IN CRITICAL PRAXIS IN EDUCATOR PREPARATION

In this section, chapters contend with the ways ableism in early childhood classrooms often gets perpetuated by the uncritical teaching of "best practices" within higher education. Authors focus on how faculty working within early childhood preparation programs can engage in critical praxis—ongoing reflection and action aimed at transforming existing power dynamics (Freire, 1970)—in their work with future educators.

The section begins with a dialogue in which we (Beneke and Love) reflect on our own compliance with early childhood pedagogical "scripts" as former teachers. In Chapter 10, we narrate our attempts to take action in our current roles as teacher educators, experimenting and pushing ourselves to think outside existing scripts. We draw on abolition and disability justice movement work to offer questions for readers to consider in their own realms of influence. In Chapter 11, Padía and Turner bring together Black feminist thought and disability critical race theory to forward a framework for critical praxis in early childhood teacher education. Drawing on examples from their own practice, they highlight ways of disrupting whiteness and normativity in early childhood teacher education and remind critical early childhood educators that this work is never done in isolation. Finally, in Chapter 12, Brea-Spahn and Soto-Boykin provide examples of their own critical praxis from their work in speech-language pathology. They showcase how students in their speech-language pathology program used collaging to critically question what counts as "good" languaging, disrupt oppressive linguistic ideologies, and envision liberated early childhood spaces in which young children's entire linguistic repertoires are valued and sustained.

Together, these chapters suggest how teacher educators can critically reflect and take action within educator preparation toward freedom and belonging.

CHAPTER 10

Unbound by the Script

Cultivating Liberatory Pedagogies Through Disability Justice and Abolition in Early Childhood

Maggie Beneke and Hailey R. Love

In early childhood, standards of teaching and learning perpetuate a culture of compliance. These technocratic processes uphold dominant notions of normalcy (constructed through racism, ableism, and other intersecting oppressions) across multiple early learning contexts (e.g., classrooms, home–school relationships, teacher education programs). In previous work, we have exposed how racism and ableism intersect in the definitions, measurements, and enactments of standardized early childhood teaching and learning—limiting young children's, their families' and their teachers' freedom (see Beneke & Love, 2022).

Here, we consider how perspectives from two social movements—abolition and disability justice—might theoretically ground our pedagogical efforts to cultivate greater freedom in early childhood teacher education. Through a "dialogic spiral" (Kinloch & San Pedro, 2016, p. 31), we think with principles from disability justice and abolition as we share letters with one another, exchanging stories that expose our own compliance with the "scripts" (Keenan, 2017) of early childhood and our ideas about how to move forward. This nonlinear, iterative process allows us to extend one another's ideas, honor each other's experiences, and elevate the perspectives of organizers who have already begun envisioning ways of moving beyond our current systems. We engage in this dialogue to agitate, undo, and imagine beyond standards of early childhood teaching and learning that keep dominant notions of normalcy intact. We asked: What can we learn from storying these moments toward cultivating greater freedom for children, families, ourselves?

. . .

Dear Hailey,

First, I am so grateful to still be on this journey with you. We have been through a lot together, haven't we? First working together in Massachusetts with 1st- and 2nd-graders, then studying inclusive early childhood education as fellow doctoral students in Kansas. And now as colleagues, collaborators, and friends who scheme across two different UWs. I have always valued your precision, your tenacity, your criticality, and your heart. Your approach to centering disability in early childhood is why I want to share with you—and explore together—teaching and learning beyond compliance with standards-based scripts.

I have long struggled with what it means to adhere to early learning standards. In my own childhood, as a young white girl labeled with a disability—I was positioned as "too loud" for school. I was trained to conform to school participation expectations—to be softer, quieter, passive. From what I remember, most of my time in intervention was spent practicing whispering. I learned to follow this school script early so that I would be perceived as a "good student." I know that my whiteness protected me in how I was perceived and treated in special education. And I also know that this early experience with intervention was pedagogical, teaching me to strive for perfection, an early lesson in white womanhood (Rao & Jackson, 2022) that has been reinforced throughout my life.

Undoing these pedagogical teachings is lifelong but necessary, work. I wonder about your early experiences with learning standards and how those have impacted the ways you approach this conversation?

With much respect and love,
Maggie

Dear Maggie,

I'm so excited to continue this work with you. It is hard to believe that we've known each other for so long! I can relate to a lot of what you described, but in slightly different ways. As a young, Black girl, I was always considered a "good" and "smart" student, and that was a really important part of my identity. I strove for perfection and expected others to do the same. I still remember that my kindergarten teacher told my mom that I was "bossy" because I would "correct" other kids. That was certainly imbued with gendered and racialized beliefs regarding who is dismissed as bossy or stereotyped as aggressive versus valued as a leader (Harris-Perry, 2011).

However, it was also indicative of the ability-related fine line I was taught to navigate early on, whereas I could and should strive for perfection, but only in certain ways. In school, doing so usually earned me good grades and accolades. Yet walking this line has affected me in other ways, including often feeling isolated in classrooms where I was the only Black student or one of very few. Reflecting on my schooling experiences now, I can see how ableism both protected me from certain forms of racism (because I was perceived as smart) and yielded what may be considered unintended consequences in the form of anxiety and some loss of racial and cultural identity that I had to later intentionally reclaim. I look forward to delving more into the complex intersections of racism and ableism and how we can envision a more just future.

Best,
Hailey

GROUNDING OUR PEDAGOGIES IN MOVEMENT

In social movements, organizers often engage in new forms of relationality, modeling ways of being and acting that defy current systems (Eagle Shield et al., 2020; Eagle Shield et al., 2021). We draw on principles of relationality that emerged from two complementary social movements: disability justice and abolition. We use these perspectives to guide pedagogical ways of being and acting beyond fidelity with ableist standards (and the intersecting oppressive ideologies that uphold them) in early childhood.

Disability Justice

First, we turn toward perspectives from disability justice movement work. Disability justice grew out of recognition that equity efforts within rights-based legal frameworks often negate the experiences of disabled people targeted by multiple intersecting oppressions (e.g., ableism, anti-Blackness, capitalism, cisheteropatriarchy; Berne et al., 2018; Kafai, 2021; Piepzna-Samarasinha, 2018; Sins Invalid, 2019). Through their activism and organizing, Patty Berne and coconspirators (e.g., Mia Mingus, Stacey Milbern, Eli Clare) forwarded a disability justice framework to guide alternative ways of being with one another. We foreground four key ideas from this framework in relation to early childhood pedagogies: *intersectionality, leadership of those most impacted, recognizing wholeness,* and *interdependence.*

Extending Black feminist conceptualizations of intersectionality (Collins, 1986; Combahee River Collective, 1977; Crenshaw, 1989; Lorde, 1984), disability justice means validating *intersectionality*—that experiences of disability are inherently shaped based on a nexus of intersecting oppressions (Gray, 2020). We apply this principle to understand how intersecting oppressions shape early learning standards, impacting the ways young children experience disability.

Next, acknowledging that efforts to resist oppressive systems should be guided by those who know these systems best, disability justice organizers prioritize *leadership of those most impacted* (Shah, 2022; Sins Invalid, 2019). As we consider what it might mean to engage in liberatory pedagogies in early childhood, we follow the leadership of disabled young children, especially those who may be targeted (and impacted) by multiple oppressive systems—this means listening to disabled children, following the ways they legitimately express agency, multiplicity, and resistance.

Third, in resistance to the fragmentation of people based on social categories, disability justice means *recognizing wholeness* or valuing the fullness of people's present lives regardless of their ability to perform or produce in capitalist society (Mingus, 2011). Instead of fragmenting children based on developmental domains or their abilities to develop academic skills (rooted in whiteness), we position young children as whole beings in the present, whose worth is not tied to standardized performance.

Finally, disability justice means honoring *interdependence* by orienting toward the support we each rely on and engaging in efforts to meet one another's needs without relying on state solutions (Piepzna-Samarasinha, 2018). We strive to disrupt the state-sanctioned myth that early childhood pedagogies should be focused on young children developing independent skills and instead honor the ways children and their communities (peers, teachers, families) meet one another's needs through practices of mutuality.

Prison Industrial Complex (PIC) Abolition

We also draw on perspectives from the prison industrial complex (PIC) abolition movement. PIC abolition emerged as prisons were being assembled and expanded to dominate, control, and profit from Black and Brown communities (Gilmore & Kilgore, 2019), in some ways replacing the enslavement of Black people (Davis, 2011). As video footage of state-sanctioned police violence circulated on social media amid the COVID-19 pandemic, the facade of institutional protection was thrown into high relief and strategies of PIC abolition received increased public attention (Kaba, 2021), including in education (Feliciano, 2021). The PIC is made up of a web of institutions that utilize punishment to uphold white supremacy (Strayhorn, 2021). Abolitionist imaginaries encourage efforts to dismantle punitive logics, change taken-for-granted carceral arrangements, and build alternative conditions so that people can safely get their needs met (e.g., Critical Resistance, 2023; Purnell, 2022; Sabati et al., 2022). Indeed, undoing the PIC means practicing abolition across multiple social, political, and economic institutions (beyond prisons themselves)—including in education (Love, 2019; Meiners, 2017; Stovall, 2018). Given the specific ways that ableism operates to perpetuate racialized systems of punishment from children's earliest moments in schools (e.g., Barrow, 2019; Beneke et al., 2022), we consider how PIC abolition might support efforts to build safe conditions for multiply marginalized disabled children in early childhood.

While there are myriad lessons to learn from PIC abolition, we draw on three key teachings that can be practiced in teacher education now: *moratorium, decarceration,* and *excarceration.*

First, we recognize *moratorium* as a key strategy of PIC abolition to end the building of cages (Prison Research Education Action Project, 2005). This means continuously dismantling logics that equate justice with punishment, including those that have been naturalized for us in educational systems and in our own realms of influence (Cullors, 2018; Lamble, 2022). Indeed, as trans abolitionist

Tourmaline tweeted, "When we say abolish police. We also mean the cop in your head and in your heart" (2020). Thus, as we strive to cultivate liberatory pedagogies in early childhood, we suspend our own investments in dominant standards of early childhood teaching and learning that allow cycles of punishment to thrive.

Next, abolitionist organizers engage in *decarceration*—seeking to release people from confinement through coordinated, collective action (Herzing, 2023). Longtime abolitionist organizer Mariame Kaba highlighted the power of doing this work in coalition, stating, "Everything worthwhile is done with other people" (Ewing, 2019). Therefore, we recognize that releasing young children from the confining power of ableist standards in early childhood requires that we build relationships across groups often pitted against one another (e.g., general education vs. special education, community vs. academia, adults vs. children). Moreover, as we operate within the existing schooling system, we reflect on how we might address and reduce the impact of harm on multiply marginalized children in the present.

Finally, PIC abolition involves strategies of *excarceration*—building alternatives to divert people away from cycles of punishment in the first place (Washington, 2018). Prison scholar Ruth Wilson Gilmore explained that regular people can engage in strategies of excarceration in the present: "It is not some pie-in-the-sky dream. It is actually something that is practical and achievable" (Democracy Now, 2020). We know that changing an early childhood system committed to standardized curricula is not going to happen overnight, but we can create alternative models with the tools we have, diverting young children away from cycles of punishment. Those alternative models must recognize multiply marginalized disabled children's provocations, play, and resistance as legitimate.

MOVING TOGETHER: DISABILITY JUSTICE AND PIC ABOLITION IN EARLY CHILDHOOD PEDAGOGIES

We bring these social movement lessons to bear on pedagogy in early childhood, recognizing—as others have—alignment between efforts to grow disability justice and PIC abolition (Hayes, 2023; Pejcha & Wang, 2021; Phuong et al., 2024). In bridging these perspectives, we contend that a moratorium on punitive standards in early childhood must recognize how ableism and racism interlock in systems of compliance (including those dominant expectations we have internalized). In doing so, we turn toward the ways multiply marginalized children might lead us toward new ways of relating to young children and early learning itself. As we take actions to release children from learning systems rooted in hyper-individualism, we work in coalition and interdependent relationships with others who share these same commitments. And in our efforts to build alternatives to punishment- to dream otherwise- we seek to honor children as fundamentally whole beings. Together, disability justice and PIC abolition help us explore ways of moving beyond adherence to restrictive standards in early childhood, and instead, build otherwise pedagogical possibilities.

A Moratorium on Pathologizing Children in the Name of Compliance

Dear Maggie,

We must reflect on ways we've promoted compliance with dominant ways of being, even as we tried to address inequities and support inclusion. In a previous role, I supervised college students volunteering in preschools primarily serving Black and Latine families who experienced poverty and multiple forms of violence. I was trained to ensure students heavily annotated and scripted how they would read books and do activities with children. The students came from a variety of racial, ethnic, and socioeconomic backgrounds. Yet their participation in the program required them to enact the "master's tools" (Lorde, 1984). I taught them to address systemic inequities through individual intervention based on dominant notions of "quality" teaching and learning. Thus, I implicate myself when discussing ways the field has perpetuated racism and ableism. How did you feel pressure to adhere to scripts imbued with dominant notions of "rigor" and "quality" as a teacher?

Best,
Hailey

Dear Hailey,

As an early educator, I too felt pressure to adhere to myriad scripted curricula, overwhelmed by expectations to maintain "order" while getting children to meet learning benchmarks. And my gosh, I put such effort into teaching children compliance: working quietly, walking in straight lines, sitting still on the rug. I think about children for whom this script never worked. There was Cole, a Black child who would playfully tell jokes; phonics interventions would send silent tears streaming down Cole's face. There was Mia, a multiracial child who expressed her zest for life by performing songs, but for whom sitting still never seemed possible. I too am implicated—I shut down children's expressions so that they would reach whatever benchmark I felt pressed to teach them. In our current roles, how can we divest from such standardization, knowing that compliance naturalizes punishment in early learning?

Your friend,
Maggie

Dominant notions of quality often allow early childhood systems (and actors within those systems) to equate goodness with compliance and justice with punishment. The argument that increasing children's access to standardized "quality" early childhood programs will ameliorate inequities in child outcomes (e.g., Heckman, 2008; Johnson-Staub, 2017) overlooks how developmental goals within such programs are problematically rooted in whiteness (Pérez, 2020) and ableism (Ferri & Bacon, 2011). Within this framing of quality, early educators are frequently encouraged to use developmental assessments and referral processes normed on white, nondisabled, and middle-class ways of knowing and being (e.g., Dyson, 2015; Souto-Manning & Rabadi-Raol, 2018) to identify children and families who might benefit from "support," meaning multiply marginalized children and families are likely to be subjected to increased surveillance, categorization, and remediation. We contend that children and families should not have to endure pedagogical surveillance and practices of "fixing" their bodies, minds, and/or behaviors to get their needs met.

Further, despite the field's commitments to inclusion, pedagogical remediation often leads to children receiving special education services in isolated settings (Grindal et al., 2019). When children with disabilities *are* included in general education settings, inclusion is often defined in relation to placement rather than a change in practices and the ability hierarchies that undergird such practices (Love & Horn, 2021). For instance, within inclusive settings, peer-mediated interventions are often touted as a way to engage children with disabilities in meaningful social interaction. Yet this practice often relies on positioning nondisabled peers as "expert learners" who are recruited to surveil and intervene on their peers with disabilities. We argue that the normalization of pedagogical surveillance promotes the isolation and separation of children labeled with disabilities for the purposes of intervention, while also breaking relationships and people.

A moratorium on pathologizing children in the name of compliance is more than needed. And, as Leah Lakshmi Piepzna Samarasinha noted, to lay the groundwork for relationships of interdependence to thrive, "there is a lot of pre-work that needs to be done" (Hayes, 2023). To move beyond compliance with the script of early childhood curricula means early educators (ourselves included) must contend with our own investments in naturalized notions of "individual skill development" that perpetuate cycles of punishment. While our dialogue above offers a beginning, we recognize that abolishing internalized and institutional messages surrounding pedagogical forms of punishment must be a continuous process. Further, to engage in the ongoing work of divesting from compliance in early childhood teaching and learning, we turn toward the brilliance of children most impacted by these systems. Indeed, the ways multiply marginalized young children express their desires to participate and meaningfully engage in their learning can release us from punitive logics. With this in mind, we offer the following questions for early educators and teacher educators as provocations toward collective efforts to dismantle the pedagogical script:

- How might my current pedagogical approach predefine normative goals for early childhood teaching and learning, ones that allow surveillance and other forms of control to thrive?
- How might alternative forms of pedagogical documentation help me see young children's wide range of emotions and expressions as meaningful resistance to normative expectations?

- How might I build from multiply marginalized children's and families' resistance to unwelcoming norms? What might their resistance help me reframe in terms of goals for teaching and learning?

Decarcerating Punitive Pedagogies Through Commitments to Young Children's Wholeness

Dear Hailey,

I am thinking about how I can support future and current teachers to begin reversing (and hopefully transforming) harmful narratives that position young children as needing "fixing." I don't have all the answers, but I know we need to try—especially in finding ways to grow alternative possibilities in our roles as early childhood teacher educators. In my previous letter to you I reflected on the ways my commitments to compliance impacted Cole and Mia. If I had oriented toward their provocations and meaning-making—what might have been different for these two children? For other children? How might we cultivate spaces of learning that embrace multiply marginalized young children's multidimensional identities and competencies, while recognizing them as already whole beings? I am curious to learn more about how you are thinking about this, Hailey, and how you think about making change in the context of teacher education.

Warmly,
Maggie

Dear Maggie,

You're asking important questions that I think can only be answered through critical praxis. When teaching, I try to orient students toward a reflexive process of engaging and learning with children. Understandably, preservice teachers often want direct answers and specific strategies. Yet implementing decontextualized strategies without a deep understanding of systemic inequities and solidarity with multiply marginalized communities only reproduces injustices. State and national teacher education program accreditation standards further challenge such an orientation as they carry assumptions about child development and learning grounded in whiteness and dominant notions of ability (Love & Hancock, 2022; Luna, 2016). I try to model and support a praxis around critical questions, such as, what does practice look like that presumes children's wholeness and explicitly counters inequities? Still, I am struck by the need for more urgent changes and wonder how I can work in solidarity with multiply marginalized children and families to effect change now.

Best,
Hailey

Children are constantly fragmented in early childhood practice, whether it be on the basis of developmental domains (Reinke et al., 2019) or social identities (Martínez-Álvarez, 2019). Even as the early childhood field acknowledges that developmental domains intersect, practice guidance, assessment, and policy continue to divide children's development into discrete domains (e.g., social–emotional, physical, cognitive; CEC & DEC, 2020; NAEYC, 2020). For instance, standardized curricula and assessments are often divided by developmental domain-specific objectives. Such fragmentation drives hierarchies whereby Black, Indignenous, Latine, Asian, and Pacific Islander children, children identified as having disabilities, and children at the intersection of those identities are subjected to intervention—often scripted or bound by expectations of "fidelity"—intended to "fix" isolated perceived deficits. These children are subject to the dismissal of their cultural and linguistic assets and often only perceived in terms of those presumed deficits (Martínez-Álvarez, 2019; Padía, 2023). Fragmenting the child also isolates families as professionals invalidate family contributions, priorities, and holistic views of the child grounded in cultural norms, community membership, and an awareness of the discrimination their communities face (Cioè-Peña, 2021; Lalvani, 2014).

Children are already whole. Accordingly, decarceration requires releasing children from the confines of fragmentation and centering connection in multiple ways. We assert that moving away from scripted curricula that isolate parts of who children are requires recognizing children's wholeness and eschewing artificial divisions—both the ways children have been disjointed (i.e., reliance on discrete developmental domains) and the ways their familial and communal bonds have been disrupted by said fragmentation. Orienting toward community can help drive this movement—relationships counter fragmentation. When we attend to the ways children are severed from their families and communities by dominant developmental norms and associated scripted curricula, we can begin to recognize and mend the artificial fractures that have been fueled by standardization.

In line with Mariame Kaba's assertion that we already have the tools needed for PIC abolition (Ewing, 2019), we contend that not only are children already whole, but they also already have the tools they need to be in community with those around them. Rather than a focus on fixing children, we can orient ourselves to their provocations, play, and resistance to identify alternatives to scripted curricula. That is, we can follow the lead of disabled children and their families as well as teachers and teacher candidates who are multiply marginalized to understand how they want to be in community. Creating community is a manifestation of care work, defined by disability justice scholars as the everyday practice of creating and ensuring safety and access for those we are in community with (Piepzna-Samarasinha, 2018). As Leah Lakshmi Piepzna-Samarasinha espoused, this entails building relationships so children and families feel comfortable expressing their needs (Hayes, 2023) and then ensuring every member of the community has their needs met, as they define their needs and the ways they should be met (Piepzna-Samarasinha, 2018).

Moreover, we must ensure everyone in the community is able to responsibly practice their freedom, exercising autonomy as they choose to be in community with, and care for, others, and respond to harm as it comes up (Shalaby, 2017). By building community with multiply marginalized children, families, and teachers using such care tactics (e.g., identifying and working against the isolation of any community members), we can immediately begin to reduce harm caused by standardization.

At the same time, we must also look to what Kaba referred to as the "500-year clock" (Ewing, 2019), organizing to reverse the harm caused by standardization and the consequential fragmentation of children and families. In recognition of the inherent wholeness of multiply marginalized children and their families and the need to follow their lead, we must advocate to abolish manifestations of standardization and deficit-based intervention (e.g., developmental norms, demands for instructional fidelity, generalized and narrowed behavioral expectations). Doing so requires disrupting hierarchies (e.g., teacher–student; teacher educator–teacher candidate) and moving away from silos (e.g., researcher–practitioner; researcher–activist; special education–general education) reinforced by standardization that only positions white, nondisabled knowledges and ways of being as valuable. At the same time, abolitionists like Kaba (Hayes, 2023) and Sultan and Herskind (2020) remind us that reversing harm and preventing future harm also requires harnessing hope to imagine and begin to build new systems that prioritize community access, safety, and accountability to each other. Likewise, as teacher educators, we must partner with multiply marginalized communities to identify programmatic changes and to advocate based on their desires. This includes making changes that facilitate and codify care for multiply marginalized teacher candidates (TCs).

With intentions to immediately prevent and reduce harm, and work toward long-term harm reversal, early educators and teacher educators may ask themselves:

- In what ways are current curriculum and assessment practices fragmenting children and families? What cultural and linguistic assets are potentially being overlooked or dismissed, including assets related to learning to navigate the world with a disability?
- What knowledge and skills do multiply marginalized children and their families prioritize, and how might those priorities drive curricula and assessment?
- How do multiply marginalized children and families define safety within the spaces I work? Based on that, how can I support safety with and for them?
- How might I be limiting avenues for multiply marginalized children and their families to lead, organize, and build for themselves and others? How can I reinstate or repair those pathways?
- What program structures are interfering with community building, and how can I advocate to amend them?

Building Alternative Pedagogies Rooted in Interdependence

Dear Maggie,

Something I continue to grapple with is our field's emphasis on independence. It is embedded in developmental milestones, children's individualized goals, and communication with families (Beneke & Love, 2022). In multiple classrooms I've observed teachers stopping children from helping each other in the name of supporting children's development and promoting independence. Yet disability justice requires interdependence. How can we support disability justice while every aspect of the early educational system is focused on intervening on the child, detached from their families; or intervening on the family, detached from their community? This isn't just a problem of how we position children and families, but how we conceptualize and respond to the relationships that shape us. I wonder how to situate relationships as central to our practice in early childhood teacher education, even as forces of hyper-individualism and standardized curriculum circulate? In what ways have you supported interdependence and engaged in coalition-building to combat intersecting oppressions?

Best,
Hailey

Dear Hailey,

YES! The primacy of independence in schools reinforces ableist expectations that young children can and should learn to perform skills on their own and overlooks how we all rely on support in our daily lives (Mingus, 2017; 2011). I have been especially interested in ways we might build early childhood classroom communities that value our dependence on one another and our environments (Shalaby, 2020). With teachers and colleagues, I have participated in inquiry spaces that honor supports we, as grown-ups, rely on, which has helped us position early learning as an interdependent endeavor (Beneke et al., 2023). Moreover, as we build such alternatives in early childhood, I continue to reflect on the support and community that sustain me in this work—I am so grateful to be growing coalitions with other critical scholars like you as we nurture more humanizing alternatives within and across fields (e.g., early childhood, disability studies, critical race studies, early literacy, etc.).

Love,
Maggie

Pivoting away from compliance-based pedagogical approaches requires that we build alternative models of teaching and learning rooted in relationships of support (Mingus, 2011; Piepzna-Samarasinha, 2018). Valuing relationships within our pedagogies affords resistance to ableism, because ableism not only requires that we value what people are able to do in relation to dominant expectations rooted in whiteness but also locates and measures that value within individual bodies, minds, and behaviors (Lewis, 2022). Early childhood pedagogies that move beyond ranking and sorting the individual bodies, minds, and behaviors of multiply marginalized children, their families, and their teachers, must define meaningful teaching and learning as happening (and sustaining relationships) *between people* (Kaba, 2021; Rogoff, 2003). Further, we must recognize that our work as teacher educators and scholars is situated within a larger ecosystem of relationships (Annamma & Morrison, 2018); our interactions (and the supportive relationships we build) with community partners, with colleagues at our institutions, and with scholars across fields necessarily impact the experiences of our TCs and the children in their care (and vice versa).

To support disability justice–driven early childhood teachers in orienting toward interdependence, and in the hopes that children might ultimately see how their learning and survival depend on one another, we strive to build early childhood pedagogies rooted in interdependence at multiple levels. That is, values for interdependence can guide how we understand meaningful teaching and learning in early childhood classrooms, in the relationships we forge with and among students in our teacher preparation programs, and in the kinds of coalitions we build with colleagues and across disciplines. And across this coalition-building work, we remain answerable to those made most vulnerable by educational systems (Patel, 2014). Thus, as we encourage TCs to imagine beyond scripts and standards, white, nondisabled teacher educators can follow the lead of and show up for multiply marginalized teacher educators and communities, recognizing that efforts to position multiply marginalized young children as whole is a communal responsibility. Further, as teacher educators encourage TCs to be subversive within educational systems (Gonzalez, 2020), we must simultaneously think about how we encourage and support the building of coalitions that protect and lift up multiply marginalized TCs. To that end, critical affinity spaces can be protected spaces for TCs (especially multiply marginalized TCs) to process the ways they can subvert ableist–racist educational systems while also supporting one another in this process (Kulkarni et al., 2022; Varghese et al., 2019).

As we practice relationships of interdependence, we can build coalitions with other teacher educators as well. For instance, we can cultivate relationships across faculty in multiple departments or units to develop preparation programs that explicitly reject the deficit-based positioning of children (Ashby, 2012; Oyler, 2011), and instead recognize, respond to, and honor multiply marginalized children's wholeness. As we do so, we can also consider how we show up for and support our justice-driven colleagues. Although academic spaces are mired in neoliberal and merit-based logics that often pit faculty against one another (Samuels, 2017; Singh, 2021), we can build people power (Madison, 2019), standing alongside one another when our pedagogies are challenged. As Leah Lakshmi Piepzna-Samarasinha (Hayes, 2023) reminds us, showing up for one another does not mean taking on a savior mentality by waiting to swoop in to fix a problem in moments of crises and then expecting thanks. Instead, we can proactively and continuously work through divides across fields (Cochran-Smith & Dudley Marling, 2012), knowing that our efforts to grow relationships of support for children are bound up in our relationships with each other. With this in mind, we offer the following questions for early educators and teacher educators as provocations toward building pedagogies rooted in interdependence:

- How might my current approaches to growing justice-driven pedagogies be upholding individualism, allowing feelings of isolation and competition to thrive?
- How can I explicitly cultivate relationships of support with and between TCs and my colleagues as an ongoing practice?
- How might I practice alternatives to deficit-based pedagogies in coalition, showing up for those most vulnerable to harm as a result of pedagogical subversion?

BUILDING TOGETHER, MOVING FORWARD

> *None of us has all the answers, or we would have ended oppression already. But if we keep building the world we want, trying new things, and learning from our mistakes, new possibilities emerge.*
>
> —Mariame Kaba (2021, p.4)

We know we do not have all the answers about how to undo and imagine beyond racist–ableist standards of early childhood teaching and learning. And still—knowing that the humanity of generations of young children, their families, and their teachers is at stake—we have to experiment, to push ourselves to think outside the current script. Through our dialogue and the writing of this chapter, including words printed here and those that did not make it into these pages, we have puzzled through ways disability justice and abolition movement work might help us mitigate, and eventually reverse, the harm of pedagogical compliance. Moving forward, we commit to staying rooted in relationships and practicing hope as we strive to build possibilities for more liberatory pedagogies in early childhood. We make this commitment knowing that the work will not be straightforward, that we have much to learn through the process, and that we must continue to try.

CHAPTER 11

Enacting Critical Epistemologies in Early Childhood Teacher Education

A Black Feminist Disability Studies Critical Race Theory Praxis

Lilly Padía and Crystasany R. Turner

As other contributors have expanded on, the field of early childhood education (ECE) historically and presently adheres to white, English-dominant, ableist, and middle-class standards of care, education, and child development (e.g., Ferri & Bacon, 2011).

In this chapter, we bring together Black feminisms and disability critical race theory (DisCrit) in the context of early childhood teacher education to advance ideas of how early educators can be prepared to combat such norms, including those working with young multilingual and/or disabled learners. Black feminism(s) provides a framework for early childhood teacher educators and teacher candidates to understand the intersectional experiences of marginalized children living within oppressive systems. DisCrit points to the particular intersections of ableism and racism (Annamma et al., 2013a). Annamma (2017) explicitly noted that DisCrit exists because of the legacy of Black feminist genealogies. However, early childhood teacher education and Black feminisms have experienced ruptures that framed the two fields as distinct rather than inextricably linked. Therefore, we argue that an early childhood Black feminist disability critical race theory praxis can help mend these ruptures and further explicate the intersections where harm is enacted on young children, as well as the possibilities of liberation for all children.

We come to this work as two teacher educators and former early childhood educators. While we advocate for more liberatory early childhood experiences for all children, we center young Black girls because our collective liberation is inherently entwined with their liberation. As the Combahee River Collective (1977) expressed, Black girls' "freedom would necessitate the destruction of all the systems of oppression" (p. 7). Lilly is a white and Latina cis woman scholar whose work is rooted in the genealogies of racialization, disablement, and languaging. Crystasany is a Black cis woman scholar whose work is rooted in Black feminist thought and spirit-centered educational practices.

THE NEED FOR BLACKFEM DISCRIT IN EARLY CHILDHOOD TEACHER EDUCATION

Teacher education traditionally requires separate coursework and licensure for early childhood, special, bilingual, and general education (as evidenced in state teacher licensure requirements). Siloing educator preparation programs fragments children and withholds from teacher candidates' understandings of the myriad ways Children of Color, multilingual/multidialectical[1] children, and/or children with disabilities develop within their cultural contexts. The erasure of the perspectives of Children of Color, multilingual/multidialectical children, immigrant children, and children with disabilities is yet another manifestation of white supremacy and a form of epistemic violence (Taylor, 2018). In this chapter, we focus on teacher education since the enactment of just pedagogy with our earliest learners necessitates socially just education of their teachers.

Black feminists have called out similar siloing in society and the need to address it for liberation. In *Feminist Theory: From Margin to Center*, bell hooks critiqued white women's call for solidarity in the feminist movement, asserting that the "sisterhood" propagated by the contemporary feminist movement discounted "racist discrimination, exploitation, and oppression of multi-ethnic women" (hooks, 2015, pp. 50–51). Because white women disregarded Black women's intersectional positionality as both women and Black, the experiences and perspectives of Black women were continually left on the margins of the feminist movement. This constant disregard of the intersectional impact of racism and sexism on the lived experiences of women and girls of Color is at the core of our argument for a Black feminist DisCrit within ECE.

DisCrit, as a theoretical framework, examines and critiques how social constructions of race and ability uphold "normalcy." It helps us understand the implications of "normalcy" on multiply marginalized children (Annamma et al., 2013b; Love & Beneke, 2021). While DisCrit builds on a legacy of Black feminist thought, we argue a need to *explicitly* reintegrate Black feminist epistemologies within DisCrit's application in teacher education. This is necessary to thoroughly discuss the intersectional ECE experiences of young children. Scholars have used DisCrit *or* Black feminisms to illuminate the experiences of Black girls in pre-K–12 education broadly (e.g., Salazar Pérez, 2017), or name Black feminists' contributions to educational practice (e.g., Annamma, 2017). However, this work is still rarely applied in ECE teacher education. For this reason, we center the experiences of Black girls—and teachers of Black girls—within early childhood teacher education. We draw on Black feminisms *and* DisCrit to name the workings of racism, anti-Blackness, linguicism, patriarchy, and capitalism as the roots of ableism from the very beginning of our educational systems. We argue that beginning this discourse in pre-K is already too late. Black feminisms and DisCrit must be integrated at birth—and, accordingly, must begin with early childhood teacher preparation.

Due to the normalization of white, middle-class ways of being, learning, thinking, and expressing, Black children are seen as atypical from early on. The persistent othering of Black girls—often through adultification (Blake et al., 2017) and sexualization—has led to their increased suspension, expulsion, and criminalization. In particular, white teachers are often threatened by Black girls' modes of communication and expression, seeing them as "sassy," "loud," and "dangerous" (Annamma et al., 2019; Morris, 2016; Wun, 2016). In early childhood settings in the United States, Black girls constitute 20% of girls enrolled in public preschool but 54% of preschool girls who have received an out-of-school suspension (Morris, 2016). Nationally, Black girls experience discipline rates six times higher than white girls and suspension rates 67% higher than boys (U.S. DOE, 2014).

These trends are not the result of Black girls engaging in more serious offenses (Annamma et al., 2019; Bradshaw et al., 2010). The hyper-punishment of Black girls reflects biased ideological stances, ones that are often reified within early childhood teacher preparation programs. Sealey-Ruiz and Greene (2015) stated,

> When preservice teachers are allowed to remain uninformed [or misinformed] about the cultures of their future students, and the role of race and racism is not discussed constructively in preservice courses, teacher education programs become complicit in producing another generation of teachers who will fail to recognize how stereotypes fuel their "understanding" of students of color. (p. 57)

We extend these perspectives in early childhood teacher education and argue preservice teachers must recognize how intersectional oppressions (e.g., race, gender, ableism) produce stereotypes about young children, and specifically Black girls. Black feminists discuss the concept of standpoint epistemologies, which privilege the expertise of those who hold lived experience rather than those who generate knowledge from an outsider's perspective (Richie, 2012). We encourage teacher educators to center Black girls' lived experiences and knowledges—a centering that is especially crucial and especially ignored in early childhood spaces.

While Black girls are disproportionately disciplined in schools, other disparities point to the ways so-called "protections" in early childhood are not extended to Black children. Black children with developmental delays are 78% less likely to receive early intervention services (Gillispie, 2021). While early intervention is problematically premised on the idea of a typical, or ideal, child, this racial discrepancy sheds light on racist, differential expectations. Thus, our call to integrate Black feminisms and DisCrit in ECE teacher education is predicated on the urgent need to protect Black girls' childhood. When ECE teachers are prepared through these perspectives, they are positioned to transform early childhood pedagogy and practices away from punishing or withholding resources from neurodivergent, multilingual, and racialized children and toward liberatory learning for all—educators and children alike.

We also call for the explication of Black feminism in early childhood teacher education because it necessitates attention to the role of capitalism in educational practice and how it intersects with misogynoir. Early childhood programs are pressured to produce "successful" learners with the understanding that, in time, the learners will become earners and consumers who repay the state for the initial costs of quality early education by requiring less governmental support and paying taxes through employment later in life (Malik et al., 2018). Perceptions of Black children's disabilities through notions of "unsuitability" stem from the understanding of Black girls and women as producers to sustain white capitalist systems. White, capitalist notions of Black girlhood informed Salazar Pérez's (2017) return to Black feminism as she states, "Black feminist thought unveils systemic reproductions of power . . . and informs transformative teacher education" (p. 55). We must name capitalism as one of the systems that configures conceptualizations of Black girls with disabilities as not deserving of resources or only worth their potential contributions to capitalism.

In early childhood teacher education, as well as in bilingual education and inclusive education spaces, words like "intersectionality" (Crenshaw, 1989) are sometimes utilized to recognize the Black feminist legacy our work stands on (Brady, 2022). However, oftentimes these mentions are just that—nods to theories that do little more than accessorize a syllabus. We situate and root early childhood teacher education firmly within a Black feminist disability critical race theory praxis (heretofore referred to as BlackFem DisCrit ECE praxis), particularly naming the unique contributions of Black feminisms as a perspective whose contributions have been obscured. We pose the question, *How can ECE teacher educators help surface, frame, and ground teachers' ECE experiences in a BlackFem DisCrit ECE pPraxis?*

BLACKFEM DISCRIT ECE PRAXIS IN TEACHER EDUCATION

In this discussion of a BlackFem DisCrit ECE praxis, we identify and critique three ideological norms that govern modern early childhood teacher education. We then offer core principles for implementing a BlackFem DisCrit ECE praxis within and beyond early childhood teacher education.

1. Early childhood teacher education in the United States has historically operated on the ideological foundation of a mythical white, neurotypical, monolingual English-speaking child. A BlackFem DisCrit ECE praxis tells us that ECE is inherently political and future early educators must interrogate, disrupt, and relearn notions of "typicality," "delay," and "normalcy" as they relate to ability, race, language, and their intersections (Meiners, 2017; Padía & Traxler, 2020; Pérez, 2017).

2. Early childhood teacher education in the United States privileges normative, spoken English as markers of success in children's development. A BlackFem DisCrit ECE praxis requires us to challenge dysconscious ableism and racism (Kulkarni et al., 2024) and expand concepts of what "counts" as communication (Padía, 2023). We must engage children's full selves rather than defaulting to disciplinary siloing that fragments them, following a legacy of critical, holistic thinking.

3. Early childhood teacher education in the United States operates on the ideological foundation that early childhood is "too young" for children—and their educators—to engage with issues of social justice and societal inequities. A BlackFem DisCrit ECE praxis recognizes that racialization and disablement are endemic to capitalist Western society and thus impact children's experiences from birth (e.g., Annamma et al., 2013a; Clark & Clark, 1947; Tatum, 2017). When early educators ignore, obscure, or erase young Children of Color's identities and experiences under the guise of children's age and capacity, they neglect children's agency and dismiss their experiences of racism and ableism as irrelevant (Brady, 2022; Green, 2024). BlackFem DisCrit ECE praxis encourages a discourse of intersectionality to understand how teachers', teacher educators', and young children's social positioning impacts the way they engage with curriculum and instruction.

TRANSFORMATIONAL TURNS TOWARD BLACKFEM DISCRIT ECE PRAXIS

A BlackFem DisCrit ECE praxis recognizes that silence in the face of white normalcy only serves to ignore multiply marginalized children's needs, thereby perpetuating inequities (Sealey-Ruiz & Greene, 2015). While it is imperative to name and dismantle oppressive ideological systems, we must also engage in radical envisioning of a more just future that is not yet created. With this intention, we share "transformational turns" that a BlackFem DisCrit ECE praxis affords in early childhood teacher education. Table 11.1 aligns each transformational turn in juxtaposition to the ideological norm that has historically governed the field.

Based on our own critical epistemologies and experiences as teacher educators, we offer guiding questions with each transformational turn to support early childhood teacher educators in applying the praxis.

1. We recognize early childhood (teacher) education is inherently political, not neutral. I (Lilly) recall a conversation with a white school leader, who had been an early childhood educator for many years before transitioning to administration. She was adamant that she did not see color, saying, "I love all children the same, I see them all the same." This school leader also said she believed that any parent,

Table 11.1. Ideological Norms and Transformational Turns

Ideological Norm	Transformational Turn
1. Centers a mythical white, neurotypical, monolingual English-speaking child	1. BlackFem DisCrit ECE praxis recognizes early childhood (teacher) education is inherently political, not neutral.
2. Privileges normative, spoken English as markers of success in children's development	2. BlackFem DisCrit ECE praxis equips early childhood educators with the knowledge that they are not alone; there is a legacy and lineage of critical, holistic thinking and activism on which they can draw.
3. Argues that early childhood is "too young" for children—and their educators—to engage with issues of social justice and societal inequities	3. BlackFem DisCrit ECE praxis disrupts the pervasive whiteness and normativity constructs of early childhood teacher education programs, even if/when the majority of the teachers are white, neurotypical women.

if given the choice, would prefer their child be "normal" and nondisabled. This simultaneous ableist and racist whitewashing of early childhood education, rooted in eugenic logic (desiring to remove the state of disability), is a dangerous trope that can be disrupted by a BlackFem DisCrit ECE praxis. A BlackFem DisCrit ECE praxis tells us that if one recognizes the significance of race when it comes to adults, then they must recognize the significance of race when working with children, families, and caregivers. It mandates that we view racialization and disablement in tandem. One must recognize that babies and young children are part of their families; the ideologies held toward their families include babies. While this line of thinking may seem rudimentary to many readers, it is an unfortunate reality that these explicit connections are not often drawn and examined in early childhood teacher education.

A BlackFem DisCrit ECE Praxis Guiding Question

What topics don't you explore with current or future teachers of young children because you have been socialized to view these topics as too advanced, too complex, or too political?

Make a list of all that come to mind. Now, using a BlackFem DisCrit ECE praxis lens, identify how each listed topic impacts young children. *How does this topic show up in children's daily experiences? How can you address this directly with educators to guide their conversations with young children?* Pay particular attention to the intersections of racism and ableism on your list. A BlackFem DisCrit ECE praxis reminds us that addressing these issues means holding space for children's full selves and helping them make meaning of the world around them and the multiple systems of power they experience. Ignoring systems of power is not protecting our children; we protect children's joy and wholeness when we honor their full identities and experiences in the world.

2. We equip early childhood educators with the knowledge that they are not alone; there is a legacy and lineage of critical, holistic thinking and activism on which they can draw. A BlackFem DisCrit praxis can support how educators are informed and guided into the field. This dovetails with how early childhood research is framed and conducted. As such, we recognize the importance of highlighting works like Love and Beneke (2021) and other early childhood scholars who ground their work in critical theories to identify inequities and ways to conduct justice-driven early childhood research.

Accordingly, as teacher educators, we use classroom conversations and coursework to explore perspectives of critical ECE theorists and philosophers. For example, in addition to building the syllabus of my (Crystasany) introductory ECE course around principles of multicultural education and social justice, students conduct research on the theories and practices of racially, linguistically, and culturally diverse critical scholars, educators, and activists who have influenced ECE. While we discuss traditional scholars, whose work still heavily influences the field, these conversations are woven with discussions about the influence of the researchers' positionality and the sociohistorical context of their work.

ECE teacher educators should encourage their students to interrogate both the theorists they study and the authors of materials presented. *Does this person identify as a member of the cultural group they are discussing? Whose perspective is being presented? Does their work suggest by omission, commission, overemphasis, or erasure that any group is superior, more capable or desirable, or more important?* (Rosenberg, 1973). Practicing critical questioning and open conversations around race, culture, and power enables teacher candidates to become critical consumers of research and instructional materials, and empowers students to engage in critical, holistic thinking and activism.

When we first started teaching, we felt the common sensation of being thrown into the deep end of a pool and having to figure out how to swim, float, and generally survive—both in terms of teaching strategies and curriculum and in building critically conscious learning communities. We found that many schools ignored issues of identity and power altogether. Many social justice educator groups recognized race but largely ignored disability; special education spaces were often governed by a sense of benign paternalism, with little to no critical analysis. A BlackFem DisCrit ECE praxis is rooted in the collective consciousness and intergenerational discourses around the intersections of our being. Crenshaw conceptualized *intersectionality* in 1989. Collins introduced us to the *matrix of domination* in 1990, integrating class as a key social stratification system. *DisCrit*, pioneered by Annamma et al. (2013a), stood on Black feminists' shoulders, urging us to explicitly consider the intersections of race and disability. With this understanding, BlackFem DisCrit ECE praxis reminds critical educators that even when we may feel isolated within the programs or institutions where we work, we are not alone in our ideological commitments.

Flag those areas. If the answer is that Black feminist thought and disability studies do not show up in your curriculum, identify where these frames are needed. A BlackFem DisCrit ECE praxis offers us a blueprint of where scholars have gone before and a map forward.

A BlackFem DisCrit ECE Praxis Guiding Question

In what ways do you feel alone in trying to address racial justice and abolish ableism in your curriculum and practice? Review your curriculum. Where are your students reading Black feminist scholars? Disability studies scholars?

3. We disrupt the pervasiveness of whiteness and normativity in early childhood teacher education, even if/when the majority of teachers are white and neurotypical (women). A BlackFem DisCrit ECE praxis disrupts whiteness and constructions of normativity to advance a liberatory learning stance. In the United States, many teacher candidates identify as monolingual, nondisabled white women. With this, much of teacher preparation is centered around the experiences of white women, even when preparing them to work with children with diverse identities and backgrounds. In my (Crystasany) teaching practice, I have been asked by monolingual teachers how they can effectively educate Children of Color whose first language is not English. When confronted with the importance of creating inclusive spaces of linguistic justice (Baker-Bell, 2020), teachers often express discomfort with having discussions in their classroom that they do not understand and cannot participate in. In these instances, I often challenge teacher candidates to step outside their own perspectives and instead view their classrooms from the perspectives of young learners who are consistently prompted to compromise their home languages and cultural ways of engagement to participate in schools.

Decentering the pervasive whiteness within teacher education challenges us to recenter the perspectives and experience of children and communities. As previously mentioned, a Black feminist genealogy encourages standpoint epistemologies, centering the expertise and experience of those with said lived experience rather than privileging outsiders' perspectives and knowledges (Richie, 2012; Turner, 2022). With this understanding, we encourage teacher candidates to interrogate their own identities and to reposition children and families as the experts in our collective learning processes.

A BlackFem DisCrit ECE Praxis Guiding Question

Have you engaged your teacher candidates in reflection on their own identities? Have you done this as a static, start-of-semester positionality activity, or do you engage their identities and positionings continually throughout their learning (Boveda & Annamma, 2023)?

A BlackFem DisCrit ECE praxis requires us to examine our own relationships to power and to support teachers in recognizing that by virtue of existing in this world, they experience racism and ableism, even if they benefit from these systems. A BlackFem DisCrit ECE praxis helps us understand that within this experience, we can be complicit or we can be disrupters. You might engage teacher candidates in questions like, *How have you experienced anti-Blackness, racism, classism, and ableism? If you have the privilege and power of not being harmed explicitly by these systems, how can you use your power and privilege to disrupt them? What does this disruption look like in early childhood spaces? How can we lean on the legacies of Black feminist thought and disability studies to engage in these disruptions?*

CONCLUSION

There is no DisCrit without Black feminist genealogies, and we must reclaim their unique contributions. Kulkarni et al. (2024) described how *dysconscious racism and dysconscious ableism* function in early childhood through a lack of attention or explicit consciousness around race, disability, multilingualism, and their intersections. Salazar Pérez (2017) reminded us that integrating class with race and gender discussions in early childhood builds on the legacy of Black feminists. Identifying how racism, classism, and ableism function, beyond the scope of individual choices, intentions, and actions, helps situate the field of ECE within broader social structures. These turns are key to rewriting early childhood teacher education as sites of liberation rather than launching pads for lifelong systems of oppression.

CHAPTER 12

Imagining Liberated Languaging in Early Childhood With Preservice Speech-Language Practitioners

María Rosa Brea-Spahn and Xigrid Soto-Boykin

Languaging, or language-as-a-verb, refers to the embodied, fluid, and active ways individuals perceive, describe, understand, and belong to the world around them (Maturana & Varela, 1973; Pennycook, 2021). A languaging stance recognizes communication as dynamic and complex, multimodal, including meaning-making symbols and signs and various "codes" (i.e., registers, dialects, nation-state languages). From this lens, moments of communication are actioned within purposes, needs, power dynamics, conversational themes, and bodily movements. They are also dependent on the disposition of the communication partner to co-build understanding (Canagarajah, 2017).

However, most fields concerning child communication and learning, including speech-language pathology (SLP), reduce language to a rule-based system of spoken sounds, words, sentences, and discourse that are positioned outside of people's bodies (Chomsky, 1988). Indeed, dominant conceptualizations of language exclude "different ways of languaging such as touch, drawing, and gesture" (Henner & Robinson, 2023, p. 9). In early childhood education (ECE), there is little positive recognition of the embodied nature of children's language use, especially those children who are racialized emergent bilinguals with "suspected or identified" disabilities. Rigid definitions of "developmentally appropriate" communication, movement, learning, and play are implemented to determine the types, intensity, location, and frequency of young children's early intervention and/or early childhood special education (EI/ECSE). In this context, SLPs are tasked with determining if academic performance concerns are due to "language differences or language disorders" (American Speech-Language-Hearing Association [ASHA], 1993). This "language difference–disorder" binary masquerades as a benevolent practice that can potentially "save" marginalized children from over- and underrepresentation in EI/ECSE (Artiles et al., 2010b). Further, this binary acts as a power-neutral and race-evasive filter that positions racialized emergent bilingual children, and others with intersecting identities, as "less than" an idealized languaging agent (nondisabled, white, monolingual, middle class, etc.; Kangas, 2021). For racialized emergent bilinguals and others who speak nonstandardized spoken English, the identification of "differences from ____ (i.e., a nondisabled, standardized, and academic version of a nation-state language)" has consequences, including the pathologizing of accents, dialects, and family cultural practices, as well as the erasure of systemic barriers to equity.

To this end, SLPs contribute to intersectional oppressive systems (e.g., nexus of racism, linguicism, and ableism) in early education. In great part, SLPs' entanglement with systemic -isms is due to the absence of critical inquiry in preservice SLP training, which traditionally focuses on disciplinary frameworks, practices, and policies based on the medical model of disability and belief systems rooted in the notion of linguistic standardization. The latter, specifically, is of importance in our chapter. The categorization of languaging as either "typical or disordered" is based on historical and political ideas about ability, race, gender, and other constructed positionalities held by members of a society, or ideologies, that can be passed down implicitly across generations and institutions to rationalize an existing social order stemming from settler colonialism (Brea-Spahn & Bauler, 2023).

To transform how language is defined and categorized into a vision of ECE that centers languaging, we must create opportunities for preservice SLPs to collectively imagine humanizing ECE spaces that do not yet exist. For preservice SLPs, the practice of imagining worlds that "might" be possible incorporates critical interrogation and unlearning of dominant and harmful beliefs about language and ability, as well as visualization of joyful learning ecosystems that respond to and sustain children's whole languaging selves. In this chapter, we introduce the construct of *liberated languaging* in early childhood as *that* space of imaginative possibility for SLPs, especially for children who are multiply marginalized (i.e., those who experience intersecting forms of discrimination based on race, ethnicity, ability/disability, home languages, etc.).

CENTERING LANGUAGING IN THE WORK OF LIBERATION

A languaging stance means communication takes place by and between humans in active and dynamic ways. Languaging can be expanded by incorporating *crip language* (Henner & Robinson, 2023), whereby the body–mind languages through signing/moving in context. Crip language depicts a child's "languaging repertoire" as encompassing the integration of multisensory and multimodal "features" as "embodiments." Further, languaging is negotiated within power dynamics based on our own and other languaging partners' positionalities and power within interpersonal and person-to-system relationships (Mignolo, 1999). Thus, to disrupt deficit frames that may be imposed on children's languaging bodies themselves, an embodied and situated view of language must consider power.

Because *liberated languaging* is not considered in educational movements, regulations, and pedagogies, there is an urgent need for creating space for its imagination. Our operationalization of liberation is an invitation to *create* worlds that *do not yet exist*—those in which "equity, fairness, and the implementation of systems for the allocation of goods and services, benefits, and rewards . . . support the full participation of each human and the promotion of their full humanness" (Love et al., 2009, p. 1). Engaging preservice SLPs in this critical work requires that barriers to liberated languaging in ECE be explicitly named. In the next sections, we begin by reflecting on questions that informed our practice as preservice SLP educators. We incorporate educational policies, learning standards, and SLP practices that sustain ableism, racism, and other forms of oppression into our inquiry.

Who Is the Child?

Envisioning liberated languaging requires pondering how children and childhood have been defined. Much of the evidence in early childhood policies and practices follows a hegemonic developmentalist perspective that originates from stage cognitive theories (e.g., Piaget's schema theory) and social constructivist views of learning (e.g., Vygotsky) (Murris, 2016). Developmentalist orientations position the child as an incomplete human, who is immature and concrete in thinking and knowing about the world. Developmentalist views are evident in lists of normative, monolingual language milestones that are used to track children's transitions from babbling to speaking in phrases. Similarly, activities are organized to help children move from simple to complex concepts.

According to developmental perspectives, the child's main role is to progress through a continuum of stages, while being guided through social situations, to become cognitively and linguistically independent. As such, the child—understood as a passive receiver—is acted on by adults (*the* full humans). Adding nuance to this perspective is the 1989 United Nations Conventions on the Rights of the Child's definition of adulthood, in which childhood is positioned as a chrono-moment in life and becoming an adult is positioned as a journey to living as an economically autonomous human, an achievement that is entangled with chronological age (i.e., 18 years), Western capitalism, and neoliberalism. Critics of developmentalism argue that describing children as simple and incomplete reduces the philosophical advantage of their creativity in problem-solving and in engaging with the world (Murris, 2016).

What Is Language Learning in Early Childhood?

Chomsky's (1966) structural and mentalist ideas about language learning were most influential in fields like early childhood education and speech-language pathology. He theorized that all languages have similar structures and that humans have innate language competence. This innate predisposition, per Chomsky, allows language acquisition to happen quickly, efficiently, and effortlessly. Because language learning was defined as observable and measurable, it could be objectified and, thus, disembodied. Chomsky's work drove the separation of language (ideas) from speech (sounds), which scaffolded its segmentation of it into subsystems, such as syntax, semantics, and phonology, views that remain prevalent in assessment and instructional practices in education writ large.

Extending Chomsky's ideas to second-language acquisition, Krashen highlighted the role of comprehensible input (CI). From this perspective, languages were acquired through perception and the senses, as defined within normative ideals, and minimized the role of conscious learning (e.g., metacognition), output or speaking practice, and correction (Krashen, 2017). Although to Krashen, input would happen in conversational interaction, communication was conceived as a process of information transmission from mind to mind; that is, the process of acquiring a language would mainly occur when input met the individual's mental levels of cognition. Similar to Chomsky, Krashen considered social and cultural dimensions of language learning to be universal.

What Counts as "Good" Languaging?

In early educational settings, spoken language is elevated as a universal, formal, and mental system of grammatical rules governed by idealized speakers. Even when SLPs introduce young disabled children to sign languages or visual communication systems like an augmentative and alternative communication (AAC) device, the goal is to use these nonspoken languages and modalities as the springboard for speech. Limited conceptualizations of "what normal development is" create harm for children whose expressions do not fit inside this standard box of normalcy.

Language standardization can be traced back to Quetelet's definition of the average man, the birth of the "extremes" in the statistical bell curve, Galton's definition of eugenics and disabled bodies, and Alexander Graham Bell's eugenicist speech in the 1880s about the consequences of deaf people procreating a deaf race (Davis, 2016). Further, the cultural deprivation model of the 1960s held that some groups of people (e.g., those who are disabled, racialized, without citizenship, nonspeakers of the majority language, living in poverty) have measurably inferior norms, values, language skills, and knowledge (Valencia, 2012).

Positioning language learning as a cumulative mental process, generalizable to all persons, disregards that language is, also, socially co-constructed (Block, 2003). This omission has serious consequences for how learning is translated into learning standards. For example, in the Office of Head Start's Early Learning Outcomes Framework (ELOF) communication and language domain, some of the expectations for preschoolers include, "*child understands, follows, and uses appropriate social and conversational rules*" (Goals PLC-4) and "*child expresses self in increasingly long, detailed, and sophisticated ways*" (Goal

PLC-5). These two learning standards implicitly create a hierarchy of normalcy and deviance, as children who are nonspeakers and whose social interactions are considered unexpected are deemed deviant based on ableist social standards (Beneke & Love, 2022; Viruru, 2001). Although nonspeaking autistic children who communicate using vocalizations develop communication outside of the margins of these standards, these standards position them as needing remediation (Viruru, 2001).

Federal and state laws also reify notions of normalcy. The Individuals with Disabilities Education Act (IDEA; 2004) was passed to protect children and youths' civil right to a "free and appropriate public education" in their "least restrictive environment," EI (Part C) for infants/toddlers and Part B 619 that offers preschoolers (3–5 year olds) ECSE. However, IDEA does not mention whether emergent bilinguals (including those children who use sign languages) labeled as disabled have the right to a dual-language education or to special education services in all of their languages (Soto-Boykin et al., 2023). Consequently, disabled multilingual children have limited access to dual-language education despite research supporting that they can develop bilingually (Cioè-Peña, 2017; Martínez-Álvarez, 2019).

A consequence of standardizing languaging is its substantiation as a window to competence. In turn, regulatory organizations can, and do, prescribe linguistic standardization through learning standards and practices. If an SLP's expectations are anchored on ideologies of "good" languaging, assessments with children will rely on normative developmental milestones that are rigid and ableist, creating inaccurate assumptions of competence.

Once children are determined eligible for services, SLPs provide EI/ECSE. For infants/toddlers, the term *early intervention* itself reveals ableist ideologies. First, the inclusion of a time designator ("early") implies that children considered to be delayed in their acquisition of standardized linguistic milestones need timely "treatment" to prevent the potential permanency of "deviance." Second, "intervention" situates children's language within the biological system, reinforcing the medical model.

THE IMPACT OF LANGUAGE IDEOLOGIES ON EARLY CHILDHOOD

Standardized linguistic beliefs lead to children's classification as "deficient communicators" (Firth & Wagner, 1997, p. 757). Through the delineation of who falls "within the normal" curve of standardized languaging, SLPs engage in co-constructing racialized, disabled, linguistically variable "others" arising from deficit-based assumptions. Thus, the centering of spoken language as the privileged mode of communication truncates children's inherent complexity and freedom. Privileging spoken language in ECE creates harm for young children, who are "given the message that using language is desirable and 'good' whereas other forms of communication are not" (Viruru, 2001, p. 37).

Similarly, children are not given the freedom to be silent, or to communicate in ways that are enigmatic to adults in their environment. Loris Malaguzzi (1996), founder of the Reggio Emilia approach, famously noted that young children have 100 languages to illustrate all the ways they express themselves, yet education systems stifle them. Viruru (2001) further explained the harm of expecting all children to communicate using spoken language—the same modality then used to describe, observe, categorize, and label young children. Children perceived as "lacking language" are considered to be limited, still developing, and needing remediation as they misalign to an adult standard. With this logic, children do not have the agency to communicate in their own way, at their own time. Extending the themes in Malaguzzi's poem to disabled children, prescribing speech as the only way robs children's freedom. The limited discussions of ableism and racism in ECE and SLP, and particularly the lack of criticality around ableist-prescribed notions of "normal" or "good language," continue to underpin practices that impact young disabled children from multiply marginalized communities.

COLLAGING TO IMAGINE LIBERATED LANGUAGING IN EARLY CHILDHOOD

Preservice SLPs' critical, liberatory consciousness can begin by acknowledging how ECE is linguistically oppressive (Love et al., 2009). But awareness is insufficient for transforming systems and disciplines. To create meaningful lever-level change, we must make space for imagining otherwise. Hill-Jarrett (2023) suggested: "Our thoughts create our reality. In a world where racism, sexism, homophobia, ageism, and other forms of oppression maintain a false social hierarchy and unequal distribution of power, the radical imagination is the foundation to re-envisioning the future and building a new, balanced world" (p. 1). To *imagine* means to generate new ideas through all the perceptual modalities in our repertoires (i.e., visual, motor, auditory, etc.).

We also understand the timelessness of *imagination* in relation to the resiliency and futurism of Black freedom dreams (Kelley, 2022). From this lens, constructs, practices, and beliefs centering social justice can be reimagined to incorporate *both* the dismantling of oppression *and* the building or rebuilding of structures from dispositions of possibility and hope. Imagination necessitates "methods and art that witness our freedoms in their very creation" (Carter, 2018, p. 41). This visioning can be integrated in the fostering of participatory social change, as individuals are invited to reclaim their vision for what they wish to see in the world.

We explored this both/and imaginative space in a graduate SLP course in the 2023–24 academic year. In this class, preservice SLPs were invited to "imagine and create an anti-ableist ECE where all forms of languaging are centered, through collaging." Collaging is an arts-based inquiry tool that is useful because it provides avenues for nonlinear thinking and ways of using language outside the spoken–written continuum (Davis & Butler-Kisber, 1999). Student collages could be digital, incorporate video narration, or be two-dimensional art pieces, utilizing materials like photographs, stickers, objects, drawings, text, and so on.

Laura Carlin's picturebook *A World of Your Own* inspired the collages' theme. In this story, a child imagines a world of her own. Prior to their collages, preservice SLPs participated in learning about the concept of languaging and completed readings about linguistic ideologies and crip linguistics (e.g., Brea-Spahn & Bauler 2023; Henner & Robinson, 2023).

Preservice SLPs' Collaging: Themes, Disruptions, Imaginations

Preservice SLPs' collages addressed themes related to the identification and disruption of oppressive linguistic ideologies and the imagining of children's linguistic liberation. We illustrate these themes by highlighting four example collages shared with authors' permission.

Disrupting Ideologies. Preservice SLPs portrayed the ways language standardization perpetuates harm. First, they were invited to reflect on the following: (1) "*Who has good language?*"; (2) "*Who is in need of intervention?*"; and (3) "*Which languagers are left out of definitions of 'good language?'*" The assignment translated to the depiction of harmful ideologies. Building on Beneke et al.'s (2022) work with early literacy teachers, we invited preservice SLPs to critically reflect on ideals of normalcy, highlighting intersections between race, language, and ability. For example, Cora's collage (Figure 12.1) reflects on the policing of bodies (e.g., "sit still") and language (e.g., saying "no Spanish"). She elaborated that her intentional conversion of the colorful collage to a monochromatic expression represents "the rigid, ableist, and conformist environments that children are expected to learn in throughout the public school system."

Sandra's collage (Figure 12.2) engaged criticality: "In the middle, I included the phrase 'Are you listening?' because there are many ways that we can share these ideas, but many are overlooked, especially now that we are existing within a time of heavy erasure (censoring/banning books, media portrayals of humanitarian issues, politics)." Sandra incorporated images depicting the pathologization of languaging, including a quote from an individual who felt they had to hide their accent, and words/images to depict the consequences of this pathologization (e.g., x's; person looking away).

Samantha's collage (Figure 12.3) intentionally used space to represent transitions between awareness of oppressive ideologies and an imagined world where these ideologies are dismantled. She noted,

> At the center, I placed an image of a cactus to symbolize the potential for new growth coming from even the most inhospitable places. The Social Determinants of Health illustration is featured at the top-center of the collage because of the importance of bringing attention to its core elements: "economic stability," "education access and quality," "health care access and quality," "neighborhood and built environment,"

Figure 12.1. "Disrupting Ideologies of Good Languaging in Early Childhood" by Cora

Figure 12.2. "Are You Listening?" by Sandra

Figure 12.3. "Decentering Perfection and Imagining the Imperfect Learning World of the Child" by Samantha

> and "social and community context." Colorful, wavy lines emanate from this image leading to a vented ceiling at the top of the collage to give the linguistic ideologies that have shaped US institutions space to evolve and change, allowing new ideas flow up and out.

Samantha situated change within systems and ideologies, showing her growing critical consciousness. This type of critical interrogation is not common in the SLP field (Brea-Spahn & Bauler, 2023). It also displays courage to envision the impossible within existing structures.

Imagining Liberation. To scaffold preservice SLPs' imagining of liberated ECE, we asked them to reflect on: (1) "*What would a learning environment that disrupts "typical" spoken output (in English) as the expectation for all children look/feel like or incorporate?*"; (2) "*How would variability in languaging be centered?*"; and (3) "*How could the activities, experiences and environments offer options for access and meaningful learning, and enable children to experience belonging while sustaining their own diverse ways of languaging?*"

Samantha depicted her imagined world of liberated languaging on the right side of her art piece, incorporating the disruption of "perfectionistic or idealistic" language use by including a series of game pieces that are represented as flying off the page (see Figure 12.3). To disrupt the standardized "order," she created her own materialist conception of freedom with symbols—which, in turn, may elicit in the art-perceiver memories about embodied and sensory experiences of play but also a representation of liberation whereby "humans are decentered and everything exists on the same plane" (Hackett & Somerville, 2017, p. 374).

Samantha explained that she incorporated text such as "Words of Welcome, Unlock Anti-Oppression Curriculum, and Full Language Story" to show how curricula can take children's full language stories into account, and she added that "'Make Room for All of You' . . . highlights that space can and should be made for the diverse cultures and intersectionalities of our students [children] . . . so they can use all of their knowledge, experience, and faculties to learn in a space that is made **just for kids**" (bolding included from her description). In Samantha's view, place is languaging and the languaging child is centered as a knowledge weaver between place and self (Murris, 2016).

Camille, in Figure 12.4, expanded on this notion of children as weavers of knowledges by explaining that in her imagined world of liberated languaging in ECE:

> Children's participation in the class/school is voluntary and they determine how often they attend . . . their bodies are free in class/at school, allowing them to choose their location, movement, focus of attention and noise level. . . . I included the word "flexible" to highlight how learning in my imagined environment can happen in a variety of ways, settings, etc. depending on the child's preferences and [their self-determined] abilities.

She continued with "participation and 'learning outputs' . . . are voluntary and the mode of delivery (verbal, song, dance, sign language, language other than English, gestures/movement, etc.) is up to the [child]."

Figure 12.4. "Transgressions" by Camille

Camille centered disabled children's agency with an example of a classroom meeting at a "free school" in Brooklyn. She also provided granularity to the idea of the child as knower: "the children discuss and decide on community agreements, school events, etc. . . . determining their own rules and making decisions for themselves about how they want their school to operate." Further, she centered plural ways of languaging:

> I highlighted the word plurilingual to show that multiple languages are sustained. I envision that the practices of the class/school [learning environment] will evolve as the children's identities and understandings of themselves change. The class/school would not only be inclusive of multiple languages and cultures and heritages, but also various abilities, skill level, modes of interacting, modes of communication, sensory processing, neurotypes, and ways of being.

Camille's imagination can be adapted to ECE; she expanded notions of languaging liberation while disrupting the nondisabled, white perceiving adult. She went beyond conceptions of which language "types" are affirmed and sustained in the learning environment, noting that liberated languaging *is* a political embodiment and can be a tool for systemic change. To do this, she provided pedagogical elements, situating children as colearners who model for each other through social interactions:

> Children who have already learned about a particular culture, language, modality, languaging share what they know with children who are just learning. This way they all help each other learn all the languages used by the children in the classroom [learning environment]. I illustrated this with a picture of two children signing to each other. I imagine one is kind of teaching or helping the other gain more fluency in this language. I also included a picture of a child and the teacher co-teaching/co-sharing a translanguaged book. . . . The words in the book weave at least two languages seamlessly to tell the story. . . . This may mean small group or pair work/interactions would work easier, but could also take the form of big group lessons [activities]. . . . The children are free to decide what they want to learn and they prioritize their interests and curiosity. The children learn each at their own pace.

While the adult is decentered, Camille alluded to the role of teachers as culturally responsive and linguistically sustaining, as flexible and open to colearning. Similar to Camille, Samantha, (Figure 12.3) defined the role of SLPs and teachers within collaborative coalitions where reflexive praxis is at the center:

> *SLPs and teachers should also remain curious and self-reflective to help prevent their positionalities and stances from negatively impacting how they interact with their students. They should be considering how to stay connected . . . using Universal Design for Learning (UDL) principles and looking towards the future by learning from the mistakes of the past.*

Figure 12.5. Liberated Languaging Imaginations

Across these collages, and others not included here, imagination gave way to nostalgic notions of fun and play as learning, creative use of the body in and through art activities, and utopian places where all body–minds and their unique co-creation of meaning-making were nurtured. That is, a common thread was the deliberate and intentional centering of love. As Love et al. (2009) poignantly articulated: "Having love for ourselves, those close to us, our communities at large, and our environment forms the basis for our liberation work and reminds us that we matter in the world and our work is important. . . . Successful liberation work stems from a love for all humans" (p. 4).

CONCLUSION

In this chapter, we engaged in disruption and imagination, much like the preservice SLPs did in their collages. In Figure 12.5, we envision liberated languaging as ideologies, practices, learning standards, and policies legitimizing and sustaining individuals' communication—be it spoken, unspoken, in conjunction with symbols, partners, and places, and in various nation-state languages. To disrupt language standardization, liberated languaging ensures that all aspects of an early childhood system, including EI/ECSE, are designed to validate and sustain children's vast ways of communicative engagement. We represent language standardization as concentric monochromatic circles, lacking in innovation in comparison to the colorful liberated languaging coming from the deaf child positioned on the bottom left.

In early childhood learning spaces, *liberated languaging* can look like children being free to express themselves while transgressing human-built borders in different ways (e.g., through vocalization, speech, drawings, incorporating multiple named languages, etc.). Liberated languaging also decenters speech as a privileged modality (Henner & Robinson, 2023). As in Figure 12.5, where the child's colorful imagination breaks through stale standards, the goal of liberated languaging is to reacquaint educational professionals, including SLPs, with the genius and joy of the *child as knower*, to create learning ecologies in which full linguistic repertoires, agency, and humanity are not only accepted but preserved and loved.

Conclusion

Hailey R. Love and Maggie Beneke

The weekend before I (Hailey) started to draft this conclusion, I flew to my hometown to take care of my 3-year-old nephew, Jonathan (pseudonym). As his aunt, I see Jonathan as an extremely curious, funny boy who loves dinosaurs, engages in play that adults often view as risky (e.g., scaling and leaping from the back of couches), and loves splashing water. As a scholar, I am all too aware that as a young Black boy, Jonathan is particularly vulnerable to educational experiences imbued with racism and ableism that may affect perceptions of his behavior, the learning opportunities he is afforded, and his risk for exclusionary discipline (e.g., Bryan, 2020; Freidus, 2020; Gilliam et al., 2016).

Before taking care of him, my mom told me that Jonathan was in a "why phase." Sure enough, during my time with him, he frequently and persistently asked "why"—about everything. Sometimes, the question was so he could understand the world around him, like "Why are my shoes wet?" the morning after we played with the water hose. Sometimes, the question was to challenge a direction, like "Why do I have to eat this?" Sometimes, the question was to understand the people around him, even if it was an unintentional insult, like asking me "Why are you sweating?" as we played outside in the Texas heat.

Each time Jonathan asked why, I explained the best I could. Sometimes that led to more whys, and sometimes my response satisfied his curiosity. When necessary (often after multiple why questions), I simply responded, "I don't know. What do you think?" We would then brainstorm possible reasons, working together to figure out what made the most sense in the moment. Or my response stopped his questioning as he worked to figure out the answer himself before exploring something else.

WHY?

As Hailey shared her reflections with me (Maggie), we discussed how, as usual, we can—and must—learn from children, especially those who are most vulnerable to being targeted by ableism and additional systems of oppression. Standardization and demands for compliance imply that an answer is singular and known, and that others should universally and unambiguously follow that answer (with "fidelity"). Moreover, compliance demands aimed toward children with disabilities and others from marginalized communities are often meant to shut down conversation, obscuring the workings of ableism and preventing marginalized communities from acting on their own desires and priorities.

At their core, the contributors in this book reject compliance and ask "why?" In Part I, Coloma Boyce and King asked, why has the early education system operated in ways that reinforce ableism, even as inclusive education has ostensibly gained prominence? In response, they trace how eugenic ideologies have led us here, offering ways early educators can disrupt said logics and resist dehumanizing control. In Part II, Meyer and colleagues asked, why has disability history been left out of early education curriculum? In response, they discuss how ableism has positioned disability as a bad thing, meant to be hidden away, and offer affirming ways to teach disability history that centers disabled activists and scholars. In Part III, Begaye-Tewa, Ruiz, and Begay asked, why have Indigenous families' stories and experiences been left out of early childhood special education scholarship and practice? In response, they offer a way to reenvision family engagement to center Indigenous culture. Finally, in Part IV, Padía and Turner asked, why do ableist and anti-Black notions of child development and early education persist? In response, they explore how whiteness and misguided notions of neutrality have obfuscated the inherently political nature of early education and offer a new framework that teacher educators can employ to build on legacies of political action that advance justice. Indeed, chapter authors have asked a variety of why questions to challenge norms that reinforce racism, ableism, colonialism, and other oppressive systems. In turn, they have offered possible ways to combat these systems and move beyond compliance based on their own scholarship, communities, and praxis.

GUIDANCE FOR MOVING BEYOND COMPLIANCE

The contributors in this book also provide guidance on ways caregivers, scholars, practitioners, and policymakers can pose their own questions and endeavor to find meaningful answers that facilitate freedom and belonging for children with disabilities and their families. We close this book with a brief discussion of our takeaways regarding the praxis that the contributors have modeled and how their work connects to other scholarly conversations and resources.

Identifying and Moving Beyond Neoliberal Reforms and Performativity

Several of the chapters in this volume point to the importance of identifying and moving beyond the allure of neoliberal reform efforts and superficial, or performative, changes. Coloma Boyce and King demonstrated how neoliberal reforms often apply a different name to the same ideas, leading to changes in practice that are still rooted in ableism and eugenics. Families of children with disabilities have also called attention to this. Park highlighted how Latina mothers critiqued and rejected paternalistic "supports" whereby school districts made recommendations intended to encourage conformity while dismissing the effects of the myriad systems of oppression that impacted the families (e.g., racism, xenophobia, linguicism, capitalism). Following the mothers' lead, Park elevated the need for family–professional relationships rooted in interdependence. Sins Invalid, the collective of disabled artists who developed a disability justice framework, included interdependence as a core principle of disability justice. Simultaneously, they argued against reliance on legal frameworks for justice (Sins Invalid, 2019). The collective's disability justice primer details specific ways readers can combat ableism through movement organizing and collective access.

Other scholars have similarly discussed the need to move beyond legal frameworks for justice, noting how that often only eschews, and therefore reinforces, inequities by promoting technical interventions (i.e., changes to practices) to adaptive, complex problems that require epistemological shifts. For instance, Handy (2024) recently detailed how colonial logics endure in special education, disrupting learning opportunities for multiply marginalized students with disabilities. While laws, such as the Individuals with Disabilities Education Act (2004), and court cases, such as *Brown v. Board of Education*, resulted in some change, they have largely only reflected "tinkering" with practices and processes. As a result, inequities endure whereby it is still acceptable to segregate children with disabilities on the basis that they do not adhere to normative standards; schools are still largely segregated by race and class; and Black, Indigenous, and Latine children are still disproportionately labeled with the most stigmatizing labels (e.g., "emotional disturbance"). Likewise, Voulgarides et al. (2024) critiqued the use of IDEA compliance measures as the predominant way to address racial disproportionality. Instead, they provided multiple recommendations to shift ways of thinking toward fixing educational systems rather than children and families, address racism and ableism, and engage in self-studies at both the personal and systemic levels. We encourage the reader to refer to these examples as touchstones that can sharpen critiques of neoliberal reform efforts and performative change.

Adopting a Praxis of Learning and Unlearning

Because we have all been socialized, and likely professionally prepared, within an ableist society and educational system, moving beyond compliance necessarily requires both unlearning limiting ways of being, educating, and relating, and learning new ways of being, educating, and relating. We (Hailey and Maggie) engaged in collaborative reflection on our own journeys of learning and unlearning in our chapter discussing liberatory pedagogies grounded in disability justice and abolition. The reflection questions we offered are ones we continuously pose to ourselves as we strive to redefine the goals of early education, change norms, and center the knowledges and priorities of multiply marginalized children and families. Similarly, Brea-Spahn and Soto-Boykin discussed the absence of critical perspectives in preservice speech and language pathologist (SLP) preparation, leading them to redefine constructions of the child, learning, and languaging to advance a liberatory approach in their work preparing SLPs. The preservice SLPs' collages are powerful examples of how reflecting on the ways children's language is pathologized can support future practitioners as they work to dismantle oppressive language ideologies.

Unlearning oppressive ideologies and practices and learning new ways of thinking and new practices that enable the freedom and belonging of multiply marginalized children with disabilities and their families is an ongoing process—a praxis that requires consistent movement between reflection and action. Like the collages included in this volume, Annamma (2016) introduced education journey mapping as a way to reflect on one's own educational journey, attending to the ways ableism and other systems of oppression have influenced it (including ways we have benefited; see Beneke, 2021). Journey mapping can disrupt notions of normalcy and prompt imagining otherwise and can be used with multiply marginalized children to center their knowledges. These examples of praxis—text-based, visual, or both—can be a guide for the reader as you examine your own experiences being indoctrinated into, and held accountable to, notions of normalcy and imagine otherwise.

Expanding What Counts as "Knowledge" and "Learning"

An overarching goal of this book was to center the perspectives of multiply marginalized children and families, shifting ideas about both *who* has knowledge that should inform practice and *what* knowledge and learning look like. Hancock and Waters did this in their chapter as they elevated the resistance of multiply marginalized families within home-visiting decision-making. Families advocated for what they believed should guide practice, shifted conversations to reorient practitioners toward their children's abilities, and asserted their expertise and knowledge of their children. Meanwhile, Christiansen made visible the ways children with disabilities are already in relation with people and place and how outdoor education can enable them to enact and build on such relations. These examples counter conceptualizations of children with disabilities as needing to learn normative behaviors to be included, as well as notions of outdoor education as only being in service of learning toward normative child development.

Similarly, other scholars have demonstrated ways to reposition children as capable beyond standardized developmental norms. Shannon and Hackett (2024) discussed the need to honor communication beyond notions of utility, clarity, or rationality and instead to recognize communication in relation to community. That is, we must recognize that children have different ways of approaching and utilizing communication and that opacity is not inherently an error, or disability, to be fixed; rather, opacity should be acknowledged as a possible assertion of agency and unpacked in relationship with children. Likewise, in her commentary, Templeton (2024) argued for expanding notions of communication to reflect the narratives children build through play and material configurations. And still, she pointed out that we must also grapple with the fact that we (as adults) sometimes *cannot* know what children mean. Rather than trying to discipline children to fit within our imagination, we should provide the freedom for them to create beyond our abilities and perceptions. This is significant for multiply marginalized children, in particular—to disrupt notions of normalcy constructed by ableism, racism, and other systems of oppression, we must honor subordinated knowledges.

Honoring the Agency and Resistance of Multiply Marginalized Children With Disabilities and Their Families

To do any of the above, we must be led by the agency and resistance of multiply marginalized children with disabilities and their families. In their chapter, Coomer, Martin, Proffitt, and Campbell exemplified what it looks like to center the experiences and perspectives of multiply marginalized children and their families. Learning from children labeled as having "emotional difficulties" and their families, they uncovered how children internalized harmful perspectives about themselves and their abilities, as well as the personhood and abilities of others, based on the messages imbued in classroom management approaches. Learning from the perspectives of children labeled with disabilities and their families leads us to question the logic of taken-for-granted ideas that have resulted in multiply marginalized children with disabilities being excluded as a form of "support" and frees us to engage in new logics that support children's freedom and belonging. That is, following the desires of children with disabilities and their families enables a new vision for inclusion. Jennifer White-Johnson (2024), a disabled, neurodivergent Afro-Latina artist and mother, similarly recalled feeling like she was "bad" because she talked during class. Now a mother of an autistic son, she enacts mothering as a radical act to combat ableism and calls on educators to be accountable to disabled children and their families to challenge ableism and white supremacy. White-Johnson created a zine to help families disrupt such deficit-based expectations and reorient the IEP process to the desires of disabled children. Her work is a powerful reminder that families are acting in solidarity with their children and are critical partners in dismantling ableism.

As Handy (2024) put it, we must realign our allegiances to children and families rather than systems or a professional field. Doing so requires creating space for, and being responsive to, the many forms of resistance that children with disabilities may enact, including those that seem counter to our knowledge systems or best intentions. Baptista de Oliveira and Gediel's account of Sofia is an excellent example of this. While trying to keep her in the classroom seemed like an act of inclusion, Sofia resisted being included into a space of discipline and control. Understanding her elopement as a display of resistance challenges educators to consider what they need to change about the classroom environment—rather than focusing on how to change Sofia and force compliance. Following the agency and resistance of multiply marginalized children and their families enables us to envision something new—new practices, new processes, new environments—outside of the existing structures that reflect and reinforce ableism and intersecting oppressions.

Questioning and Finding Answers in Community

Finally, we must recognize that this work must happen in community with others. It is evident how community has been critical to so much of the work reflected in this volume, and there is strength in sharing these stories, testimonies, and arguments together—scholars working together, building on years-long relationships; scholars working with educators, children, and families; caregivers partnering with and honoring their children. Importantly, attending to children and families' agency is not a promotion of capitalistic ideals of independence. Campano and colleagues (2020) asserted that agency is realized through collectives, particularly intergenerational collectives and coalitions of members from different marginalized groups. In these collectives, community members take care of each other's needs, freeing space for challenging the status quo, and imagining and enacting a state of justice that has not been experienced. Unadkat and Cuenca's case study of Kit illustrates this. The authors detailed how they worked together to design a series of literacy lessons that move beyond standardized curriculum or restrictive ideas of literacy. They then consulted with children (working intergenerationally) after each project to inform subsequent projects. They particularly attended to how Kit was positioned and empowered in the lessons, working with his mother to lead a lesson about ADHD and frequently checking in with him. In doing so, they were able to design a space in which Kit both enjoyed the activities and could capitalize on his strengths to help others. Thus, Kit's belonging was a result of collaborative lesson development that built on his strengths and addressed his support needs based on his own and his mother's perspectives, while eschewing standardized curriculum.

I DON'T KNOW. WHAT DO YOU THINK?

The authors in this volume asked multiple "why?" questions and offered rich examples of ways to move beyond compliance based on their contexts, experiences, and communities. Perhaps it is therefore appropriate to now end this book with "I don't know. What do you think?" In doing so, we invite you, the reader, to reflect, explore the scholarly and activist lineages of work presented here, and consider new questions and answers based on your own contexts, experiences, and communities. We invite you to join or persist in conversations about why things are the way they are and dream up ways to move forward, sharing responsibility for both the harm that has been perpetuated by ableism and the need to counter it. Most importantly, we invite you to be led by the knowledges of multiply marginalized children with disabilities and their families, forfeiting notions of expertise and positions of power. Both asking "why" in place of compliance and working from a position of "I don't know" in place of standardization can be powerful tools to counter ableism and intersecting systems of oppression, cultivate interdependence, and enable multiply marginalized children with disabilities and their families to lead the way forward. Indeed, we believe multiply marginalized children's and their families' answers to "What do you think?" can guide us toward new understandings of disability, freedom, and belonging in early childhood education.

Notes

Introduction

1. Following Schalk (2018), we use "bodyminds" to highlight the intertwinement of mental and physical being.

2. We use "disability" or "disabilities" to signify ascriptions of impairment based on historically and culturally defined expectations, tasks, and categorizations. We use "disabled" to connote a personal and political identity with a history of resistance to injustice.

Chapter 1

1. We use the term "multiply marginalized" to refer to children impacted by multiple oppressions (e.g., ableism, racism).

2. Many of these images were retrieved from the Image Archive on the American Eugenics Movement, which were sourced from the Eugenics Record Office at Cold Spring Harbor, the center of eugenics research until the 1940s. Other images were found via Science Photo Library.

3. Dena Simmons is the former assistant director of the Yale Center for Emotional Intelligence and founder of LiberatED.

4. See Jen White Johnson's work on "Hack[ing] the IEP" at https://jenwhitejohnson.com/The-Advocazine-Hack-The-IEP.

Chapter 2

1. *Sanism* is the devaluation and marginalization of people perceived to be mentally and emotionally deviant from white, middle class, cisheternormative constructions of sanity and rationality (Perlin, 1992) and the means by which aggression toward "insane" people in clinical settings is normalized (Poole, 2011).

Chapter 3

1. In Brazil, education for the d/Deaf is structured into two models: inclusive education and bilingual schools. Inclusive education has been implemented in all Brazilian cities since early 2000, spanning all educational levels. Bilingual education for the d/Deaf is an independent teaching modality, previously included as part of special education (Brasil, 2021). In this approach, Brazilian Sign Language (Libras) is recognized as the first language and written Portuguese as the second language.

Chapter 8

1. The participants described themselves as Latina or Latina mothers. Hence, I keep their language in the book chapter. When I refer to parents or families in the more general sense, I use Latine parents and families.

2. I name Black children, Indigenous children, and other children of Color, which includes Latine, Asian, and Pacific Islander children. This language, while inclusive, does not homogenize the experiences of different racial groups in white supremacist structures. I do not capitalize white children. The *Columbia Journalism Review* notes that "White carries a different set of meanings; capitalizing the word in this context risks following the lead of white supremacists." https://www.cjr.org/analysis/capital-b-black-styleguide.php

3. I use their first names with permission.

Chapter 9

1. Navajo translation (speaking to all): Let us talk to you: We will start with a story.

2. We use the terms Native, Indigenous, and Native American interchangeably to refer to Native peoples in the present-day United States.

3. Navajo translation: We are done talking to you, thank you.

Chapter 11

1. We use the term multidialectical in tandem with multilingual to recognize and honor multiple dialects of one named language as just as valuable as mutlilingualism with multiple named languages.

Glossary

Ableism—following T. L. Lewis's (2022) definition, ableism is an oppressive system of assigning value to people's bodies based on socially constructed ideas of normalcy, productivity, desirability, intelligence, excellence, and fitness; reflects the devaluation of disability and discrimination of people with disabilities or those perceived to have a disability or otherwise differ from social norms

Abolition (in reference to the prison industrial complex)—the movement to dismantle punitive systems, institutions, processes, and ways of thinking that operate to uphold white supremacy

Accessibility—process or practice of making environments, materials, information, and services usable by people regardless of their abilities or circumstances, particularly people with disabilities

Ageism—a system of discrimination, or oppression, based on age

Augmentative and Alternative Communication (AAC)—forms, or systems, of communication other than oral language; augmentative systems supplement oral speech, while alternative systems largely replace oral speech

Black feminist theory—a theoretical perspective that centers the experiences and knowledges of Black women in order to name and dismantle systemic oppression at the intersection of racism and sexism, in particular, but also classism

Bodymind—a word to reflect the physical body and mind as being both integral pieces of oneself and intricately linked; Dr. Sami Schalk has elevated the use of this term in disability studies to highlight the multiple intertwined ways that oppression has both mental and physical effects for people with disabilities, broadly, and, more specifically, people with disabilities who are additionally marginalized by racism

Capitalism—an economic system primarily characterized by individuals' pursuit of private wealth and property through competition and a free market approach (e.g., setting resource values based on supply and demand); this pursuit is at the expense of collective care and well-being and results in the further marginalization of oppressed groups

Carceral—relating to, or replicating, punitive systems and approaches, including the mass incarceration of Black, Indigenous, and Latine people and the pathologization and criminalization of young children based on race, disability, language, and other markers of difference

(Cis)heteropatriarchy—a system of oppression that values cisgender, heterosexual men over others and perceives them as the arbiters of social norms; this leads to the marginalization of those who do not align with those identities

Cisheterosexism—a system of oppression based on the belief that individuals should align their gender identity and expression with their sex assignment at birth (i.e., cisgender) and maintain heterosexual relationships and associated gender roles

Classism—a system of oppression or discrimination placing value on individuals based on their ability to produce and attain wealth

Collective access—a principle of disability justice, as delineated by Sins Invalid, in which people recognize inequities and power dynamics in order to identify and meet access needs through community and collective action; this principle recognizes that communities share responsibility to ensure individuals' needs and desires for participation and care can be expressed without shame or stigma and are met in ways that honor autonomy and the group's capacity

Colonialism (settler)—a system of oppression in which settlers displace and take control of Indigenous peoples; can also broadly be understood to reflect the general practice of forcibly acquiring and taking control of another entity or community—this can manifest in multiple ways, resulting in approaches, spaces, relationships, and ways of thinking that reinforce a similar power dynamic

Convivir—within *mujerismo* (theory of Latina womanism), a praxis of living together

Counternarrative—a narrative, or story, that presents the experiences and perspectives of a group who have been marginalized, with the intention of challenging dominant narratives that disparage or stereotype the marginalized group and promoting equity grounded in the perspectives of the marginalized group

Criminalization—the act of turning an activity into a criminal offense that can result in punishment, including incarceration; alternately, this can refer to the characterization of an individual or group as criminals or deserving of punishment and exclusion

Crip linguistics/language—a framework or understanding of language that rejects narrow, normative expectations of language (i.e., norms grounded in ableism and linguicism) that result in the characterization of certain groups' ways of communicating as disordered; crip linguistics elevates the diverse language and communication means of people with disabilities, in particular, as valid

Critical literacy/literacies—an approach or way of thinking about literacy that argues for expansive understandings of children's meaning-making (i.e., honoring children's expressions beyond reading and writing); can also be used to reflect practices promoting children's abilities to analyze information and ideas in the world around them to understand their social reality (i.e., reading the word and the world)

Critical race theory (CRT)—a theory that recognizes race as a social construct intended to uphold white supremacy; the theory is used to name and combat racism embedded in systems and policies and to center the experiences of groups marginalized by racism

Cultural capital—the social relationships and resources an individual may have that help them navigate society

Cultural cognitive structures—a representation of knowledge regarding one's cultural environment

Cultural model—a set of assumptions that define a social reality and what are considered appropriate ways of being and behaving

Cultural model of disability—a framework that views disability as a cultural identity in which those who identify as disability share some similar experiences and a history of both marginalization and resistance; under this framework, disability is understood as a part of human diversity and a source of pride and shared cultural norms

Decarceration (in the context of abolition)—an approach within abolitionist movements to release people from incarceration and confinement through coordinated, collective action

Decolonialize—to upend colonialism by freeing oppressed groups, particularly Indigenous peoples, from settlers who have forcibly removed them from land and spaces that they inhabited and cared for; as a result, said land and spaces are returned, and the marginalized group is enabled to reclaim, sustain, and grow their cultural norms, including their language and ways of being

Developmentally appropriate practice—a set of teaching practices and methods within early childhood education that are intended to support children's learning and development; these practices are generally grounded in white, middle-class norms and developmental theory that has been found to be marginalizing to children who fall outside of these norms

Disability critical race theory (DisCrit)—a theory grounded in Black feminism, disability studies, and critical race theory; its tenets theorize about how race, racism, disability, and ableism are constructed in society in ways that uniquely marginalize Black, Indigenous, Latine, Asian, and Pacific Islander people with disabilities and others subject to multiple forms of oppression

Disability justice—a framework and movement articulated by Sins Invalid, a collective of disabled artists, that seeks to enable inclusion and liberation of people with disabilities; it includes principles that recognize the intersection of multiple forms of oppression, center the perspectives of disabled people, combat capitalism, and argue for solidarity and community

Disproportionality—a group's representation in a particular category (e.g., disabled or not; certain disability labels) exceeds or is below what is expected or predicted based on their percentage of the wider population

Epistemology—a theory of knowledge or way of thinking about how something is, or comes to be, known

Eugenics/eugenic ideologies—a movement and related perspectives that aim to improve the quality of the human population through selective breeding, forced sterilization, institutionalization, intervention, and otherwise preventing certain groups (e.g., racialized people, disabled people, others deemed "unfit") from living, proliferating, or exercising control over their lives while increasing the power and control of those who are considered more valuable and superior

Excarceration (in the context of abolition)—a strategy to build alternatives to incarceration and control of marginalized groups, diverting them away from punishment and enabling self-determination based on their desired goals and resistance

Free and appropriate public education (FAPE)—a principle of the Individuals with Disabilities Education Act (IDEA) that argues that students with disabilities should receive an education that is free of cost and individualized to their abilities and support needs to enable their progress

Holism—human interrelatedness among the intellectual, spiritual, emotional, and physical realms that form the person as a whole

Inclusive education—a form of, or approach to, education that combats multiple systems of oppression in order to redistribute access to educational spaces and opportunities, value and be responsive to a variety of differences, and ensure marginalized groups are able to represent themselves in decision-making

Individualized education program (IEP)—a legal document, facilitated by an associated process, that documents and guides special education service provision for students (3–21 years old) identified with disabilities under IDEA Part B

Individualized family service plan (IFSP)—a legal document, facilitated by an associated process, that documents and guides early intervention service provision for young children (0–3 years old) identified as having developmental delays or disabilities, or otherwise qualifying, for services under IDEA Part C

Individuals with Disabilities Education Act (IDEA)—a federal law in the United States that was intended to improve access to public education for students with disabilities

Interdependence—recognizing and meeting each other's needs as a community imperative and form of care

Intersectionality—a lens for understanding how multiple systems of oppression interact to create unique experiences of discrimination, or marginalization, and privilege; a principle of disability justice and feature of Black feminist thought

La facultad—the concept of knowing through experience and intuition, within mujerismo (Latina womanism)

Least restrictive environment (LRE)—a principle of the Individuals with Disabilities Education Act that dictates that students with disabilities should be placed in the environment that is considered to be least restrictive to their learning opportunities, based on their individual abilities and support needs

Linguicism—discrimination on the basis of how a person speaks or expresses themselves; this may particularly marginalize people with disabilities and multilingual children and families

Mad studies—a form of activist scholarship that attends to the lived experiences, cultural histories, and epistemologies of madness and those who experience or are perceived to be affected by mental illness or mental disabilities

Marginalization—discrimination, unfair treatment, or exclusion of a group or individual based on their identities or perceived identities

Medical model of disability—an understanding of disability as an individual abnormality, or impairment, that must be "fixed"; the focus of educational approaches grounded in the medical model of disability is to provide intervention to decrease the experience or impact of disability

Moratorium (in the context of abolition)—to end punitive logics and practices that aid in the incarceration, punishment, and control of individuals and groups

Mujerismo—Latina womanism, a critical feminist perspective that recognizes Latina women's everyday experiences as sources of knowledge; addresses gendered dimensions of pedagogy as well as motherhood

Neurodivergent—individuals whose brain functions, cognitive processes, or behavioral patterns differ from what is considered the norm or "typical"; this term has often been used as a more inclusive, or encompassing, label that reflects multiple different ways of being, behaving, learning, and relating

Normalcy—a social construction that dictates the behaviors, knowledge, and ways of being that are considered normal or typical

Pesadora—creative thinkers that drive mujerismo (Latina womanism)

Positive behavioral interventions and supports (PBIS)/Schoolwide PBIS—an approach, or framework, for behavior management in which a set of behavior expectations are established and upheld as the standard for all children; children's compliance with these behavior expectations are monitored, assessed, and supported in various ways and noncompliance results in escalated intervention at the school, classroom, and/or individual child level

Praxis—following Paulo Freire, an iterative cycle of reflection and action in order to transform the world toward greater justice

Prison industrial complex (PIC)—the system of governmental, public, and private entities and processes that benefit from, and therefore sustain and grow, incarceration in various forms

Raciolinguistic ideologies—perspectives on the ways race and language intersect and influence each other, as described by Nelson Flores and Jonathan Rosa

Racism—a belief that race is a fundamental determinant of human traits and capacities and that racial differences produce an inherent superiority of those deemed to belong to the white race; race is a social construction based on perceived biological differences rooted in appearance, skin tone, and ancestral homelands

Sanism—a system of oppression that devalues and marginalizes people perceived to be mentally and emotionally deviant from white, middle class, cisheternormative constructions of sanity and rationality; accordingly, justifies intervention and violence toward those deemed "insane"

Schema theory—a theory of cognitive development formulated by Jean Piaget that argues that children come to understand and interpret the world through the development and revision of schemas (i.e., mental categories of knowledge)

Settler colonialism—a system of oppression that forcibly displaces a population, particularly Indigenous peoples, from the land and spaces they have historically inhabited and care for and puts new (predominately, white) settlers in their place and/or in positions of power over them; this is often done through genocide and various eugenic practices to end the colonized group's cultural ways of being and communicating

Sexism—discrimination against women and femmes, often also upholding traditional notions of masculinity as the ideal

Social construction—the name, meaning, and/or value assigned to objects or characteristics based on dominant social norms, values, and expectations

Social model of disability—an understanding of disability as the result of environmental barriers; the focus of educational approaches grounded in the social model of disability is to change environments, supports, and expectations to increase access and support the inclusion of children with disabilities

Solidarity—to act in unity or agreement with an oppressed group based on shared values, common interests, and mutual support

System of oppression—a set of practices, processes, and perspectives that are used together by a group in power to exercise control over and discriminate against another group or community

Technocratic—a way of characterizing an approach, practice, or discourse that focuses on technicalities (i.e., specific actions) to the exclusion of considering and addressing entrenched values and systems of oppression

Testimonios—first-person narratives of those with lived experiences of racist, classist, sexist, and/or nativist injustices, particularly among the Latine community

Universal design for learning (UDL)—an approach to teaching that attempts to account for diversity in the ways children learn and express themselves; principles dictate that teachers represent information in multiple ways, offer multiple options for engagement in learning activities, and allow children to express their knowledge in multiple ways

White civility—the establishment of white, middle-class beliefs, values, and behaviors as the normative standard to which all else is compared; originally related specifically to colonialist methods in Canada

White supremacy—oppressive system that upholds racism, ableism, and other systems of oppression by centering whiteness (i.e., ways of being, expressing, and behaving valued and enacted by white people) as "normal" and ideal

Xenophobia—the fear or discrimination against anyone who is, or is considered to be, foreign to a place or country

References

Allan, J. (1996). Foucault and special educational needs: A "box of tools" for analysing children's experiences of mainstreaming. *Disability & Society, 11*(2), 219–234.

Allen, A. (2002). Power, subjectivity, and agency: Between Arendt and Foucault. *International Journal of Philosophical Studies, 10*(2), 131–149.

Alvarez, A. (2020). Experiential knowledge as capital and resistance among families from Mexican immigrant backgrounds. *Equity & Excellence in Education, 53*(4), 482–503.

American Speech-Language-Hearing Association (ASHA). (1993). *Definitions of communication disorders and variations* [Relevant Paper]. https://www.asha.org/policy

Annamma, S., & Morrison, D. (2018). DisCrit classroom ecology: Using praxis to dismantle dysfunctional education ecologies. *Teaching and Teacher Education, 73*, 70–80.

Annamma, S. A. (2016). Disrupting the carceral state through education journey mapping. *International Journal of Qualitative Studies in Education, 29*(9), 1210–1230.

Annamma, S. A. (2017). *The pedagogy of pathologization: Dis/abled girls of color in the school-prison nexus*. Routledge.

Annamma, S. A., Anyon, Y., Joseph, N. M., Farrar, J., Greer, E., Downing, B., & Simmons, J. (2019). Black girls and school discipline: The complexities of being overrepresented and understudied. *Urban Education, 54*(2), 211–242.

Annamma, S. A., Boelé, A. L., Moore, B. A., & Klingner, J. (2013b). Challenging the ideology of normal in schools. *International Journal of Inclusive Education, 17*(12), 1278–1294.

Annamma, S. A., Connor, D., & Ferri, B. (2013a). Dis/ability critical race studies (DisCrit): Theorizing at the intersections of race and dis/ability. *Race, Ethnicity and Education, 16*(1), 1–31.

Annamma, S. A., Connor, D., & Ferri, B. (2023). Disability critical race theory as asset pedagogy. In F. R. Waitoller & K. K. Thorius (Eds.), *Sustaining disabled youth: Centering disability in asset pedagogies* (pp. 74–85). Teachers College Press.

Annamma, S. A., Ferri, B. A., & Connor, D. J. (2018). Disability critical race theory: Exploring the intersectional lineage, emergence, and potential futures of DisCrit in education. *Review of Research in Education, 42*(1), 46–71.

Archibald, J. A. (2008). *Indigenous storywork: Educating the heart, mind, body, and spirit*. UBC Press.

Artiles, A. (2009). Re-framing disproportionality research: Outline of a cultural-historical paradigm. *Multiple Voices for Ethnically Diverse Exceptional Learners, 11*(2), 24–37.

Artiles, A. J. (2011). Toward an interdisciplinary understanding of educational equity and difference: The case of the racialization of ability. *Educational Researcher, 40*(9), 431–445.

Artiles, A. J. (2019). Fourteenth annual Brown lecture in education research: Reenvisioning equity research: Disability identification disparities as a case in point. *Educational Researcher*, *48*(6), 325–335.

Artiles, A. J., Harris-Murri, N., & Rostenberg, D. (2006). Inclusion as social justice: Critical notes on discourses, assumptions, and the road ahead. *Theory Into Practice, 45*(3), 260–268.

Artiles, A. J., Kozleski, E. B., Trent, S. C., Osher, D., & Ortiz, A. (2010a). Justifying and explaining disproportionality, 1968–2008: A critique of underlying views of culture. *Exceptional Children*, *76*(3), 279–299.

Artiles, A. J., Waitoller, F. R., & Neal, R. (2010b). Grappling with the intersection of language and ability differences. In R. R. Valencia (Ed.), *Chicano school failure and success: Past, present, and future* (pp. 213–244). Routledge.

Arvey, S., & Rosenberg, A. (2020). One out of five: Disability history and pride project. https://oeo.wa.gov/en/education-issues/one-out-five-disability-history-and-pride-project

Ashby, C. (2012). Disability studies and inclusive teacher preparation: A socially just path for teacher education. *Research and Practice for Persons with Severe Disabilities, 37*(2), 89–99.

Au, W. (2007). High-stakes testing and curricular control: A qualitative metasynthesis. *Educational Researcher*, *36*(5), 258–267.

Australian Broadcasting Corporation [ABC] Radio Melbourne. (2022, July 11). *Darebin creek fish ladder is Sammy J's "Watergate."* https://www.abc.net.au/listen/programs/melbourne-breakfast/darebin-river/13969236

Australian Children's Education and Care Quality Authority (ACECQA). (2017). *Guide to the education and care services national law and the education and care services national regulations, 2011.* https://www.acecqa.gov.au/sites/default/files/2018-01/NQF-Resource-02-Guide-to-ECS-Law-Regs.pdf

Baglieri, S., Bejoian, L. M., Broderick, A. A., Connor, D. J., & Valle, J. (2011). [Re]claiming "inclusive education" toward cohesion in educational reform: Disability studies unravels the myth of the normal child. *Teachers College Record*, *113*(10), 2122–2154.

Baker, D., Ackerman, L., Pohl, P., & Kim, H. (2020). Somali American boys with autism: Examining three educational transitions through capital theory. *Journal of International Special Needs Education*, *23*(2), 57–68.

Baker-Bell, A. (2020). *Linguistic justice: Black language, literacy, identity, and pedagogy.* Routledge.

Bal, A., Betters-Bubon, J., & Fish, R. E. (2019). A multilevel analysis of statewide disproportionality in exclusionary discipline and the identification of emotional disturbance. *Education and Urban Society*, *51*(2), 247–268.

Banks, J. (2017). "These people are never going to stop labeling me": Educational experiences of African American male students labeled with learning disabilities. *Equity & Excellence in Education*, *50*(1), 96–107.

Baquedano-López, P., Alexander, R. A., & Hernandez, S. J. (2013). Equity issues in parental and community involvement in schools. *Review of Research in Education*, *37*(1), 149–182.

Barad, K. (2007). *Meeting the universe halfway: Quantum physics and the entanglement of matter and meaning*. Duke University Press.

Bardin, L. (1977). *Análise de conteúdo* (L. A. Reto & A. Pinheiro, Trans.). Edições 70.

Baynton, D. C. (2013). Disability and the justification of inequality in American history. *The Disability Studies Reader*, *17*(33), 33–50.

Beneke, M. R. (2021). Mapping socio-spatial constructions of normalcy: Whiteness and ability in teacher candidates' educational trajectories. *Whiteness and Education*, *6*(1), 92–113.

Beneke, M. R., Collins, S., & Powell, S. (2021). Who may be competent? Mothering young children of color with disabilities and the politics of care. *Equity & Excellence in Education*, *54*(3), 328–344.

Beneke, M. R., & Love, H. R. (2022). A DisCrit analysis of quality in early childhood: Toward pedagogies of wholeness, access, and interdependence. *Teachers College Record*, *124*(12), 192–219.

Beneke, M. R., Machado, E., & Taitingfong, J. (2022). DisCrit literacies: Early childhood teachers critically reading school as text and imagining an otherwise. *Reading Research Quarterly*, *57*(4), 1237–1257.

Beneke, M. R., Machado, E., & Taitingfong, J. (2024). Dismantling carceral logics in the urban early literacy classroom: Towards liberatory literacy pedagogies with/for multiply-marginalized young children. *Urban Education, 59*(6), 1871–1904.

Beneke, M. R., Machado, E., Taitingfong, J., Dhoot, S., Nagarajan, J., & Rupert, M. (2023). "'Together' means I am not the only one": Educators reclaiming interdependence in early literacy through narratives of struggle. *Language Arts*, *100*(5), 365–377.

Berne, P., Morales, A. L., Langstaff, D., & Invalid, S. (2018). Ten principles of disability justice. *WSQ: Women's Studies Quarterly, 46*(1), 227–230.

Blake, J. J., Keith, V. M., Luo, W., Le, H., & Salter, P. (2017). The role of colorism in explaining African American females' suspension risk. *School Psychology Quarterly: The Official Journal of the Division of School Psychology, American Psychological Association*, *32*(1), 118–130.

Blanchett, K., Klingner, J. K., & Harry, B. (2009). The intersection of race, culture, language, and disability: Implications for urban education. *Urban Education*, *44*(4), 389–409.

Block, D. (2003). *The social turn in second language acquisition*. Georgetown University Press.

Bolden, G. B., & Hepburn, A. (2018). Transcription for conversation analysis. In G. B. Bolden, & A. Hepburn (Eds.), *Oxford research encyclopedia of communication*. Oxford University Press. https://doi.org/10.1093/acrefore/9780190228613.013.131.

Boveda, M., & Annamma, S. A. (2023). Beyond making a statement: An intersectional framing of the power and possibilities of positioning. *Educational Researcher, 52*(5), 306–314.

Boveda, M., & Bhattacharya, K. (2019). Love as de/colonial onto-epistemology: A post-oppositional approach to contextualized research ethics. *Urban Review*, *51*(1), 5–25.

Boveda, M., Reyes, G., & Aronson, B. (2019). Disciplined to access the general education curriculum: Girls of color, disabilities, and specialized education programming. *Curriculum Inquiry*, *49*(4), 405–425.

Bradshaw, C. P., Mitchell, M. M., O'Brennan, L. M., & Leaf, P. J. (2010). Multilevel exploration of factors contributing to the overrepresentation of Black students in office disciplinary referrals. *Journal of Educational Psychology*, *102*(2), 508.

Brady, J. (2022). Exploring the role of Black feminist thought in pre-service early childhood education: On the possibilities of embedded transformative change. *Contemporary Issues in Early Childhood, 23*(4), 392–407.

Brasil (2021). Lei n° 14.191 de 3 de agosto de 2021. *Altera a Lei n° 9.394, de 20 de dezembro de 1996 (Lei de Diretrizes e Bases da Educação Nacional), para dispor sobre a modalidade de educação bilíngue de surdos.* https://www.planalto.gov.br/ccivil_03/_ato2019-2022/2021/lei/l14191.htm

Brea-Spahn, M. R., & Bauler, C. V. (2023). Where do you anchor your beliefs? An invitation to interrogate dominant ideologies of language and languaging in speech-language pathology. *Language, Speech, and Hearing Services in Schools*, *54*(3), 675–687.

Bredekamp, S., & Copple, C. (1997). *Developmentally appropriate practice in early childhood programs* (Rev. ed.). National Association for the Education of Young Children.

Broderick, A. A., & Leonardo, Z. (2016). What a good boy: The deployment and distribution of "goodness" as ideological property in schools. In D. J. Connor, B. A. Ferri, & S. A. Annamma (Eds.), *DisCrit: Disability studies and critical race theory in education* (pp. 55–67). Teachers College Press.

Brown, K. (2022). *Sam's super seats.* Penguin Random House.

Brownell, C. J., & Parks, A. N. (2022). When the clips are down: How young children negotiate a classroom management system. *Anthropology & Education Quarterly*, *53*(1), 5–26.

Bruhn, S. (2023). "Me cuesta mucho": Latina immigrant mothers navigating remote learning and caregiving during COVID-19. *Journal of Social Issues*, *79*(3), 1035–1056.

Bryan, N. (2017). White teachers' role in sustaining the school-to-prison pipeline: Recommendations for teacher education. *Urban Review, 49*, 326–345.

Bryan, N. (2020). Shaking the bad boys: Troubling the criminalization of Black boys' childhood play, hegemonic white masculinity and femininity, and the school playground-to-prison pipeline. *Race Ethnicity and Education*, *23*(5), 673–692.

Bulmer, M. G. (2003). *Francis Galton: Pioneer of heredity and biometry.* Johns Hopkins University Press.

Burman, E. (2015). Developmental psychology: The turn to deconstruction. In I. Parker (Ed.), *Handbook of critical psychology* (pp. 70–78). Routledge.

Campano, G., Ghiso, M. P., Badaki, O., & Kannan, C. (2020). Agency as collectivity: Community-based research for educational equity. *Theory Into Practice, 59*(2), 223–233.

Canagarajah, S., (2017). *Translingual practices and neoliberal policies.* Springer International.

Carter, D. (2018). Black study. In L. Sealey-Huggins, A. Johnson, R. Joseph-Salisbury, & B. Kamunge (Eds.), *The fire now: Anti-racist scholarship in times of explicit racial violence* (pp. 38–43). Zed Books.

Casey, Z. A., Lozenski, B. D., & McManimon, S. K. (2013). From neoliberal policy to neoliberal pedagogy: Racializing and historicizing classroom management. *Journal of Pedagogy, 4*(1), 36–58.

Centers for Disease Control (CDC). (2018, August 16). CDC: 1 in 4 US adults live with a disability. *CDC Newsroom.* https://archive.cdc.gov/#/details?url=https://www.cdc.gov/media/releases/2018/p0816-disability.html

Centers for Disease Control (CDC). (2024, May 22). Learn the signs. Act early. https://www.cdc.gov/ncbddd/actearly/index.html

Chomsky, N. (1966). Explanatory models in linguistics. *Studies in Logic and the Foundations of Mathematics*, *44*, 528–550.

Chomsky, N. (1988). *Language and problems of knowledge*. MIT Press.

Christiansen, A., Hannan, S., Anderson, K., Coxon, L., & Fargher, D. (2018). Place-based nature kindergarten in Victoria, Australia: No tools, no toys, no art supplies. *Journal of Outdoor & Environmental Education*, *21*(1), 61–75.

Christiansen, A. L. (2022). *Reconceptualising disability and inclusion: Enacting relational ways of knowing, being and doing with Bush Kinder*. http://hdl.handle.net/11343/326845

Cioè-Peña, M. (2017). The intersectional gap: How bilingual students in the United States are excluded from inclusion. *International Journal of Inclusive Education*, *21*(9), 906–919.

Cioè-Peña, M. (2021). From pedagogies to research: Engaging with culturally and linguistically diverse families of students with dis/abilities. *Teachers College Record*, *123*(12), 38–66.

Cioè-Peña, M., Migliarini, V., & Beneke, M. R. (2024). DisCrit mothering: interrogating consequential education for our children's lives and humanity. *International Journal of Qualitative Studies in Education*, *37*(9), 2489–2492.

Clark, C., Chrisman, A. C., & Lewis, S. G. (2022). (Un)standardizing emotions: An ethical critique of social and emotional learning standards. *Teachers College Record*, *124*(7), 131–149.

Clark, K., & Clark M. (1947). *Racial identification and preference in Negro children*. Bobbs-Merrill.

Cochran-Smith, M., & Dudley-Marling, C. (2012). Diversity in teacher education and special education: The issues that divide. *Journal of Teacher Education, 63*(4), 237–244.

Cochran-Smith, M., & Lytle, S. L. (2015). *Inquiry as stance: Practitioner research for the next generation*. Teachers College Press.

Coleman, D. (1996). *White civility: The literary project of English Canada*. University of Toronto Press.

Collins, K., & Ferri, B. (2016). Literacy education and disability studies: Reenvisioning struggling students. *Journal of Adolescent & Adult Literacy, 60*(1), 7–12.

Collins, P. H. (1986). Learning from the outsider within: The sociological significance of Black feminist thought. *Social Problems*, *33*(6), 14–32.

Collins, P. H. (1990). *Black feminist thought: Knowledge, consciousness, and the politics of empowerment*. Routledge.

Collins, P. H. (2019). *Intersectionality as critical social theory*. Duke University Press.

Cologon, K., & Thomas, C. (2014). Ableism, disablism and the early years. In K. Cologon (Ed.), *Inclusive education in the early years: Right from the start* (pp. 27–48). Oxford University Press.

Combahee River Collective. (1977). *The Combahee River Collective statement: Black feminist organizing in the seventies and eighties*. Women of Color Press.

Combahee River Collective. (1981). A Black feminist statement. In G. Anzaldúa & C. Moraga (Eds.), *This bridge called my back: Writings by radical women of color* (2nd ed., pp. 210–218). Kitchen Table/Women of Color Press.

Comber, B., & Woods, A. (2018). Pedagogies of belonging in literacy classrooms and beyond: What's holding us back? In C. Halse (Ed.), *Interrogating belonging for young people in schools* (pp. 263–281). Palgrave Macmillan.

Cooc, N. (2022). Disparities in general education inclusion for students of color with disabilities: Understanding when and why. *Journal of School Psychology*, *90*, 43–59.

Coomer, M. N. (2021). *Figuring the emotionally disturbed child: The function of teacher talk on special education referrals of elementary aged children with emotional and behavioral disorders* [Doctoral dissertation, Indiana University].

Cope, B., & Kalantzis, M. (2009). "Multiliteracies": New literacies, new learning. *Pedagogies: An International Journal, 4*(3), 164–195.

Council for Exceptional Children and Division for Early Childhood [CEC & DEC]. (2020). *Initial practice-based professional preparation standards for early interventionists/early childhood special educators*. https://exceptionalchildren.org/standards/initial-practicebased-standards-early-interventionists-early-childhood-special-educators

Counsell, S. L., & Wright, B. L. (2018). High-stakes accountability systems: Creating cultures of fear. *Global Education Review, 5*(2), 189–202.

Crenshaw, K. (1989). *Demarginalizing the intersection of race and sex: A Black feminist critique of antidiscrimination doctrine, feminist theory and antiracist politics* (pp. 139–167). University of Chicago Legal Forum.

Creswell, J. W. (2013). *Qualitative inquiry and research design: Choosing among five approaches*. Sage.

Critical Resistance. (2023). How we organize. *Critical Resistance*. https://criticalresistance.org/how-we-organize/

Cruz, R. A., Kulkarni, S. S., & Firestone, A. R. (2021). A QuantCrit analysis of context, discipline, special education, and disproportionality. *AERA Open*, *7*(1), 1–16. https://doi.org/10.1177/23328584211041354

Cullors, P. (2018). Abolition and reparations: Histories of resistance, transformative justice, and accountability. *Harvard Law Review*, *132*, 1684.

Cumpston, Z., Fletcher, M., & Head, L. (2022). *First knowledges plants: Past, present and future*. Thames & Hudson Australia.

D'Andrade, R. (2005). Studying cultural cognitive structures. In N. Quinn (Ed.), *Finding culture in talk* (pp. 82–104). Palgrave Macmillan.

Darebin Creek Management Committee [DCMC]. (n.d.). *Darebin parklands spiritual healing trail*. https://dcmc.org.au/wp-content/uploads/2022/05/Spiritual-Healing-Brochure-compressed2.pdf

Darebin Creek Management Committee. (2025). Darebin Creek nature calendar. https://dcmc.org.au/plan/nature-calendar/

Davis, A. Y. (2011). *Are prisons obsolete?* Seven Stories Press.

Davis, D., & Butler-Kisber, L. (1999). *Arts-based representation in qualitative research: Collage as a contextualizing analytic strategy*. Paper presented at the Annual Meeting of the American Educational Research Association (Montreal, Quebec, Canada, April 19–23).

Davis, L. J. (1995). *Enforcing normalcy: Disability, deafness, and the body*. Verso.

Davis, L. J. (2016). *The disability studies reader*. Routledge.

Democracy Now. (2020, May 5). *The case for prison abolition: Ruth Wilson Gilmore on COVID-19, racial capitalism & decarceration*. https://www.democracynow.org/2020/5/5/ruth_wilson_gilmore_abolition_coronavirus

Dorey, A. K. V. (1999). *Better baby contests: The scientific quest for perfect childhood health in the early twentieth century*. McFarland & Company.

Dow, J. (2021). *The witness tree*. From Small Beginnings. https://www.fromsmallbeginnings.org/the-witness-tree

Duarte, R. (2004). Interviews in qualitative research. *Educar em Revista*, *24*, 213–225.

Dudley-Marling, C., & Dippo, D. (1995). What learning disability does: Sustaining the ideology of schooling. *Journal of Learning Disabilities*, *28*(7), 408–414.

Dyrness, A. (2008). Research for change versus research as change: Lessons from a *mujerista* participatory research team. *Anthropology & Education Quarterly*, *39*(1), 23–44.

Dyson, A. H. (2015). The search for inclusion: Deficit discourse and the erasure of childhoods. *Language Arts*, *92*(3), 199–207.

Eagle Shield, A., Munson, M. M., & San Pedro, T. (2021). Dreams, healing, and listening to learn: Educational movements in the everyday. *Equity & Excellence in Education*, *54*(1), 39–49.

Eagle Shield, A., Paris, D., Paris, R., & San Pedro, T. (Eds.). (2020). *Education in movement spaces: Standing Rock to Chicago Freedom Square*. Routledge.

Emmerich, K. (2023). Translating for language justice, across the disciplines. *PMLA*, *138*(3), 682–697.

Erevelles, N. (2011). *Disability and difference in global contexts: Enabling a transformative body politic*. Palgrave Macmillan.

Ewing, E. L. (2019). Mariame Kaba: Everything worthwhile is done with other people. *Adi Magazine*. https://adimagazine.com/articles/mariame-kaba-everything-worthwhile-is-done-with-other-people/

Fadus, M. C., Ginsburg, K. R., Sobowale, K., Halliday-Boykins, C. A., Bryant, B. E., Gray, K. M., & Squeglia, L. M. (2020). Unconscious bias and the diagnosis of disruptive behavior disorders and ADHD in African American and Hispanic Youth. *Academic Psychiatry*, *44*(1), 95–102.

Faircloth, S. (2006). Early childhood education among American Indian/Alaskan Native children with disabilities: Implications for research and practice. *Rural Special Education Quarterly, 25*(1), 25–31.

Feliciano, T. (2021, May 12). The case for abolitionist pedagogy. *Visible Pedagogy: A Teach@CUNY Project*. https://vp.commons.gc.cuny.edu/2021/05/12/the-case-for-abolitionist-pedagogy/

Ferri, B. A., & Bacon, J. (2011). Beyond inclusion: Disability studies in early childhood teacher education. In B. S. Fennimore & A. L. Goodwin (Eds.), *Promoting social justice for young children* (pp. 137–146). Springer.

Ferri, B. A., & Connor, D. J. (2005). Tools of exclusion: Race, disability, and (re)segregated education. *Teachers College Record*, *107*(3), 453–474.

Firth, A., & Wagner, J. (1997). On discourse, communication, and (some) fundamental concepts in SLA research. *The Modern Language Journal*, *81*(3), 285–300.

Fletcher, M.-S., Dressler, W., Palmer, L., & Hamilton, R. (2021, October 11). Indigenous knowledge and the myth of "wilderness." *Pursuit*. https://pursuit.unimelb.edu.au/articles/indigenous-knowledge-and-the-myth-of-wilderness

Flores, N., & Rosa, J. (2015). Undoing appropriateness: Raciolinguistic ideologies and language diversity in education. *Harvard Educational Review*, *85*(2), 149–171.

Forber-Pratt, A. J., Lyew, D. A., Mueller, C., & Samples, L. B. (2017). Disability identity development: A systematic review of the literature. *Rehabilitation Psychology*, *62*(2), 198.

Foucault, M. (1975). *Discipline and punish—The birth of the prison*. Vintage Books.

Freidus, A. (2020). "Problem children" and "children with problems": Discipline and innocence in a gentrifying elementary school. *Harvard Educational Review, 90*(4), 550–572.

Freire, P. (1970). *Pedagogy of the oppressed*. Continuum.

Freire, P. (1987). *Pedagogia do oprimido* (29th ed.). Paz e Terra.

Freire, P. (2014) *Pedagogy of the oppressed: 30th anniversary edition* (M. B. Ramos, Trans., 3rd ed.). Bloomsbury Academic. (Original work published 1968)

Freire, P., & Macedo, M. (2005*). Reading the word and the world*. Routledge.

Fricker, M. (2007). *Epistemic injustice: Power and the ethics of knowing*. Oxford University Press.

Fritsch, K., McGuire, A., & Trejos, E. (2021a). *A learning guide for we move together.* https://wemovetogether.ca/resources/WMT-LearningGuide-v01.pdf

Fritsch, K., McGuire, A., & Trejos, E. (2021b). *We move together.* AK Press.

Fritzgerald, A. (2020). *Antiracism and universal design for learning: Building expressways to success*. CAST.

Fuchs, L. S., Seethaler, P. M., Fuchs, D., & Espinas, D. (2023). Severe pandemic learning loss and the promise of remotely delivered intervention in students with comorbid reading and mathematics learning difficulty. *Journal of Learning Disabilities*, *56*(4): 278–294.

Galván, R. T. (2005). Transnational communities en la lucha: Campesinas and grassroots organizations "globalizing from below." *Journal of Latinos and Education*, *4*(1), 3–20.

Garbes, A. (2002). *Essential labor: Mothering as social change*. Harper Wave.

Garcia, J. (2019). Critical and culturally sustaining Indigenous family and community engagement in education. In S. B. Shelson & T. A. Turner-Vorbeck (Eds.), *The Wiley handbook of family, school, and community relationships in education* (pp. 71–90). John Wiley & Sons.

Garcia, N. M., & Delgado Bernal, D. (2021). Remembering and revisiting pedagogies of the home. *American Educational Research Journal*, *58*(3), 567–601.

García, O., Johnson, S. I., Seltzer, K., & Valdés, G. (2017). *The translanguaging classroom: Leveraging student bilingualism for learning*. Caslon.

Gee, J. P. (1996). *Social linguistics and literacies: Ideology in discourses*. Routledge.

Gee, J. P. (2014). *An introduction to discourse analysis: Theory and method* (4th ed.). Routledge.

Gill, T. (2014). The benefits of children's engagement with nature: A systematic literature review. *Children Youth and Environments*, *24*(2), 10–34.

Gillborn, D. (2006). Rethinking white supremacy: Who counts in "whiteworld." *Ethnicities*, *6*(3), 318–340.

Gillborn, D., Rollock, N., Vincent, C., & Ball, S. (2016). The Black middle classes, education, racism, and dis/ability. In D. Connor, B. Ferri, & S. A. Annamma (Eds.), *DisCrit: Disability studies and critical race theory in education* (pp. 35–54). Teachers College Press.

Gilliam, W. S., Maupin, A. N., Reyes, C. R., Accavitti, M., & Shic, F. (2016). Do early educators' implicit biases regarding sex and race relate to behavior expectations and recommendations of preschool expulsions and suspensions. *Yale University Child Study Center*, *9*(28), 1–16.

Gillispie, C. (2021). Our youngest learners: Increasing equity in early intervention. Education Trust (American Association for Higher Education). https://edtrust.org/wp-content/uploads/2014/09/Increasing-Equity-in-Early-Intervention-May-2021.pdf

Gilmore, R. W., & Kilgore, J. (2019, June 19). The case for abolition. *The Marshall Project.* https://www.themarshallproject.org/2019/06/19/the-case-for-abolition

Godínez, R. & Baquedano-López, P. (2022). Mother pedagogies of migration: Multiplicitous identities and pedagogies. *Diaspora, Indigenous, and Minority Education*, *16*(3), 185–199.

Gonzales, G. C., Machado, E., & Plitkins, L. (2023). "I bring them here to tell their stories": Transnational Latina mothers' critical literacy practices in an intergenerational storytelling workshop. *Journal of Adolescent & Adult Literacy*, *66*(5), 308–318.

Gonzalez, J. (2020, October 12). Subversion: An essential tool of a master teacher [Podcast episode]. *Cult of Pedagogy*. https://www.cultofpedagogy.com/subversion/

Goodley, D. (2014). *Dis/ability studies: Theorising disablism and ableism*. Routledge.

Gray, K. (2020, July 23). Intersectionality and disability, featuring Keri Gray, the Keri Gray Group. *Ford Foundation*. https://www.fordfoundation.org/news-and-stories/videos/disability-demands-justice/intersectionality-disability-featuring-keri-gray-the-keri-gray-group/

Green, M. L. (2024). Building culturally situated relationships with BIPOC children through a communal ethic of care. *Early Childhood Education Journal*, *52*(5), 935–948.

Grindal, T., Schifter, L. A., Schwartz, G., & Hehir, T. (2019). Racial differences in special education identification and placement: Evidence across three states. *Harvard Educational Review*, *89*(4), 525–553.

Guzmán, B. (2012). Cultivating a guerrera spirit in Latinas: The praxis of mothering. *Association of Mexican American Educators Journal*, *6*(1), 45–51.

Hackett, A., & Somerville, M. (2017). Posthuman literacies: Young children moving in time, place and more-than-human worlds. *Journal of Early Childhood Literacy*, *17*(3), 374–391.

Hagan, J. F., Shaw, J. S., & Duncan, P. M. (2017). *Bright futures: Guidelines for health supervision of infants, children, and adolescents: Pocket guide*. American Academy of Pediatrics/Bright Futures.

Halse, C. (2018). Theories and theorizing of belonging. In C. Halse (Ed.), *Interrogating belonging for young people in schools* (pp. 1–28). Palgrave Macmillan.

Hamm, C., & Boucher, K. (2017). Engaging with place: Foregrounding Aboriginal perspectives in Early Childhood Education. In N. Yelland & D. F. Bentley (Eds.), *Found in translation: Connecting reconceptualist thinking with Early Childhood Education practices* (1st ed.). Routledge.

Hammond, T. (2023). *A day with no words*. Simon & Schuster.

Hancock, C. L., & Cheatham, G. A. (2024). How Early Head Start home visitors foster or impede shared decision-making with families. *Journal of Research in Childhood Education*, *38*(1), 80–103.

Handy, T. (2024). Disrupting durabilities of colonial logics in the field of special education: Toward abolitionist futures. *Teachers College Record*, *126*(8), 63–95, 01614681241276949.

Haraway, D. J. (2016). *Staying with the trouble: Making kin in the Chthulucene*. Duke University Press.

Harris-Perry, M. V. (2011). *Sister citizen: Shame, stereotypes, and Black women in America*. Yale University Press.

Harry, B., & Klingner, J. (2022). *Why are so many students of color in special education? Understanding race and disability in schools* (3rd ed.). Teachers College Press.

Harry, B., & Ocasio-Stoutenburg, L. (2020). *Meeting families where they are: Building equity through advocacy with diverse schools and communities*. Teachers College Press.

Harry, H. Laughlin Papers. (1921). Schedule and apparatus for Binet Test. Truman State University (Papers C-2-4-8).

Hayes, K. (Host). (2023, February 23). Disability justice organizers dream big and resist a culture of disposability [Audio podcast episode]. *Movement memos. Truthout.* https://truthout.org/audio/disability-justice-organizers-dream-big-and-resist-a-culture-of-disposability/

Heckman, J. J. (2008). The case for investing in disadvantaged young children. *CESifo DICE Report*, *6*(2), 3–8.

Hehir, R., Schifter, L., Grindal, T., Ng, M., & Eidelman, H. (2014). *Review of special education in the Commonwealth of Massachusetts: A synthesis report.* MA Department of Elementary and Secondary Education Report. https://www.kurzweiledu.com/files/special-education-ma-thomas-hehir-reseff.pdf

Hehir, T. (2002). Eliminating ableism in education. *Harvard Educational Review*, *72*(1), 1–33.

Henner, J., & Robinson, O. (2023). Unsettling languages, unruly bodyminds: A crip linguistics manifesto. *Journal of Critical Study of Communication & Disability*, *1*(1), 7–37.

Herzing, R. (2023, July 11). Here's how organizing to abolish the prison industrial complex works in practice. *Truthout.* https://truthout.org/articles/heres-how-organizing-to-abolish-the-prison-industrial-complex-works-in-practice/

Heumann, J. (2020). *Being Heumann: An unrepentant memoir of a disability rights activist.* Beacon Press.

Hill-Jarrett, T. G. (2023). The Black radical imagination: A space of hope and possible futures. *Frontiers in Neurology*, *14*, 1241922.

Hoffman, D. M. (2009). Reflecting on social emotional learning: A critical perspective on trends in the United States. *Review of Educational Research*, *79*(2), 533–556.

Hong, S. (2019). *Natural allies: Hope and possibility in teacher-family partnerships*. Harvard Education Press.

Hong, S., Baloch, M. H., Conklin, K. H., & Warren, H. W. (2022). Teacher-family solidarity as culturally sustaining pedagogy and practice. *Urban Education*, *60*(1), 90–122. https://doi.org/10.1177/00420859221131809

hooks, b. (2014). *Ain't I a woman: Black women and feminism*. Routledge.

hooks, b. (2015). *Feminist theory: From margin to center*. Routledge.

Howe, K. R., Boelé, A. L., & Miramontes, O. B. (2018). *The ethics of special education.* Teachers College Press.

Hughes, F., Elliott, S., Anderson, K., & Chancellor, B. (2022). *Early years learning in Australian natural environments*. Oxford University Press.

Individuals with Disabilities Education Act [IDEA], 34 C.F.R § 300.39. (2004). Legal Information Institute. https://www.law.cornell.edu/cfr/text/34/300.39

Ishimaru, A. M. (2019). *Just schools: Building equitable collaborations with families and communities*. Teachers College Press.

Jackson, A., & Mazzei, L. (2017). Thinking with theory in qualitative research. In N. K. Denzin & Y. Lincoln (Eds.), *The Sage handbook of qualitative research* (5th ed.). Sage.

Jackson, P. W. (1990). *Life in classrooms*. Teachers College Press.

Johnson-Staub, C. (2017). Equity starts early: Addressing racial inequities in child care and early education policy. *Center for Law and Social Policy (CLASP)*. https://www.clasp.org/publications/report/brief/equity-starts-early-addressing-racial-inequities-child-care-and-early

Johnstone, E. R. (1915). [Illustration in printed 1915 report *Mental Defectives in Virginia*]. Internet Archive and Brandeis University Libraries.

Jordan, J. V. (2017). Relational-cultural theory: The power of connection to transform our lives. *Journal of Humanistic Counseling, 56*(3), 228–253.

Kaba, M. (2021). *We do this 'til we free us: Abolitionist organizing and transforming justice*. Haymarket Books.

Kafai, S. (2021). *Crip kinship: The disability justice and art activism of Sins Invalid*. Arsenal Pulp Press.

Kaler-Jones, C. (2020). *When SEL is used as another form of policing*. Communities for Just Schools Fund.

Kalyanpur, M., & Harry, B. (2012). *Cultural reciprocity in special education: Building family-professional relationships*. Paul H. Brookes.

Kangas, S. E. (2021). "Is it language or disability?" An ableist and monolingual filter for English learners with disabilities. *TESOL Quarterly, 55*(3), 673–683.

Keenan, H. B. (2017). Unscripting curriculum: Toward a critical trans pedagogy. *Harvard Educational Review, 87*(4), 538–556.

Keilty, B., Trivette, C. M., & Gillespie, J. (2022). Parent agency in promoting child learning: Family perceptions of focusing on family strengths during early childhood assessment and planning practices. *Journal of Early Childhood Research, 20*(3), 397–412.

Kelley, R. D. (2022). *Freedom dreams: The Black radical imagination*. Beacon Press.

Kids in Nature Network. (2018). *The state of nature play, outdoor learning and bush kinder in Victoria*. https://docs.wixstatic.com/ugd/c8e3a7_a8a8b070b9624525b0f660e9143be700.pdf

Kim, R. M., & Venet, A. S. (2023). Unsnarling PBIS and trauma-informed education. *Urban Education*, 1–29. https://doi.org/10.1177/00420859231175670

Kinloch, V., & San Pedro, T. (2016). The space between listening and storying: Foundations for projects in humanization. In D. Paris & M. T. Winn (Eds.), *Humanizing research: Decolonizing qualitative inquiry with youth and communities* (pp. 21–42). Sage.

Kirkness, V. J., & Barnhardt, R. (1991). First Nations and higher education: The four R's—Respect, relevance, reciprocity, responsibility. *Journal of American Indian Education, 30*(3), 1–15. https://www.jstor.org/stable/24397980

Kleinman, R., Ayoub, C., Del Grosso, P., Harding, J. F., Hsu, R., Gaither, M., Mondi-Rago, C., Kalb, M., O'Brien, J., Roberts, J., Rosen, E., & Rosengarten, M. (2023). *Understanding family engagement in home visiting: Literature synthesis* (OPRE Report #2023-004). Office of Planning, Research, and Evaluation, Administration for Children and Families, U.S. Department of Health and Human Services.

Knight, H. (2019). Centering the problem child: Temporality, colonialism, and theories of the child. *Global Studies of Childhood, 9*(1), 72–83.

Krashen, S. (2017). The case for comprehensible input. *Language Magazine, 7*(1), 1–6.

Krawek, P. [@daanis]. (2022, February 9). *There is no word for disabled in Anishinaabemowin . . .* [Tweet]. Twitter. https://twitter.com/gindaanis/status/1491421165000138757?s=20&t=BX3KdJVch0cJIlJOJJkWLg

Kulkarni, S. S., Bland, S., & Gaeta, J. M. (2022). From support to action: A critical affinity group of special education teachers of color. *Teacher Education and Special Education, 45*(1), 43–60.

Kulkarni, S. S., Miller, A. L., Nusbaum, E. A., Pearson, H., & Brown, L. X. (2024). Toward disability-centered, culturally sustaining pedagogies in teacher education. *Critical Studies in Education, 65*(2), 107–127.

Kwaymullina, A. (2018). You are on Indigenous land: Ecofeminism, Indigenous peoples and land justice. In L. Stevens, P. Tait, & D. Varney (Eds.), *Feminist ecologies: Changing environments in the anthropocene* (pp. 193–208). Springer International.

Kwaymullina, A. (2020). *Living on stolen land.* Magabala Books Aboriginal Corporation.

Lacy, J. (1998). *Director, Community Resources for Independent Living: An African-American woman's perspective on the independent living movement in the Bay Area, 1960s–1980s, an oral history conducted in 1998 by David Landes* [Interview]. The Bancroft Library, University of California. https://oac.cdlib.org/view?docId=hb8x0nb6d8;NAAN=13030&doc.view=frames&chunk.id=div00001&toc.depth=1&toc.id=div00001&brand=oac4

Ladson-Billings, G. (1995). Toward a theory of culturally relevant pedagogy. *American Educational Research Journal*, *52*(3), 465–491.

Lalvani, P. (2014). The enforcement of normalcy in schools and the disablement of families: Unpacking master narratives on parental denial. *Disability & Society*, *29*(8), 1221–1233.

Lamble, S. (2022, April 14). Resisting the cop in our heads. *New Internationalist.* https://newint.org/features/2022/02/07/everyday-abolition-resisting-cop-our-heads

Laureano, B. I., Turman, A., Kallen, K., Silverberg, C., & Snell, S. (n.d.). *Crip Camp curriculum.* https://cripcamp.com/curriculum/

Le François, B., Menzies, R., & Reaume, G. (2013). *Mad matters: A critical reader in Canadian mad studies.* Canadian Scholars.

Lea, D. (2006). "You don't know me like that": Patterns of disconnect between adolescent mothers of children with disabilities and their early interventionists. *Journal of Early Intervention*, *28*(4), 264–282.

Lee, M. (Elder), Diné Nation. *Perceptions and definition of disability in the Diné culture.* personal communication. 2024, February 18. Shared on the unpreceded territory of the Diné Peoples.

Leonardo, Z., & Broderick, A. A. (2011). Smartness as property: A critical exploration of intersections between whiteness and disability studies. *Teachers College Record (1970)*, *113*(10), 2206–2232.

Lewis, T. (2022, January 1). Working definition of ableism—January 2022 update [Blog post]. https://www.talilalewis.com/blog/working-definition-of-ableism-january-2022-update

Li, D., Larsen, L., Yang, Y., Wang, L., Zhai, Y., & Sullivan, W. C. (2019). Exposure to nature for children with autism spectrum disorder: Benefits, caveats, and barriers. *Health & Place*, *55*, 71–79.

Lipkin, P. H., & Macias, M. M. (2020). Promoting optimal development: Identifying infants and young children with developmental disorders through developmental surveillance and screening. *Academy of Pediatrics, 145*(1): e20193449.

Locke, M. A., Guzman, V., Hallaran, A. E., Arciniegas, M., Friedman, T. E., & Brito, A. (2022). Counternarratives as DisCrit praxis: Disrupting classroom master narratives through imagined composite stories. *Teachers College Record*, *124*(7), 150–173.

Loeppky, J. (2021, June 30). There's a shortage of special-ed teachers in the US. Advocates say the system isn't set up to support disabled educators when schools need them most. *Business Insider.* https://www.businessinsider.com/special-education-disabled-teachers-shortage-lack-support-us-school-system-2021-6

Lomawaima, K. T., & McCarty, T. L. (2006). *To remain an Indian: Lessons in democracy from a century of Native American education.* Teachers College Press.

Lonigan, C. J., & Shanahan. T. (2008). *Executive summary of the report of the National Early Literacy Panel.* Developing Early Literacy: Report of the National Early Literacy Panel. https://files.eric.ed.gov/fulltext/ED508381.pdf

Lorde, A. (1984). Age, race, class, and sex. In A. Lorde (Ed.), *Sister outsider: Essays and speeches by Audre Lorde* (pp. 114–123). Crossing.

Love, B. J., De Jong, K., & Hughbanks, C. (2009). *Critical liberation theory.* NCORE. University of Massachusetts, Amherst. https://english1bnicolas.wordpress.com/wp-content/uploads/2013/10/criticalliberationtheory.pdfs

Love, B. L. (2019). *We want to do more than survive: Abolitionist teaching and the pursuit of educational freedom.* Beacon Press.

Love, H. R., Annamma, S., & Miller, A. L. (2021a). Whose parenting is legitimate? School positioning of multiply-marginalized Black families and consequences for Black girls. In D. E. Hines, M. Boveda, & E. J. Lindo (Eds.), *Racism by another name. Black students, overrepresentation and the carceral state of special education* (pp. 183–203). Information Age.

Love, H. R., & Beneke, M. R. (2021). Pursuing justice-driven inclusive education research: Disability critical race theory (DisCrit) in early childhood. *Topics in Early Childhood Special Education, 41*(1), 31–44.

Love, H. R., & Hancock, C. L. (2022). Tensions as opportunities for transformation: Applying DisCrit resistance to early childhood teacher education programs. *Contemporary Issues in Early Childhood, 23*(4), 483–499.

Love, H. R., & Horn, E. (2021). Definition, context, quality: Current issues in research examining high-quality inclusive education. *Topics in Early Childhood Special Education, 40*(4), 204–216.

Love, H. R., Nyegenye, S. N., Wilt, C. L., & Annamma, S. A. (2021b). Black families' resistance to deficit positioning: Addressing the paradox of Black parent involvement. *Race Ethnicity and Education, 24*(5), 637–653.

Luke, A. (2012). Critical literacy: Foundational notes. *Theory Into Practice, 51*(1), 4–11.

Luna, S. M. (2016). (Re)defining "good teaching": Teacher performance assessments and critical race theory in early childhood teacher education. *Contemporary Issues in Early Childhood, 17*(4), 442–446.

Mackenzie, M., Cologon, K., & Fenech, M. (2016). "Embracing everybody": Approaching the inclusive early childhood education of a child labelled with autism from a social relational understanding of disability. *Australasian Journal of Early Childhood, 41*(2), 4–12.

Madison, M. P. R. (2019). Building just ecologies for educators and young children. *Young Exceptional Children, 22*(2), 101–111.

Malaguzzi, L. (1996). *The hundred languages of children: The Reggio Emilia approach to early childhood education.* Ablex.

Malik, R., Hamm, K., Schochet, L., Novoa, C., Workman, S., & Jessen-Howard, S. (2018, December). America's child care deserts in 2018. *Center for American Progress.* https://www.americanprogress.org/wp-content/uploads/sites/2/2018/12/AmericasChildCareDeserts20182.pdf

Martin, K. (2016). *Voices & visions: Aboriginal early childhood education in Australia.* Pademelon Press.

Martínez-Álvarez, P. (2019). Dis/ability labels and emergent bilingual children: Current research and new possibilities to grow as bilingual and biliterate learners. *Race Ethnicity and Education, 22*(2), 174–193.

Massey, G. C., Scott, M. V., Dornbusch, S. M. (1975). Racism without racists: Institutional racism in urban schools. *The Black Scholar, 7*(3), 10–19.

Maturana, H., & Varela, F. (1973). *The tree of knowledge. The biological roots of human understanding*. Shambhala.

Maxwell, J. (2013). *Qualitative research design: An interactive approach* (3rd ed.). Sage.

McKinney de Royston, M., & Vossoughi, S. (2021). *Fixating on pandemic "learning loss" undermines the need to transform education.* [Op-Ed]. Truthout. https://truthout.org/articles/fixating-on-pandemic-learning-loss-undermines-the-need-to-transform-education/

Meerai, S., Abdillahi, I., & Poole, J. (2016). An introduction to anti-Black sanism. *Intersectionalities: A Global Journal of Social Work Analysis, Research, Polity, & Practice, 5*(3), 18–35.

Meiners, E. R. (2017). The problem child: Provocations toward dismantling the carceral state. *Harvard Educational Review, 87*(1), 122–146.

Melbourne Water. (2023, June 23). *Darebin Creek fish ladder.* https://www.melbournewater.com.au/services/projects/darebin-creek-fish-ladder

Menzies, R., LeFrançois, B. A., & Reaume, G. (Eds.). (2013). Introducing mad studies. In B. A. LeFrançois, R. Menzies, & G. Reaume (Eds.), *Mad matters: A critical reader in Canadian mad studies* (pp. 1–22). Canadian Scholars.

Microsoft. (2020). *Judy Heumann: Disability is a strength: Simple things count episode 3* [Video]. Youtube. https://www.youtube.com/watch?v=TOy8vYnPKhA

Mignolo, W. D. (1999). I am where I think: Epistemology and the colonial difference. *Journal of Latin American Cultural Studies, 8*(2), 235–245.

Miles, M. B., Huberman, A. M., & Saldaña, J. (2014). *Qualitative data analysis: A methods sourcebook* (3rd ed). Sage.

Minayo, M. C. D. S. (2012). Qualitative analysis: Theory, steps and reliability. *Ciencia & Saude Coletiva, 17*, 621–626.

Mingus, M. (2011, February 12). Changing the framework: Disability justice [Blog post]. *Leaving Evidence.* https://leavingevidence.wordpress.com/2011/02/12/changing-the-framework-disability-justice/

Mingus, M. (2017, April 12). Access intimacy, interdependence, and disability justice. *Leaving Evidence.* https://leavingevidence.wordpress.com/2017/04/12/access-intimacy-interdependence-and-disability-justice

Morris, M. (2016). *Pushout: The criminalization of Black girls in schools.* New Press.

Mrs. Frank deGarmo Papers. (Circa 1910). [Photograph of Better Babies contest contestant with trophy, Louisiana State Fair, Shreveport, LA]. Special Collections (MS# 1879) University of Tennessee. http://www.eugenicsarchive.org/

Mueller, C. (2019). Adolescent understandings of disability labels and social stigma in school. *International Journal of Qualitative Studies in Education, 32*(3), 263–281.

Mueller, C. (2021). "I didn't know people with disabilities could grow up to be adults": Making the case for disability history, curriculum, and identity in school. *Teacher Education & Special Education, 44*(3), 189–205.

Mueller, C. O., & Beneke, M. R. (2022). Whiteness and ability: Discourses in disability history curriculum legislation. *Educational Policy, 37*(7), 1823–1856.

Muhammad, G. (2023). Unearthing joy: A guide to culturally and historically responsive curriculum and instruction. *Scholastic Teaching Solutions.*

Murphy, J. W., & Kennedy, L. (2016). *Welcome to country.* Walker Books.

Murris, K. (2016). *The posthuman child: Educational transformation through philosophy with picturebooks.* Routledge.

Mygind, L., Kjeldsted, E., Hartmeyer, R., Mygind, E., Bølling, M., & Bentsen, P. (2019). Mental, physical and social health benefits of immersive nature-experience for children and adolescents: A systematic review and quality assessment of the evidence. *Health & Place, 58,* 102–136.

National Association for the Education of Young Children. (2020). *Developmentally appropriate practice (DAP) position statement.* https://www.naeyc.org/resources/positionstatements/dap/contents

National Early Literacy Panel. (2008). *Developing early literacy: Report of the National Early Literacy Panel.* Institute for Literacy. http://lincs.ed.gov/publications/pdf/NELPReport09.pdf

NBC News. (2016). *NBC Asian America presents life stories: Disability activist Alice Wong* [Video]. YouTube. https://www.youtube.com/watch?v=h9JfY0tkCqU

Neumeier, S. M., & Brown, L. X. (2020). Torture in the name of treatment: The mission to stop the shocks in the age of deinstitutionalization. In S. K. Kapp (Ed.), *Autistic community and the neurodiversity movement: Stories from the frontline* (pp. 195–210). Springer.

New London Group. (1996). A pedagogy of multiliteracies: Designing social futures. *Harvard Educational Review, 66*(1), 60–93.

New York Times Editorial Board. (2023, November 18). The startling evidence on learning loss is in. [Opinion]. *The New York Times.* https://www.nytimes.com/2023/11/18/opinion/pandemic-school-learning-loss.html

Newland, B. T. (2022). *Federal Indian boarding school initiative investigative report.* United States Department of the Interior, Office of the Secretary.

Newton, J. R., Batz, R., O'Grady, C., Vinh, M., & Blanchard, S. B. (2024). Beyond omission: Analysing the erasure of disability and inclusion in the developmentally appropriate practices. *International Journal of Early Years Education, 32*(3), 647–657.

Nishida, A. (2024). We survive together: Interviews with organizations fighting against disaster ableism and injustices: Part 1. *Disability Visability.* https://disabilityvisibilityproject.com/2024/01/31/we-survive-together-interviews-with-organizations-fighting-against-disaster-ableism-and-injustices-part-one/

Nuñez, I., & García-Mateus, S. (2021). Ruptures of possibility: Mexican origin mothers as critical border pedagogues. *Association of Mexican American Educators Journal, 15*(3), 107–125.

Nxumalo, F. (2019). *Decolonizing place in Early Childhood Education.* Routledge.

Nygreen, K., Saba, M., & Moreno, A. P. (2016). Mujerista research: Integrating body, emotion, spirit, and community. In T. Bryant-Davis & L. Comas-Díaz (Eds.), *Womanist and mujerista psychologies: Voices of fire, acts of courage* (pp. 41–65). American Psychological Association.

Office of Head Start. (2022). *About the Early Head Start program.* https://eclkc.ohs.acf.hhs.gov/programs/article/about-early-head-start-program

Okazawa-Rey, M. (2015). Solidarity with Palestinian women: Notes from a Japanese Black US feminist. In J. Sudbury & M. Okazawa-Rey (Eds.), *Activist scholarship* (pp. 205–223). Routledge.

Okun, T., & Jones, K. (2000). White supremacy culture. *Dismantling racism: A workbook for social change groups.* https://www.thc.texas.gov/public/upload/preserve/museums/files/White_Supremacy_Culture.pdf

Oliver, M. (1990). *The politics of disablement: A sociological approach.* St. Martin's Press.

Oliver, M. (1996). *Understanding disability from theory to practice.* MacMillan.

Oliver, M., Sapey, B., & Thomas, P. (2012). *Social work with disabled people.* Bloomsbury.

Ortner, S. B. (2001). Specifying agency: The Comaroffs and their critics. *Interventions, 3*(1), 76–84.

Oyler, C. (2011). Teacher preparation for inclusive and critical (special) education. *Teacher Education and Special Education, 34*(3), 201–218.

Pacini-Ketchabaw, V., Nxumalo, F., Kocher, L., Elliot, E., & Sanchez, A. (2015). *Journeys: Reconceptualizing early childhood practices through pedagogical narrations.* University of Toronto Press.

Padía, L. (2023). Toward a model of reciprocal carryover: Learning from communication systems of families of nonspeaking bilingual children. *Language, Speech, and Hearing Services in Schools, 54*(3), 716–728.

Padía, L., & Traxler, R. E. (2020). (Special) education is political; (special) education is social justice. *Journal of Critical Thought and Praxis, 10*(1), 1–9. https://doi.org/10.31274/jctp.11613

Paratore, J. R., Cassano, C. M., & Schickedanz, J. A. (2011). Supporting early (and later) literacy development at home and at school: The long view. In M. L. Kamil, P. D. Pearson, E. B. Moje, & P. P. Afflerbach (Eds.), *Handbook of reading research* (Vol. IV, pp. 107–135). Routledge.

Park, S. (2024). Reframing deficit narratives to honor the community cultural wealth of immigrant families of children with disabilities. *Journal of Family Diversity in Education, 6*(1), 27–46.

Park, S., & Paulick, J. (2024). An inquiry into home visits as a practice of culturally sustaining pedagogy in urban schools. *Urban Education, 59*(1), 124–154.

Patel, L. (2014). Countering coloniality in educational research: From ownership to answerability. *Educational Studies, 50*(4), 357–377.

Patel, L. (2016). *Decolonizing educational research: From ownership to answerability.* Routledge.

Paul, D. B. (1995). *Controlling human heredity: 1865 to the present.* Humanities Press.

Paulick, J., Park, S., & Cornett, A. (2022). Power dynamics and positioning in teacher home visits with marginalized families. *American Journal of Education, 129*(1), 53–78.

Pejcha, L., & Wang, R. (2021, May 5). *Abolition is a disability justice issue, a digital zine.* https://issuu.com/rashellwang/docs/abolition___disability_justice_zine

Pennycook, A. (2021). *Critical applied linguistics: A critical re-introduction.* Routledge.

Pérez, M. S. (2017). Black feminist thought in early childhood studies: (Re)centering marginalized feminist perspectives. In K. Smith, K. Alexander, & S. Campbell (Eds.), *Feminism(s) in early childhood: Using feminist theories in research and practice* (pp. 49–62). Springer.

Pérez, M. S. (2020). Dismantling racialized discourses in early childhood education and care: A revolution toward reframing the field. In F. Nxumalo & C. P. Brown (Eds.), *Disrupting and countering deficits in early childhood education* (pp. 20–36). Routledge.

Pérez, M. S., Medellin, K., & Rideaux, K. S. (2016). Repositioning childhood lived experiences within adult contexts: A Black feminist analysis of childhood/s regulation in early childhood care and education. *Global Studies of Childhood*, *6*(1), 67–79.

Perlin, M. L. (1992). On sanism. *SMU Law Review, 46*(2), 373–407.

Phuong, J., Padía, L., & Beneke, M. R. (2024). Struggling toward abolition and dreaming beyond ableism in teacher education. *Theory Into Practice, 63*(4), 340–352.

Picton, C., & Tufue-Dolgoy, R. (2019). Designing futures of identity: Navigating agenda collisions in Pacific disability. In L. T. Smith, E. Tuck, & K. W. Yang (Eds.), *Indigenous and decolonizing studies in education* (pp. 189–203). Routledge.

Piepzna-Samarasinha, L. L. (2018). *Care work: Dreaming disability justice*. Arsenal Pulp Press.

Piepzna-Samarasinha, L. L. (2022). *The future is disabled*. Arsenal Pulp Press.

Plank, L. (2018, December 14). *Inaccessibility has very real consequences for people living with disabilities* [Video]. Facebook. https://www.facebook.com/consideritshow/videos/inaccessibility-has-very-real-consequences-for-people-living-with-disabilities/379466219482605/

Poole, J. (2011). *Behind the rhetoric: Mental health recovery in Ontario*. Fernwood.

Porter, J. E., Sullivan, P., Blythe, S., Grabill, J. T., & Miles, L. (2000). Institutional critique: A rhetorical methodology for change. *College Composition and Communication 51*(4), 610–642.

Posey-Maddox, L. (2017). Schooling in suburbia: The intersections of race, class, gender, and place in Black fathers' engagement and family–school relationships. *Gender and Education*, *29*(5), 577–593.

Powell, T., & Keeney Parks, S. (2021). "They never listen to the parent": Parent narratives at the intersection of anti-Black racism, disability, and school discipline. In D. E. Hines, M. Boveda, & E. J. Lindo (Eds.), *Racism by another name. Black students, overrepresentation and the carceral state of special education* (pp. 183–203). Information Age.

Pratt, M. L. (1998). Arts of the contact zone. In V. Zamel & R. Spack (Eds.), *Negotiating academic literacies: Teaching and learning across languages and cultures* (pp. 171–186). Routledge.

Price, M. (2009). *Mad at school: Rhetorics of disability and academic life*. University of Michigan Press.

Prison Research Education Action Project. (2005). *Instead of prisons*. Critical Resistance.

Purnell, D. (2022). *Becoming abolitionists: Police, protests, and the pursuit of freedom*. Astra.

Quality Assessment and Regulation Division (QARD). (2023, June 28). *Qualification and training requirements for educators in early childhood services*. State Government of Victoria. https://www.vic.gov.au/training-and-qualifications-staff-early-childhood-services

Rao, S., & Jackson, R. (2022, December 3). White women must do more to confront racism. *Time*. https://time.com/6227993/white-women-perfection-anti-racism/

Reaume, G. (2006). Mad people's history. *Radical History Review, 94*, 170–182.

Reese, L., & Gallimore, R. (2000). Immigrant Latinos' cultural model of literacy development: An evolving perspective on home-school discontinuities. *American Journal of Education*, *108*(2), 103–134.

Reinke, W. M., Smith, T. E., & Herman, K. C. (2019). Family-school engagement across child and adolescent development. *School Psychology*, *34*(4), 346.

Richie, B. E. (2012). *Arrested justice: Black women, violence, and America's prison nation*. New York University Press.

Rogoff, B. (2003). *The cultural nature of human development*. Oxford University Press.

Romero, N., & Yellowhorse, S. (2021). Unschooling and Indigenous education. *Humanities, 10*(4), 125. https://doi.org/10.3390/h10040125

Sabati, S., Pour-Khorshid, F., Meiners, E. R., & Hernandez, C. A. (2022). Dismantle, change, build: Lessons for growing abolition in teacher education. *Teachers College Record, 124*(3), 177–206.

Sabzalian, L. (2019). *Indigenous children's survivance in public schools*. Routledge.

Salazar Pérez, M. (2017). Black feminist thought in early childhood studies: (Re)centering marginalized feminist perspectives. In K. Smith, K. Alexander, & S. Campbell (Eds.), *Feminism(s) in early childhood: Using feminist theories in research and practice* (pp. 49–62). Springer.

Samuels, R. (2017). Introduction: Teaching critical university studies. *Radical Teacher, 108*, 1–4.

Sanchez, L., & Ensor, T. (2020). "We want to live": Teaching globally through cosmopolitan belonging. *Research in the Teaching of English, 54*(3), 254–280.

Santamaría Graff, C., & Vazquez, S. L. (2014). Family resistance as a tool in urban school reform. In E. B. Kozleski & K. A. K. Thorius (Eds.), *Ability, equity, and culture: Sustaining inclusive urban education reform* (pp. 80–104). Teachers College Press.

Schalk, S. (2018). *Bodyminds reimagined: (Dis)ability, race, and gender in Black women's speculative fiction*. Duke University Press.

Schalk, S. (2022). *Black disability politics*. Duke University Press.

Schwartz, I. S., & McBride, B. (2021). Developmentally appropriate practice (DAP). In F. R. Volkmar (Ed.), *Encyclopedia of autism spectrum disorders* (pp. 1383–1384). Springer International.

Scribner, S., & Cole, M. (1981). *The psychology of literacy*. Harvard University Press.

Sealey-Ruiz, Y., & Greene, P. (2015). Popular visual images and the (mis)reading of Black male youth: A case for racial literacy in urban preservice teacher education. *Teaching Education, 26*(1), 55–76.

Shah, V. (2022, July 22). Leading toward disability justice. *Unleading*. https://www.yorku.ca/edu/unleading/podcast-episodes/leading-towards-disability-justice/

Shakespeare, T. (2006). The social model of disability. *The Disability Studies Reader, 2*(3), 197–204.

Shalaby, C. (2017). *Troublemakers: Lessons in freedom from young children at school*. New Press.

Shalaby, C. (2020). Classroom management as a curriculum of care. *Educational Leadership, 78*(3), 40–45.

Shalaby, C. (2021). Imagining classroom management as an abolitionist project. In The Education for Liberation Network & Critical Resistance Editorial Collective (Ed.), *Lessons in liberation: An abolitionist toolkit for educators* (pp. 104–112). AK Press.

Shannon, D. B., & Hackett, A. (2024). Opaque reciprocity: Or theorising Glissant's "right to opacity" as a communication and language praxis in early childhood education. *Discourse: Studies in the Cultural Politics of Education, 45*(1), 118–130.

Shifrer, D. (2018). Clarifying the social roots of the disproportionate classification of racial minorities and males with learning disabilities. *Sociological Quarterly, 59*(3), 384–406.

Simmons, D. (2019). Why we can't afford whitewashed social-emotional learning. *ASCD Education Update, 61*(4), 2–3.

Singh, V. (2021). "Never waste a good crisis": Critical university studies during and after a pandemic. *American Quarterly, 73*(1), 181–193.

Sins Invalid. (2019). *Skin, tooth and bone: The basis of movement is our people* (2nd ed.). Sins Invalid.

Skiba, R. J., Michael, R. S., Nardo, A. C., & Peterson, R. L. (2002). The color of discipline: Sources of racial and gender disproportionality in school punishment. *Urban Review, 34*(4), 317–342.

Skiba, R. J., Poloni-Staudinger, L., Gallini, S., Simmons, A. B., & Feggins-Azziz, R. (2006). Disparate access: The disproportionality of African American students with disabilities across educational environments. *Exceptional Children, 72*(4), 411–424.

Smith, I. (2023, April 20). The criminalization of the feebleminded [Lecture]. LEND Program, University of Washington.

Smith, L. T. (2012). *Decolonizing methodologies* (2nd ed.). Zed Books.

Soltero-González, L., & Gillanders, C. (2021). Rethinking home-school partnerships: Lessons learned from Latinx parents of young children during the COVID-19 era. *Early Childhood Education Journal, 49*(5), 965–976.

Soto, L. D., & De Moed, S. T. (2011). Toward "our ways of knowing" in the age of standardization. *Contemporary Issues in Early Childhood, 12*(4), 327–331.

Soto-Boykin, X., Brea-Spahn, M. R., Perez, S., & McKenna, M. (2023). A critical analysis of state-level policies impacting racialized emergent bilinguals suspected or labeled as disabled. *Language, Speech, and Hearing Services in Schools, 54*(3), 729–745.

Soto-Boykin, X. T., Larson, A. L., Olszewski, A., Velury, V., & Feldberg, A. (2021). Who is centered? A systematic review of early childhood researchers' descriptions of children and caregivers from linguistically minoritized communities. *Topics in Early Childhood Special Education, 41*(1), 18–30.

Souto-Manning, M., Ghim, H., & Madu, M. K. (2021). Toward early literacy as a site of belonging. *Reading Teacher, 74*(5), 483–492.

Souto-Manning, M., & Rabadi-Raol, A. (2018). (Re)centering quality in early childhood education: Toward intersectional justice for minoritized children. *Review of Research in Education, 42*(1), 203–225.

Speldewinde, C. (2022). STEM teaching and learning in bush kinders. *Canadian Journal of Science, Mathematics and Technology Education, 22*(2), 444–461.

St. Pierre, E. A. (2007). Writing as method. In G. Ritzer (Ed.), *The Blackwell encyclopedia of sociology* (pp. 5304–5306). John Wiley & Sons.

State Government of Victoria. (2024, February 13). *Kindergarten: Quick guide for parents*. Best Start Best Life. https://www.vic.gov.au/kinder-quick-guide-parents

Stern, A. M. (2002). Making better babies: Public health and race betterment in Indiana, 1920–1935. *American Journal of Public Health, 92*(5), 742–752.

Stovall, D. (2018). Are we ready for "school" abolition? Thoughts and practices of radical imaginary in education. *Taboo: The Journal of Culture and Education, 17*(1), 51–61.

Strayhorn, T. L. (2021). "I know why the caged bird sings," too: Carceral logics and sense of belonging of Black and Brown bodies in education. *Peabody Journal of Education, 96*(5), 598–606.

Street, B. V. (1984). *Literacy in theory and practice*. Cambridge University Press.

Street, B. V. (2003). What's "new" in New Literacy Studies? *Current Issues in Comparative Education*, *5*(2), 77–91.

Styres, S. (2019). Literacies of land. In L. Tuhiwai Smith, E. Tuck, & W. Yang (Eds.), *Indigenous and decolonizing studies in education: Mapping the long view* (pp. 24–37). Routledge.

Sultan, R. & Herskind, M. (2020, July 23). What is abolition and why do we need it? *Vogue*. https://www.vogue.com/article/what-is-abolition-and-why-do-we-need-it

Szech, L. (2023). Mixed-lens family visits: An examination of sharing power between school and home. *International Journal of Qualitative Studies in Education*, *36*(2), 220–233.

Tachine, A. R. (2018). Story rug: Weaving stories into research. In R. S. Minthorn & H. J. Shotton (Eds.), *Reclaiming Indigenous research in higher education* (pp. 64–75). Rutgers University Press.

Tatum, B. D. (2017). *Why are all the Black kids sitting together in the cafeteria? And other conversations about race*. Basic Books.

Taylor, A. (2018). Knowledge citizens? Intellectual disability and the production of social meanings within educational research. *Harvard Educational Review*, *88*(1), 1–25.

Taylor, A., & Giugni, M. (2012). Common worlds: Reconceptualising inclusion in early childhood communities. *Contemporary Issues in Early Childhood*, *13*(2), 108–119.

Templeton, T. N. (2024). Tableaux (and children) that resist reading. *Studies in Art Education*, *65*(2), 248–254.

Thomas, C. (1999). *Female forms: Experiencing and understanding disability*. Open University Press.

Thomas, C. (2004). Rescuing a social relational understanding of disability. *Scandinavian Journal of Disability Research*, *6*(1), 22–36.

Thomas, G., & Glenny. G. (2000). Emotional and behavioural difficulties: Bogus needs in a false category. *Discourse: Studies in the Cultural Politics of Education, 21*(3), 283–298.

Thompson, V. (2020, October 10). Why Black disability history matters. Ramp Your Voice! https://www.vilissathompson.com/blog/why-black-disability-history-matters

Thorius, K. A. K. (2019). Facilitating en/counters with special education's cloak of benevolence in professional learning to eliminate racial disproportionality in special education. *International Journal of Qualitative Studies in Education, 32*(3), 323–340.

Thorpe, L., & Zerella, A. (2023). Identity: An Aboriginal perspective of supporting children's strong and proud Aboriginal identities and self-determination through connecting them with country. In C. Warden & D. Fargher (Eds.), *Beyond the gate: Respecting the relationship of children, culture and the natural world* (pp. 153–162). Pademelon Press.

Timmer, S. G., Hawk, B. N., Washington, A. M. L., & Urquiza, A. J. (2022). Trauma-informed care for maltreated children: Evidence-based treatments from a developmental perspective. In R. D. Krugman & J. E. Korbin (Eds.), *Handbook of child maltreatment* (2nd ed., pp. 483–523). Springer.

Torres, L. E. (2024). A litany for survival in pandemic times—DisCrit mothering and radical love. *International Journal of Qualitative Studies in Education*, *37*(9), 2567–2581. https://doi.org/10.1080/09518398.2024.2348779

Tourmaline [@tourmaliiine]. (2020, June 7). *When we say abolish police. We also mean the cop in your head and in your heart* [Tweet]. Twitter. https://twitter.com/tourmaliiine/status/1269774567637213190?lang=en#:~:text=🐝Tourmaline🐝%20on%20X,in%20your%20heart.%22%20%2F%20X

Trainor, A. A. (2010). Reexamining the promise of parent participation in special education: An analysis of cultural and social capital. *Anthropology & Education Quarterly, 41*(3), 245–263.

Tremain, S. (2006). *Foucault and the government of disability.* Taylor & Francis.

Truesdale, S. P. (1990). Whole-body listening: Developing active auditory skills. *Language, Speech, and Hearing Services in Schools, 21*(3), 183–84.

Turner, C. R. (2022). Black family childcare providers' roles as community mothers during the COVID-19 pandemic. In J. Pattnaik & M. Renck Jalongo (Eds.), *The impact of COVID-19 on early childhood education and care: International perspectives, challenges, and responses* (pp. 313–332). Springer.

Turner, M. K., Palmer, L., Ryder, T., Hayes, F., Gorey, L., Turner, V., Sharpe, R., & Vadiveloo, J. (2023). Intertwined Akaltyirrme Ntheenhele Apeke: Learning is everywhere. In C. Warden & D. Fargher (Eds.), *Beyond the gate: Respecting the relationship of children, culture and the natural world* (pp. 5–16). Pademelon Press.

U.S. Department of Education, EDFacts Data Warehouse (EDW): IDEA Part B Child Count and Educational Environments Collection, 2018–19. https://go.usa.gov/xdp4T

U.S. Department of Education Office of Civil Rights. (2021). Student discipline and school climate in U.S. public schools. https://www2.ed.gov/about/offices/list/ocr/docs/crdc-discipline-school-climate-report.pdf

Valencia, R. R. (2012). *The evolution of deficit thinking: Educational thought and practice.* Routledge.

Varghese, M., Daniels, J. R., & Park, C. C. (2019). Structuring disruption within university-based teacher education program1: Possibilities and challenges of race-based caucuses. *Teachers College Record, 121*(6), 1–34.

Verlie, B. (2020). From action to intra-action? Agency, identity and "goals" in a relational approach to climate change education. *Environmental Education Research, 26*(9–10), 1266–1280.

Victoria State Government Department of Education. (2024, March 25). *Kindergarten Inclusion Support (KIS).* State Government of Victoria. https://www.vic.gov.au/kindergarten-inclusion-children-disabilities

Victorian Government. (2023, August 22). *Bush kinders.* http://www.vic.gov.au/bush-kinders

Villenas, S. A., Godinez, F. E., Bernal, D. D., & Elenes, C. A. (2006). Chicanas/Latinas building bridges. In D. D. Bernal, F. E. Godinez, C. A. Elenes, & S. Villenas (Eds.), *Chicana/Latina education in everyday life: Feminista perspectives on pedagogy and epistemology* (pp. 1–9). SUNY Press.

Viruru, R. (2001). Colonized through language: The case of early childhood education. *Contemporary Issues in Early Childhood, 2*(1), 31–47.

Voulgarides, C. K., Jacobs, J., Lopez, D., & Barrio, B. L. (2024). Moving beyond compliance and toward equity to address racial disproportionality. *Intervention in School and Clinic, 60*(2), 108–118. https://doi.org/10.1177/10534512241258721

Waitoller, F. R., & King Thorius, K. A. (2016). Cross-pollinating culturally sustaining pedagogy and universal design for learning: Toward an inclusive pedagogy that accounts for dis/ability. *Harvard Educational Review, 86*(3), 366–389.

Wall Kimmerer, R. (2021). *Gathering moss: A natural cultural history of mosses*. Penguin Books.

Washington, J. (2018, July 31). What is prison abolition? *The Nation*. https://www.thenation.com/article/archive/what-is-prison-abolition/

Welsh, R. O., & Little, S. (2018). The school discipline dilemma: A comprehensive review of disparities and alternative approaches. *Review of Educational Research, 88*(5), 752–794.

Wertsch, J. V. (1998). *Mind as action*. Oxford University Press.

White-Johnson, J. (2024). DisCrit mothering as a radical act. *International Journal of Qualitative Studies in Education, 37*(9), 2493–2506. https://doi.org/10.1080/09518398.2024.2326823

Windchief, S., & Joseph, D. H. (2015). The act of claiming higher education as Indigenous space: American Indian/Alaska Native examples. *Diaspora, Indigenous, and Minority Education, 9*(4), 267–283.

Wong, A. (2020). *Disability visibility: First-person stories from the twenty-first century*. Vintage.

Wun, C. (2016). Against captivity: Black girls and school discipline policies in the afterlife of slavery. *Educational Policy, 30*(1), 171–196.

Yaden, D. B., Rowe, D. W., & MacGillivray, L. (2000). Emergent literacy: A matter (polyphony) of perspectives. In M. L. Kamil, P. B. Mosenthal, P. D. Pearson, & R. Barr (Eds.), *On reading books to children* (pp. 177–202). Erlbaum.

Yoon, H. S., & Templeton, T. N. (2019). The practice of listening to children: The challenges of hearing children out in an adult-regulated world. *Harvard Educational Review, 89*(1), 55–84.

Yosso, T. J. (2005). Whose culture has capital? A critical race theory discussion of community cultural wealth. *Race Ethnicity and Education, 8*(1), 69–91.

Yuval-Davis, N. (2006). Belonging and the politics of belonging, *Patterns of Prejudice, 40*(3), 197–214.

Yuval-Davis, N. (2011). *The politics of belonging: Intersectional contestations*. Sage.

Zdeblick, M. N. (2024). "Play my clip!" Arts-mediated agency in disability-centered learning and research. *International Journal of Qualitative Studies in Education, 37*(7), 2110–2128.

Zhang, D., Katsiyannis, A., Ju, S., & Roberts, E. (2014). Minority representation in special education: 5-year trends. *Journal of Child and Family Studies, 23*(1), 118–127.

Index

About the Editors and Contributors

Maggie Beneke is an associate professor in the College of Education at the University of Washington. She qualitatively examines how racism and ableism intersect in the context of everyday practices, as well as how young children, their families, and early educators negotiate, resist, and imagine beyond oppressive notions of "normalcy."

Hailey R. Love is an assistant professor in the Department of Rehabilitation Psychology and Special Education within the School of Education at the University of Wisconsin-Madison. She utilizes mixed methods and qualitative research to examine manifestations of racism and ableism in early childhood and explore how we can combat those oppressive systems through justice-driven inclusive education.

Bárbara Baptista de Oliveira is an English teacher with a master's degree in the postgraduate program in languages, field of applied linguistics, at Federal University of Viçosa (UFV), in MG State, Brazil. Her research focuses on teacher training and teaching strategies regarding accessible practices in the educational context.

Elizabeth A. Barcay is a former elementary school teacher, a current DECC member, and a PhD student in counseling psychology at Boston University. Her research and professional interests include harnessing transformative social–emotional learning in pursuit of building caring communities and a more equitable and inclusive world.

Nicole S. Begay is an enrolled member of the Dinè (Navajo) Tribe and a doctoral student at Arizona State University. Her research focuses on the family/kinship advocacy needs of Indigenous families for equitable access to special education. She is Dzíł ááh áí táách'íini born for Naakaii dine'é.

Rae L. Begaye-Tewa is Diné from Smoke Signal, Arizona. She is Bįįhbitoodnii born for Tótsohnii. Rae is a doctoral student at Mary Lou Fulton Teachers College at Arizona State University. Her research explores the narratives and issues of educational equity affecting Native families and students with disabilities by applying Indigenous ways of knowing.

April Coloma Boyce is a doctoral student at the University of Washington. She is a neurodivergent first-generation college graduate and Filipino immigrant. Her research explores racism and ableism in early childhood, particularly the goodness/badness binary and how young children envision a world where these labels used to categorize people no longer exist.

María Rosa Brea-Spahn, PhD, is a Dominican critical teacher-scholar-learner in the Department of Communicative Sciences and Disorders at New York University. Her work is focused on decentering English in speech and language assessment and interventions, interrogating ideologies of standardization in languaging, and reclaiming all languaging as valid and necessary.

Colleen Campbell (they/she) is a doctoral student at UC Santa Cruz in the Graduate School of Education. They are interested in work at the theoretical and material intersections of raciolinguisitics and critical disability studies in early childhood education settings.

Ame Christiansen is a researcher and lecturer in the Early Childhood Studies Academic Group and Global Childhoods Research Hub at the University of Melbourne Faculty of Education. Her doctoral thesis was awarded the John Smyth award for research excellence in the doctor of education in 2024. Ame has been a lecturer in initial teacher education since 2009 and is a founding member of Australia's Early Childhood Outdoor Learning Network.

M. Nickie Coomer is an assistant professor of education at Colorado College. In her research she analyzes the social and discursive constructions of emotions and behavior in early elementary settings through critical disability and mad studies theoretical lenses. She hopes that through her work, parents and children who have been marginalized in and by schools can find solidarity and community.

Caroline Cuenca is a doctoral student in the Learning and Instruction Department at the University of San Francisco. Her research interests include inclusive pedagogies and critical literacy. She is also an elementary educator and a reading specialist who has taught in grades kindergarten through 3rd grade.

Brianna Doherty (she/her) has a degree in early childhood education and is completing her master's degree in special education. She works in a multiage early elementary school classroom in a collaborative school. Her focus is on helping her students grow strong self-advocacy skills and improve their access to communication.

Ana Luisa Gediel is an associate professor in the Department of Languages at Federal University of Viçosa (UFV), in MG State, Brazil. She is in the postgraduate program in languages, field of applied linguistics. Her research focuses on teacher training and teaching strategies regarding accessible practices in the educational context.

Christine L. Hancock is an assistant professor of early childhood special education at Wayne State University. Her scholarship explores power dynamics in family–professional partnerships. She focuses on how to transform hierarchical relationships and foster equitable decision-making between home visitors and marginalized families.

Malcom L. King is a doctoral student at the University of Washington. His research examines how ableism and racism influence adult perceptions of childhood and the identity formation of Black boys. A Black, first-generation college graduate with lived experience being expelled from preschool, he currently enjoys hiking, swimming, painting, meditation, and time with family.

Teukie Martin is a doctoral student in inclusive special education in the School of Education at Syracuse University. They have an MS in early childhood special education and have completed advanced study in disability studies and women's and gender studies. Their work is interdisciplinary, with a particular focus on bringing mad, queer, and abolitionist frameworks to educational research.

Rosie Tuffour-Mercedat has a master's in early childhood education and has been a 1st-grade teacher for over 10 years in a multicultural setting She is interested in providing inclusive curricula to students, particularly students from systemically underserved groups and communities.

Kathryn M. Meyer teaches in the Teaching, Learning, and Educational Leadership Department at Binghamton University. Her scholarship focuses on enacting critical pedagogy to honor the strengths, lived experiences, and access needs of disabled and multiply marginalized teachers and students across pre-K–12 and higher education systems. Kathryn enjoys spending time with her cat, Linda, and watching *Jeopardy*.

Chelsea W. Morgan is an associate researcher at the University of Kansas Center for Public Partnerships and Research. Her scholarship explores special education philosophy and policy with particular concern for equitable family–professional partnerships and inclusive practice in early childhood settings.

Lilly Padía is an assistant professor of raciolinguistic justice in early childhood teacher education at Erikson Institute in Chicago. Her scholarship and community work explore liberation for children, families, and communities through disability, language, and race. Her work centers nonspeaking bilingual children and reimagines bilingual special and inclusive education.

Jie Y. Park is an associate professor of education at Clark University. A former high school teacher, she draws on socio-critical theories and community-engaged methodologies in her research, and works with classroom teachers and multilingual youth and families to design linguistically and racially affirming educational spaces.

William Proffitt is an assistant professor of inclusive education in the Department of Teaching and Learning at Montclair State University. William's research addresses cultural and systems change for the purpose of advancing inclusive education and emancipation for historically marginalized children, especially Black children labeled with disabilities.

Elizabeth A. Ruiz is a doctoral graduate of the Mary Lou Fulton Teachers College at Arizona State University. Elizabeth's research focuses on training preservice teachers to equitably engage children and families from historically marginalized communities, particularly those with disabilities. She is a special education teacher focused on transition.

A.R.Shearer (she/her) holds two master's degrees from two New York universities. School is cool and all, but her true passion is sitting on the couch playing *Animal Crossing* with the dogs watching the rabbits destroy the kitchen. RIP Lavender.

Xigrid Soto-Boykin, PhD, is a Puerto Rican critical scholar at the Children's Equity Project in Arizona State University. Her work focuses on dismantling raciolinguistic and ableist ideologies, policies, and practices in early childhood that sustain harm to children with multiply marginalized identities, including those who are emergent bilinguals and disabled.

Jasmin Stoffer (she/they) is a multiply neurodivergent/disabled and chronically ill PhD candidate (St. FX) and educator in Nova Scotia. A member of DECC, they are also a member of the Disability Rights Coalition of Nova Scotia (DRC), and the Nova Scotia Association of Teachers for Equity in Education (NSATEE).

Tran Nguyen Templeton is an assistant professor of early childhood and a faculty co-director of the Rita Gold Early Childhood Center at Teachers College, Columbia University. Taking up a critical childhood studies framework and image-based methods, Tran's work positions young children as active knowledge-producers as they take photographs, narrate, and co-produce their own stories and identities.

Crystasany R. Turner, PhD, is an assistant professor of teacher education at the University of Wisconsin-Milwaukee. Her teaching and research focus includes Black feminist epistemologies, early childhood education for social justice, and spirit-centered pedagogies. Her work interrogates imbalanced social power, institutional inequities, and systemic oppression affecting diverse children and families.

Devanshi Unadkat is an assistant professor at San Diego State University. Her research focuses on the use of digital technologies as tools for learning in various contexts with a focus on antibias and inclusive education. Devanshi has taught preschool through 2nd-grade classrooms and was a pre-K–12 special educator.